OLD ENGLISH

Grammar & Reader

OLD ENGLISH

Grammar & Reader

BY ROBERT E. DIAMOND

University of Nevada, Reno

A SAVOYARD BOOK

Wayne State University Press, Detroit

1970

Published simultaneously in Canada
By The Copp Clark Publishing Company
517 Wellington Street, West
Toronto 2B, Canada

Library of Congress Catalog Card Number: 79-79477
International Standard Book Number: 0-8143-1510-0
First paperback reprint, September, 1973
Wayne book number 38

Robert E. Diamond is professor of English at the University of Nevada, Reno. He received his B.A. and M.A. degrees from the University of Iowa (1941, 1948), and his Ph.D. from Harvard (1954).

The manuscript was edited by Robert H. Tennenhouse. The book was designed by Sylvia Winter. The type face for the text is Mergenthaler Linotype Times Roman, designed by Stanley Morison in 1931. The display face is Monotype Janson originally cut by Nicholas Kis about 1690. The book is printed on S. D. Warren's Olde Style Antique paper and bound in Bancroft's Oxford cloth over boards. Manufactured in the United States of America.

CONTENTS

5

PREFACE

THIS book is intended to make learning Old English as easy as possible. Since Old English is almost always taught in connection with a graduate program in English, it has seemed sensible to abandon the assumption that the study of the language is an adjunct to Indo-European philology. There seems to be no reason why Old English should not be presented as simply and attractively as a modern language, with a minimum of phonology and a maximum of clarity. The guiding principle of this book is to give students as much help as possible.

The book includes several features, many of them innovations:

1. Because beginners in a language have enough trouble without being obliged to wrestle with a shifting and often irrational orthography, all Old English texts are presented here in regularized spelling, a consistent orthography based on a modified form of Early West Saxon.

2. Because it is a waste of time for students to guess and to wonder if they have hit on the correct translation, all Old English texts here are provided with literal facing-page translations.

3. The grammar is as simple as possible. It is an attempt to lay before beginning students all that they need to know in order to learn to read the language.

4. Phonology is kept to a minimum: there is a section on

7

i-umlaut, designed to help students recognize words that are in umlaut relationship to each other.

5. The prose selections are only from works composed in Old English, because word-for-word translations out of Latin are not representative of any period of English style. Since a great deal of what usually passes as Old English prose is really Latin prose, students may as well read it in Latin or in Modern English; it seems pointless to read it in Old English.

6. The reader consists mostly of generous selections from Old English poetry. Since most students take an introductory course in Old English, followed by a course in *Beowulf*, it usually happens that if they do not read the good shorter poems during the first course, they never get to read them at all. Accordingly, the reader includes most of the usually anthologized and most admired short Old English poems. (No heroic poems are included, because most students are likely to use a *Beowulf* text that includes *Widsith, Deor, Waldere,* and *Finnsburg.*) Some of the poems included here, such as the *Physiologus* poems (*The Panther* and *The Whale*) are a bit farther from the beaten path. The aim has been to present complete poems wherever possible; only one poem, the *Exeter Gnomes,* now known as *Maxims I,* is given in part only: 29 of the 204 lines have been selected, the most attractive portion of the poem, including the celebrated passage about the Frisian wife.

7. A simplified and up-to-date explanation of Old English metrics is included.

8. Every attempt has been made to make the glossary as helpful as possible. For example, all strong-verb and other irregular forms are cross-referenced.

9. In order to keep this book simple, it has seemed best to dispense with notes, which students are unlikely to consult anyway. The help that the students need is provided by the translations and the glossary.

R. E. D.

GRAMMAR

THE language spoken in England before the Norman Conquest is known by two names, "Anglo-Saxon" and "Old English." Either is acceptable, although many people now tend to prefer "Old English," because it indicates the continuity of the history of the language, especially when placed alongside the terms "Middle English" and "Modern English."

PRONUNCIATION AND SPELLING

Although the spelling system of Old English was not fixed or regular, it seems best to introduce beginning students to the language in a regularized spelling system, a modified form of the Early West Saxon dialect in use at the time of King Alfred, in the late ninth century.

Vowels and diphthongs in Old English are either long or short. This feature, vowel length, is difficult for students to grasp, because Modern English no longer has it. Although it was formerly the practice in grammars and discussions of metrics to describe the vowels of Modern English as long or short, linguists tend now mostly to characterize them as simple vowels or diphthongs. For a recent study of the sounds of Old English which rejects the traditional classification of long and short vowels and analyzes them as simple vowels or diphthongs, interested students may wish to refer to Robert P. Stockwell, "The phonology of Old English: a structural sketch," *SIL,* XIII (1958), 13–24.

9

We will indicate a long vowel by placing an acute accent over it, thus: á, ǽ, é, í, ó, ú, ý. A very few words, such as the nominative singular masculine form of the definite article, will have a vowel marked ˘ to indicate that the vowel is sometimes long and sometimes short, thus: sĕ.

Old English has seven vowels and three diphthongs, as follows:

VOWEL	PRONUNCIATION	EXAMPLES
a	like the first *a* in *aha* or the *a* in German *Mann* or the *a*'s in French *à la mode*	ac, dagum, mann
á	like the *a* in *father*	ác, bán, lást
æ	like the *a* in *bat*	mæst, æfter, wæs
ǽ	like the *a* in *jazz*	mǽst, rǽd, wǽron
e	like the *e* in *set*	ʒe, bedd, setl
é	like the *a* in *made*	ʒé, hér, lét
i	like the *i* in *bit*	ride, inn, wiste
í	like the *i* in *machine*	ríde, wín, scír
o	like the *au* in *audacious* or the *o* in *pot* pronounced with a Boston or British accent	god, oft, on
ó	like the *o* in *rode*	gód, óðer, bót
u	like the *u* in *put*	full, sumor, upp
ú	like the *oo* in *boot*	fúl, tún, brúcan
y	like the *ü* in German *füllen* (round the lips to pronounce an *o* and say the *i* of *bit*)	cyme, dydon, fyllan

ý   like the *ü* in German
kühn or the *u* in French
vu (round the lips to pronounce an *o* and say the
i of *machine*)   cýme, brýd, lýt

The second element of the Old English diphthongs is the sound /ə/, like the second *a* in *drama*.

DIPHTHONG	PRONUNCIATION	EXAMPLES
ea	æ + ə	ȝeaf, heard, eall
éa	ǽ + ə	ȝéafon, déaþ, néah
eo	e + ə	beorn, feoh, seolh
éo	é + ə	béor, léof, séo
ie	i + ə	hierde, scield, bierhtan
íe	í + ə	híerde, líesan, þríe

Most of the consonants in Old English are pronounced in about the same way as in Modern English, with a few exceptions, as follows.

c

The letter *c* represents two sounds, the *k* sound of *kiss* and the *ch* sound of *chap*. The palatalized *c* sound (*ch*) will be indicated by the letter *c* with a diacritic mark over it, thus: *č*. Examples: *lič* (pronounced about like the Modern English word *leech*), *čiriče, dreččan*.

The letter *c* without any diacritic mark over it represents the *k* sound. Examples: *cynn, camp, clúd*.

g

In Old English spelling, the letter **g** represented four different sounds. Of these, the most frequent and important are the *g* sound of *gun* and the *y* sound of *yot*.

1. As an aid to beginning students, the palatalized *g* sound (*y*) will be represented by a distinct form of the letter, the flat-topped ᵹ. Examples: ᵹéar, ᵹieldan, on-ᵹinnan.

2. The ordinary round *g* will be used to indicate the voiced back stop, as in *gold*. Examples: *gamol, gráp, gód*.

In some words, *g* in combination with *n* indicated the sound /ŋg/, as in Modern English *finger* (it was never simply the sound /ŋ/, as in Modern English *singer*). In such Old English words, the ordinary round *g* will be used. Examples: *singan, wang, leornung*.

3. In many words, *g* in combination with *n* indicated the sound /nĵ/, as in the Modern English word *hinge*. In such Old English words, the flat-topped ᵹ in combination with *n* will be used. Examples: *henᵹest, enᵹel, lenᵹ*.

4. A fourth sound represented by *g* in Old English is the sound of *g* between back vowels. This sound is something like the *g* in German *sagen*, somewhere between an ordinary *g* and a *w* sound. Examples: *fugol, dagum*.

f, s, þ/ð

Three consonants are either voiced or unvoiced, depending on their position in a word: *f, s,* and *þ/ð*. (The so-called *th* sound, when unvoiced, is represented by the letter *þ* in our regularized spelling.) The unvoiced *f, s,* and *þ* (pronounced like the *f* of *fit*, the *s* of *sit*, and the *th* of *think*) are found at the beginning of a word, at the end of a word, and internally between a vowel and an unvoiced consonant, thus:

INITIALLY	INTERNALLY	FINALLY
full	æfter	hláf
sunu	lást	gós
þéaw	brecþa	wiþ

The voiced *f, s,* and *ð* (pronounced like the *v* of *over*, the *z* of *razor*, and the *th* of *that*) are found between two vowels or between a vowel and a voiced consonant, thus:

BETWEEN TWO VOWELS	BETWEEN A VOWEL AND A VOICED CONSONANT
heofon	hæfde
rísan	ræsde
cweðan	cwiðdon

Doubling *f, s,* or *þ* indicate unvoicing in any position. Examples: *Offa, blissian, oþþe.*

h

The letter *h* represents three sounds.

1. At the beginning of a word, it is pronounced about like *h* in Modern English. Examples: *hund, hláf, hréam.*

2. Following a back vowel or diphthong, such as *o, u,* or *eo,* the letter *h* represents the velar fricative sound of Scottish *loch* or German *Achtung.* Examples: *fohten, fuhton, eahta, feoh.*

3. Following a front vowel or diphthong, such as *æ, i,* or *ie,* the letter *h* represents the palatal fricative sound of German *dich,* something like the *y* sound of *you* unvoiced or the initial sound of the name *Hugh.* Examples: *riht, liehtan.*

sc

With very few exceptions, the letters *sc* represent the *sh* sound of *she.* Examples: *scolde, fersc, scrúd.* The most frequently encountered exception is the verb *áscian,* the first syllable of which is pronounced something like the Modern English word *ask.*

cg

The sound /ĵ/, spelled *dg* in Modern English, as in the word *edge,* is represented in Old English by the letters *cg.* Examples: *ecg, fricgan, brycg.* Note in this connection that, as indicated above, the sound /nĵ/, as in the Modern English word *hinge,* is indicated in Old English by the letter *n* in combination with the flat-topped ʒ, as in *honʒest.*

Bear in mind that, as indicated above, in Old English the combination *ng* is pronounced /ŋg/, as in the Modern English word *finger*, never simply /ŋ/, as in the Modern English word *singer*. Both the nasalized back stop and the voiced back stop are heard. Examples: *hungor, lang, fangen.*

Silent consonants, such as the *g* in the Modern English word *gnaw* and the *k* in the Modern English word *knee,* are not found in Old English. Thus, we pronounce the *g* in *gnornian* and the *c* in *cnáwan.*

When a consonant is doubled, both of them should be pronounced. Thus, the difference between *læde* and *lædde* is about the same as the difference between the pronunciation of the *d*'s in *lady* and in *good deal.*

INFLECTION AND WORD ORDER

Old English is an inflected language, much like Latin and Russian. The essential system of the language is that grammatical relationships are indicated by inflections. Nouns, pronouns, adjectives, and verbs have sets of endings. Grammars of Old English and histories of the English language have traditionally described Old English as a synthetic language, one in which word order is free and plays little meaningful part. Recent studies* indicate, however, that the order of the words in Old English sentences tends to follow certain patterns, much as in Modern English. Old English thus often provides a double set of signals, both inflections and word order.

* Charles R. Carleton, "Syntax of the Old English Charters," unpubl. diss. (University of Michigan, 1959); Ann Shannon, *A Descriptive Syntax of the Parker Manuscript of the Anglo-Saxon Chronicle from 734 to 891* (The Hague, 1964); Faith F. Gardner, "An Analysis of Syntactic Patterns of Old English," unpubl. diss. (Wayne State University, 1967).

GENDER, NUMBER, AND CASE

In Old English, nouns, pronouns, and adjectives fit into three categories at the same time: they have grammatical gender; they are singular, dual, or plural; and they must be in one of four (or five) cases.

Gender

Old English has grammatical gender. Any noun must be masculine, feminine, or neuter, without necessarily any reference to the nature of the thing the noun may refer to. For example, the Old English word for "woman," *wíf,* is a neuter noun.

In Modern English we have natural gender. That is, the only things that are, for example, masculine grammatically are male biologically. There are a few exceptions to this rule, such as our custom of referring to ships and countries as "she."

Many things that we think of as being neutral, neither male nor female, are masculine or feminine in Old English, just as in French or German. Consequently, where we would say "it" to refer to things in Modern English, Old English very often says the equivalent of "he" or "she." This is another way of saying that in translating Old English into Modern English we must often translate what looks like "he" or "she" with the Modern English word "it."

Anyone who has studied a language such as French or German knows that grammatical gender does not add anything to comprehension or to linguistic subtlety in any way; it merely provides the learner with a set of mistakes to make. Bear in mind, however, that in learning Old English, you will not be learning to speak the language; you will only be learning to read it. You will not be asked to have a recall knowledge of these words and their genders; you will be asked only to have a recognition knowledge of them.

Number

In Old English, nouns, adjectives, and verbs are singular or plural. In addition, Old English has a third number category known as "dual," which is found only in the personal pronouns. The dual number was formerly used throughout the language, but by the time of Old English only a vestige of it remained, in the first and second persons of the pronouns. (These forms will be given later.) Instead of thinking of all things as being either one-thing or more-than-one-thing, Old English had thought of things as being one-thing, two-things, or more-than-two-things.

Case

The case system of Old English is similar to that of Latin or Russian, although not identical. The first thing that a student must realize is that in Old English a noun, for example, can never appear except in one of its cases. When we say that a noun is *in* a certain case, we mean that it has the ending that marks it as being in that case. Following the practice of Latin grammar, we use the nominative singular of nouns and adjectives as the dictionary form.

The ambiguity of the Modern English pattern N V N N (noun-verb-noun-noun) is illustrated by a sentence that fills the pattern: The king called the man a servant. This sentence can mean either that the king said things about the man that indicated that the man was a servant, or it can mean that the king summoned a servant for the man. If this sentence were translated into Old English, the noun "king" would be in the nominative case, indicating that it is the subject of the verb; the noun "man" could be in the dative case, indicating that it is the indirect object of the verb; the noun "servant" would be in the accusative case, indicating that it is the direct object of the verb. It would thus be impossible to misunderstand the meaning of the sentence in Old English, because the case endings would show how the words operate in the sentence.

THE CASES

Nouns, pronouns, and adjectives have grammatical case in Old English. The four cases are

> Nominative
> Genitive
> Dative
> Accusative.

A possible fifth case is the Instrumental, to be explained under Dative.

Each of the cases has a primary function and several secondary functions.

In the following explanation of the case system in Old English, the examples are in Modern English wherever possible.

Nominative Case

1. The primary function of the nominative case is to indicate that a noun, for example, is the subject of the verb.

Example: The king gave the man a sword.

In Old English, "king" would be in the nominative case, indicating that it is the subject of the verb "gave."

2. The complement of a linking verb is in the nominative case.

Example: The man is a soldier.
The man is cold.

In Old English, "soldier" and "cold" would be in the nominative case as complements of the linking verb "is."

3. Words in direct address are in the nominative case.

Example: Be careful, son.

In Old English, the noun "son" would be nominative.

17

Genitive Case

1. The primary function of the genitive case is to indicate possession.

Example: Edward's sword.

In Old English, Edward would be in the genitive case and would have the genitive ending, as it does in Modern English.

2. A noun or adjective in the genitive case can be used adverbially.

Example: In Old English, the word meaning "all" can have the genitive ending and be used to mean "entirely."

Here belongs also the genitive of time.

Example: In Old English, the word for "night" in the genitive case would mean "at night."

3. The partitive genitive.

Example: In Old English, the expression "one of the men" would be just the word for "one" and the word for "man" in the genitive plural.

The words for numbers in Old English also take the genitive case.

Example: In Old English, the expression "thirty ships" would be the word for "thirty" followed by the word for "ship" in the genitive plural.

The Old English word *fela,* meaning "much" or "many," takes the genitive case:

fela plus a noun in the genitive singular means "much";

fela plus a noun in the genitive plural means "many."

4. Some verbs take their direct object in the genitive case. Some of the commonest are:

> be-dǽlan (deprive)
> be-niman (deprive)
> bídan (await)
> brúcan (enjoy)
> néosian (visit)

néotan (use)
þurfan (need)
wénan (expect).

5. The genitive case has a number of other idiomatic uses, just as in Modern English:

The genitive of relationship (Edward's brother);
The genitive of measure (an acre of land);
The subjective genitive (the king's command);
The objective genitive (the king's murderer);
The descriptive genitive (a man of honor).

Dative Case

1. The primary function of the dative case is to indicate the indirect object of the verb.

Example: The king gave the man a sword.

In Old English, the noun "man" would be in the dative.

2. The object of a preposition is usually in the dative case.

Example: She is in the house.

In Old English, "house" would be dative, because it is the object of the preposition "in."

3. The instrumental use of the dative case indicates the thing *by means of which* the action is performed.

Example: She stabbed him with a knife.

In Old English, the preposition "with" would not be needed; the noun "knife" would be in the dative case.

The instrumental used to be a separate case in Old English, as it is in Russian, but it fell together with the dative case, so that we may say that the instrumental is now a function of the dative case. That is, the instrumental endings are indistinguishable from the dative endings for almost all words. But some very common words still have separate forms for the instrumental case. For example, the definite article in Old English has a masculine and neuter instrumental singular form that is distinct from the masculine and neuter dative

singular form. If it were not for this and a few other instrumental forms, we could stop referring to the instrumental as
a separate case and merely think of it as the by-means-of-
which function of the dative case.

4. The dative case is used in expressions of time.

Example: The Modern English expression "at times"
would be translated by an Old English word for "time" in the
dative plural.

5. Some adjectives are used with the dative case.

Example: The Modern English expression "loyal to the
king" would be translated by the word for "loyal" followed
by the word for "king" in the dative case.

Some of the commonest adjectives that take the dative are:

> ȝe-líč (similar)
> hold (loyal)
> léof (dear)
> néah (near).

6. Some verbs take their direct object in the dative case.
Some of the commonest are:

> and-swarian (answer)
> ȝe-líefan (believe)
> helpan (help)
> híer-sumian (obey)
> lícian (please)
> þynčan (seem)
> wísian (guide).

7. The dative of possession: sometimes Old English uses a
dative where we might expect a genitive.

Example: Instead of saying the equivalent of "at his feet,"
as we might expect, Old English sometimes says the equivalent of "at the feet (to) him."

Accusative Case

1. The primary function of the accusative case is to indicate the direct object of the verb.

Example: They built a ship.

In Old English, the word "ship" would be in the accusative case, because it is the direct object of the verb.

2. The object of a preposition may be in the accusative case.

Example: He rode into the forest.

In Old English, the word "forest" could be in the accusative case.

3. A noun in the accusative can be used adverbially.

Example: I went home.

In Old English, the word "home" would be in the accusative.

Here belongs also the accusative of time.

Example: We stayed there a week.

In Old English, the word "week" would be in the accusative.

4. The subject of an infinitive is in the accusative case.

Example: In Modern English, we can say, "I saw the man do it."

In Old English, we would have to say the equivalent of "I saw the man to do it," selecting the infinitive form of the verb "do"; the word for "man" would be in the accusative.

THE DEFINITE ARTICLE

The definite article in Old English performed much the same function as it does in Modern English, but it also doubled as a demonstrative pronoun and a relative pronoun. That is, it could mean not only "the" but also "this" or "that"; or it could be used as a relative pronoun to introduce a subordinate clause.

When the definite article is used as a relative pronoun, it agrees with its antecedent in gender and number, but it takes whatever case is required by its role in the subordinate clause it introduces. For example, in the sentence "I saw the man who was there," the relative pronoun "who" would be translated *sé*, masculine singular to agree with the word for "man" and nominative because it is the subject of the verb "was" in the subordinate clause.

The forms of the definite article are given here. Note that instrumental forms will be given throughout the grammar only when they differ from the dative forms. The slash mark / is used to indicate variant forms.

SINGULAR

	masc.	*fem.*	*neut.*
nom.	sĕ	séo	þæt
gen.	þæs	þǽre	þæs
dat.	þǽm	þǽre	þǽm
acc.	þone	þá	þæt
instr.	þý/þon		þý/þon

PLURAL (*all three genders*)

nom.	þá
gen.	þára
dat.	þǽm
acc.	þá

THE RELATIVE PARTICLE

The word *þe* can be used as a relative pronoun, alone or in combination with the definite article. This word is indeclinable; that is, it never changes its form but can be used to refer to any gender, number, or case. It works something like the pronoun *that* in Modern English, which can be used as a relative pronoun in almost any situation.

When *þe* is combined with the definite article, the form of the article precedes it and agrees with the antecedent in gender, number, and case. For example, in the sentence "I saw the man who was there," the relative pronoun "who" could be translated *þone-þe;* it is as if Old English said "I saw the man, him who was there."

PRONOUNS

The Personal Pronouns

FIRST PERSON SINGULAR		FIRST PERSON PLURAL
nom.	ič	wé
gen.	mín	úser/úre
dat.	mé	ús
acc.	mé/meč	ús/úsič

SECOND PERSON SINGULAR		SECOND PERSON PLURAL
nom.	þú	ʒé
gen.	þín	éower
dat.	þé	éow
acc.	þé/þeč	éow/éowič

The genitive forms of the first- and second-person pronouns *mín, þín, úre, éower* are also used as pronominal adjectives, to which case endings are added. One encounters such forms as *mínra* (*mín* with the genitive plural ending) and *úrne* (*úre* with the masculine accusative singular ending).

	THIRD PERSON SINGULAR		
	masc.	*fem.*	*neut.*
nom.	hé	héo	hit
gen.	his	hire	his
dat.	him	hire	him
acc.	hine	híe	hit

23

THIRD PERSON PLURAL (*all three genders*)

nom.	híe
gen.	hira
dat.	him
acc.	híe

The dual forms of the personal pronoun are less commonly used and are found only in the first and second persons. The dual pronouns, translated "we two" or "you two," select plural verb forms.

FIRST PERSON DUAL		SECOND PERSON DUAL
nom.	wit	ʒit
gen.	uncer	incer
dat.	unc	inc
acc.	unc	inc

The Interrogative Pronoun

The interrogative pronoun is translated "who" or "what." It is not used as a relative pronoun, only as a question word.

WHO (*masc. and fem.*)		WHAT (*neut.*)
nom.	hwá	hwæt
gen.	hwæs	hwæs
dat.	hwǽm	hwǽm
acc.	hwone	hwæt
instr.		hwí

The Demonstrative Pronoun þes

The demonstrative pronoun is translated "this, that, these, those."

	SINGULAR		
	masc.	*fem.*	*neut.*
nom.	þes	þéos	þis
gen.	þisses	þisse	þisses

dat.	þissum	þisse	þissum
acc.	þisne	þás	þis
instr.	þýs		þýs

PLURAL (*all three genders*)
nom. þás
gen. þissa
dat. þissum
acc. þás

INTRODUCTION TO THE VERB

The verb in Old English is inflected to indicate distinctions of person, number, and tense. The number distinctions are only between singular forms and plural forms, as there are no dual verb endings; the dual pronouns select plural verb forms.

The tense system is simpler than in Modern English. There are only two tenses, present and past, usually called preterite. There is no future tense in Old English, with the possible exception of the verb "to be," which will be explained later; ordinarily the present tense is used with the force of the future wherever there is a need to express futurity.

The preterite tense in Old English includes the semantic territory occupied in Modern English by the past progressive (I was doing), the present perfect (I have done), and the past perfect (I had done), although those tenses, composed of a form of the verb "be" or the verb "have" and a participle, are being developed during the course of the Old English period, and the student will encounter compound forms that look exactly like, for example, the present perfect.

The Old English verbs fall into two major groupings or conjugations, traditionally called *weak* verbs and *strong* verbs. These coincide roughly with the terms "regular" (weak) and "irregular" (strong), although by no means always. The system is much the same as in Modern English: the weak verbs form their past tense by adding a dental (usually a "d" or a "t") to the stem; the strong verbs form their past tense by varying the vowel of the stem.

The Old English verb also observes distinctions of mood: indicative, imperative, and subjunctive (sometimes called optative). Generally speaking, the indicative mood is used for statements of fact, the imperative for commands, and the subjunctive for hypothetical situations.

A Sample Weak Verb

The Old English weak verbs are traditionally divided into three classes, of which the most regular is Class II. A verb from this class can serve as an example of how the weak verbs work.

folgian (follow)

The principal parts are: **folgian** (infinitive)
folgode (preterite)
folgod (past participle)

PRESENT INDICATIVE

	singular	*plural (all three persons)*
1st. pers.	ič **folgie**	wé ⎫
2nd. pers.	þú **folgast**	ʒé ⎬ **folgiaþ**
3rd. pers.	hé **folgaþ**	híe ⎭

PRETERITE INDICATIVE

	singular	*plural (all three persons)*
1st. pers.	ič **folgode**	wé ⎫
2nd. pers.	þú **folgodest**	ʒé ⎬ **folgodon**
3rd. pers.	hé **folgode**	híe ⎭

PRESENT SUBJUNCTIVE

singular (all three persons)		*plural (all three persons)*	
1st. pers.	ič ⎫	wé ⎫
2nd. pers.	þú ⎬ **folgie**	ʒé ⎬ **folgien**
3rd. pers.	hé ⎭	híe ⎭

PRETERITE SUBJUNCTIVE

singular (all three persons)		*plural (all three persons)*	
1st. pers.	ič ⎫	wé ⎫	
2nd. pers.	þú ⎬ **folgode**	ʒé ⎬ **folgoden**	
3rd. pers.	hé ⎭	híe ⎭	

IMPERATIVE

singular **folga**   *plural* **folgiaþ**

There are also two adjectives derived from the verb: one, usually called the present participle, is truly an active verbal adjective; the other, usually called the past participle, is truly a passive verbal adjective. The past participle usually has the prefix ʒe-.

The passive is formed by combining the appropriate form of the verb *béon/wesan* (be) or of *weorðan* (become) with the past participle.

> present participle: **folgiende** (following)
> past participle: **ʒe-folgod** (followed)
> the inflected infinitive, often called the
> gerundive: **to folgienne.**

A Sample Strong Verb

The strong verbs in Old English are traditionally divided into seven classes, of which more later. We will take the verb **rídan** (ride) from the first class as an example of how the strong verbs work.

The strong verbs have four principal parts:

> first principal part, infinitive
> second principal part, preterite singular
> third principal part, preterite plural
> fourth principal part, past participle.

The principal parts of our sample verb are:

> **rídan** (infinitive)
> **rád** (preterite singular)

27

ridon (preterite plural)

ʒe-riden (past participle).

From the first principal part, we derive the present tense (both indicative and subjunctive), the imperative, the present participle, and the inflected infinitive.

PRESENT INDICATIVE

	singular	*plural (all three persons)*
1st. pers.	ič **ríde**	wé ⎫
2nd. pers.	þú **rídest**	ʒé ⎬ **rídaþ**
3rd. pers.	hé **rídeþ**	híe ⎭

PRESENT SUBJUNCTIVE

singular (all three persons)		*plural (all three persons)*
1st. pers.	ič ⎫	wé ⎫
2nd. pers.	þú ⎬ **ríde**	ʒé ⎬ **ríden**
3rd. pers.	hé ⎭	híe ⎭

IMPERATIVE

singular **ríd**   *plural* **rídaþ**

PRESENT PARTICIPLE **rídende**

INFLECTED INFINITIVE **to rídenne**

From the second principal part, we derive the first and third persons singular preterite indicative. From the third principal part, we derive the second person singular preterite indicative and all three persons plural preterite indicative, and the preterite subjunctive, both singular and plural, all three persons.

PRETERITE INDICATIVE

	singular	*plural (all three persons)*
1st. pers.	ič **rád**	wé ⎫
2nd. pers.	þú **ride**	ʒé ⎬ **ridon**
3rd. pers.	hé **rád**	híe ⎭

PRETERITE SUBJUNCTIVE

singular (all three persons)		*plural (all three persons)*	
1st. pers.	ič ⎫	wé ⎫	
2nd. pers.	þú ⎬ ride	3é ⎬ riden	
3rd. pers.	hé ⎭	híe ⎭	

Note that when the pronouns *wé* and *3é* follow the verb, the ending can be *-e* instead of *-aþ*, *-on*, or *-en*. Example: *ríde wé*, where one would ordinarily expect *rídaþ wé*.

THE ADJECTIVE

The adjective in Old English is inflected to indicate distinctions of gender, number, and case. There are two main declensions of the adjective, traditionally called strong and weak. The weak set of endings of the adjective is chiefly used when the adjective accompanies the definite article (or a form of *þes* or *mín* or *þín*). The strong set of endings is used in most other situations.

The adjective **swift** (swift) in the weak declension:

SINGULAR

	masc.		*fem.*		*neut.*	
nom.	se	swifta	séo	swifte	þæt	swifte
gen.	þæs	swiftan	þǽre	swiftan	þæs	swiftan
dat.	þǽm	swiftan	þǽre	swiftan	þǽm	swiftan
acc.	þone	swiftan	þá	swiftan	þæt	swifte

PLURAL (*all three genders*)

nom.	þá	swiftan
gen.	þára	swiftena/swiftra
dat.	þǽm	swiftum
acc.	þá	swiftan

The adjective **swift** in the strong declension:

SINGULAR

	masc.	*fem.*	*neut.*
nom.	swift	swift	swift
gen.	swiftes	swiftre	swiftes
dat.	swiftum	swiftre	swiftum
acc.	swiftne	swifte	swift
instr.	swifte		swifte

PLURAL

	masc.	*fem.*	*neut.*
nom.	swifte	swifta	swift
gen.	swiftra	swiftra	swiftra
dat.	swiftum	swiftum	swiftum
acc.	swifte	swifta	swift

COMPARATIVE AND SUPERLATIVE

The comparative of *swift* is *swiftra*.
The superlative of *swift* is *swiftost*.

ADVERBS

Adverbs can be formed from adjectives by adding *-líče, -e,*
or *-inga.*

ADJECTIVE	ADVERB
swift	swift-líče
wíd (wide)	wíde
eall (all)	eallinga (entirely)

INTRODUCTION TO THE NOUN

Every noun in Old English is masculine, feminine, or neuter.
Nouns are inflected to indicate distinctions of number and
case.

Of the various noun declensions, two will serve as an in-
troduction to the noun, one of the strong declension and one

of the weak declension. The so-called strong and weak declensions or sets of endings are parallel to the strong and weak
declensions of the adjective; note, however, that a noun always uses the same set of endings (either strong or weak)
and does not shift from one to the other, as adjectives do.

wer (man, a masculine noun)

	SINGULAR	PLURAL
nom.	wer	weras
gen.	weres	wera
dat.	were	werum
acc.	wer	weras

guma (man, a masculine noun)

	SINGULAR	PLURAL
nom.	guma	guman
gen.	guman	gumena
dat.	guman	gumum
acc.	guman	guman

MORE ABOUT STRONG VERBS

The strong verbs in Old English are divided into seven ablaut classes. The following is a list of the types to be found in
each class. The four principal parts are given in four columns.
The meaning of each verb is given in parentheses. The past
participle is given without any prefix. Although there are
four principal parts for strong verbs, a fifth form, the third
person singular present indicative, is given for a few verbs.

CLASS I

infinitive	*pret. sg.*	*pret. pl.*	*past. ppl.*	*3rd. pers. sg.* *pres. indic.*
rísan (rise)	rás	rison	risen	
líðan (go)	láþ	lidon	liden	
wréon (cover)	wráh	wrigon	wriȝen	hé wríehþ

31

CLASS 2

béodan (offer)	béad	budon	boden	
čéosan (choose)	čéas	curon	coren	
séoðan (boil)	séaþ	sudon	soden	
brúcan (enjoy)	bréac	brucon	brocen	
téon (draw)	téah	tugon	togen	hé tíehþ

CLASS 3

drincan (drink)	dranc	druncon	druncen	
helpan (help)	healp	hulpon	holpen	hé hilpþ
weorpan (throw)	wearp	wurpon	worpen	hé wierpþ
weorðan (become)	wearþ	wurdon	worden	
friȝnan (inquire)	fræȝn	frugnon	frugnen	
ȝieldan (pay)	ȝeald	guldon	golden	hé ȝielt

CLASS 4

beran (carry)	bær	bǽron	boren	hé birþ/bireþ
scieran (cut)	scear	scéaron	scoren	
niman (take)	nam	námon	numen	
cuman (come)	cóm	cómon	cumen	hé cymþ/cymeþ

CLASS 5

ȝiefan (give)	ȝeaf	ȝéafon	ȝiefen	
cweðan (say)	cwæþ	cwǽdon	cweden	hé cwiþ
séon (see)	seah	sáwon	sewen	hé siehþ
biddan (ask)	bæd	bǽdon	beden	
licgan (lie)	læȝ	lágon	leȝen	hé liȝeþ
wesan (be)	wæs	wǽron		

CLASS 6

faran (go)	fór	fóron	faren	hé færeþ
weaxan (grow)	wéox	wéoxon	weaxen	
standan (stand)	stód	stódon	standen	hé stent
sléan (strike)	slóg	slógon	slæȝen	hé sliehþ
hebban (lift)	hóf	hófon	hæfen	
scieppan (create)	scóp	scópon	scæpen	
scieþþan (injure)	scód	scódon	sceaðen	

CLASS 7

hátan (call)	hét	héton	háten	
slǽpan (sleep)	slép	slépon	slǽpen	
héawan (hew)	héow	héowon	héawen	
cnáwan (know)	cnéow	cnéowon	cnáwen	
gangan (go)	ʒéong	ʒéongon	gangen	
feallan (fall)	féoll	féollon	feallen	hé fielþ
blówan (bloom)	bléow	bléowon	blówen	
wépan (weep)	wéop	wéopon	wópen	
fón (seize)	féng	féngon	fangen	hé féhþ

ANOMALOUS VERBS

Four verbs, usually called the anomalous verbs, are of such high frequency that it will be helpful to have their forms given.

béon/wesan (be)

This suppletive verb is extremely irregular but very important. In the present indicative, there are two sets of forms which were used interchangeably, although there was a tendency to use the forms *béo, hist, biþ, béoþ* for the future tense.

PRESENT INDICATIVE
singular

1st. pers.	ič **eom**	ič **béo**
2nd. pers.	þú **eart**	þú **bist**
3rd. pers.	hé **is**	hé **biþ**

plural (all three persons) **sind/sindon/sint**   **béoþ**

PRETERITE INDICATIVE
singular   *plural*

1st. pers.	ič **wæs**	wé	
2nd. pers.	þú **wǽre**	ʒé	**wǽron**
3rd. pers.	hé **wæs**	híe	

33

PRESENT SUBJUNCTIVE
singular (*all three persons*) **síe**   *plural* (*all three persons*) **síen**

PRETERITE SUBJUNCTIVE
singular (*all three persons*) **wǽre**
plural (*all three persons*) **wǽren**

IMPERATIVE
singular **wes/béo**   *plural* **wesaþ/béoþ**

PRESENT PARTICIPLE   **wesende**

willan (wish)
PRESENT INDICATIVE

	singular	*plural*	
1st. pers.	ič **wille**	wé	
2nd. pers.	þú **wilt**	ȝé	**willaþ**
3rd. pers.	hé **wile**	híe	

PRETERITE   **wolde**
PRESENT SUBJUNCTIVE   **wille**

dón (do)
PRESENT INDICATIVE

	singular	*plural*	
1st. pers.	ič **dó**	wé	
2nd. pers.	þú **dést**	ȝé	**dóþ**
3rd. pers.	hé **déþ**	híe	

PRETERITE   **dyde**
PRESENT SUBJUNCTIVE
singular **dó**   *plural* **dón**
IMPERATIVE
singular **dó**   *plural* **dóþ**
PAST PARTICIPLE   **ȝe-dón**

34

gán (go)

PRESENT INDICATIVE

	singular	*plural*	
1st. pers.	ič gá	wé	
2nd. pers.	pú gǽst	ʒé	gáþ
3rd. pers.	hé gǽþ	híe	

PRETERITE **éode**

PRESENT SUBJUNCTIVE

singular **gá**   *plural* **gán**

IMPERATIVE

singular **gá**   *plural* **gáþ**

PAST PARTICIPLE **ʒe-gán**

MORE ABOUT WEAK VERBS

The weak verbs in Old English are traditionally grouped
under three classes.

Class I

Examples of the various types of verbs to be found in Class
I are given here. The three principal parts of a weak verb
are the infinitive, the preterite, and the past participle. The
past participles will be given without any prefix.

fremman (do)   **fremede**   **fremed**

PRESENT INDICATIVE

	singular	*plural*	
1st. pers.	ič **fremme**	wé	
2nd. pers.	þú **fremest**	ʒé	**fremmaþ**
3rd. pers.	hé **fremeþ**	híe	

PRETERITE INDICATIVE

	singular	*plural*	
1st. pers.	ič **fremede**	wé	
2nd. pers.	þú **fremedest**	ʒé	**fremedon**
3rd. pers.	hé **fremede**	híe	

35

nerian (save)   nerede   nered

PRESENT INDICATIVE

	singular		plural	
1st. pers.	ič **nerie**		wé	
2nd. pers.	þú **nerest**		ȝé	**neriaþ**
3rd. pers.	hé **nereþ**		híe	

PRETERITE INDICATIVE

	singular		plural	
1st. pers.	ič **nerede**		wé	
2nd. pers.	þú **neredest**		ȝé	**neredon**
3rd. pers.	hé **nerede**		híe	

lǽran (teach)   lǽrde   lǽred

PRESENT INDICATIVE

	singular		plural	
1st. pers.	ič **lǽre**		wé	
2nd. pers.	þú **lǽrest**		ȝé	**lǽraþ**
3rd. pers.	hé **lǽreþ**		híe	

PRETERITE INDICATIVE

	singular		plural	
1st. pers.	ič **lǽrde**		wé	
2nd. pers.	þú **lǽrdest**		ȝé	**lǽrdon**
3rd. pers.	hé **lǽrde**		híe	

Some other types belonging to Class I are the following:

hreddan (rescue)	hredde	hredd
cwellan (kill)	cwealde	cweald
dreččan (oppress)	dreahte	dreaht
rǽčan (reach)	rǽhte	rǽht
séčan (seek)	sóhte	sóht
þenčan (think)	þóhte	þóht
þynčan (seem)	þúhte	þúht
bycgan (buy)	bohte	boht

wyrčan (work)	worhte	worht
lecgan (lay)	leȝde	leȝd
settan (set)	sette	sett/seted

Class II

Some more examples of this large class of weak verbs:

bifian (tremble)	bifode	bifod
bodian (announce)	bodode	bodod
clipian (call)	clipode	clipod
lufian (love)	lufode	lufod
macian (make)	macode	macod
þolian (endure)	þolode	þolod
wunian (dwell)	wunode	wunod

Class III

habban (have)   hæfde   hæfd

PRESENT INDICATIVE

singular   *plural*

1st. pers.	ič hæbbe	wé ⎫
2nd. pers.	þú hæfst/hafast	ȝé ⎬ habbaþ
3rd. pers.	hé hæfþ/hafaþ	híe ⎭

libban (live)   lifde   lifd

PRESENT INDICATIVE

singular   *plural*

1st. pers.	ič libbe	wé ⎫
2nd. pers.	þú lifast	ȝé ⎬ libbaþ
3rd. pers.	hé lifaþ	híe ⎭

secgan (say)   sæȝde   sæȝd

PRESENT INDICATIVE

singular   *plural*

1st. pers.	ič secge	wé ⎫
2nd. pers.	þú sæȝst	ȝé ⎬ secgaþ
3rd. pers.	hé sæȝeþ	híe ⎭

hycgan (think)   hogde hogod

PRESENT INDICATIVE

	singular	*plural*	
1st. pers.	ič **hycge**	wé	
2nd. pers.	þú **hyʒst**	ʒé	**hycgaþ**
3rd. pers.	hé **hyʒþ**	híe	

MORE ABOUT NOUNS

Further examples of noun declensions will alert the beginning student to the various types of endings he is most likely to encounter in his reading. These paradigms are merely a sampling of the many sets of endings to be found. The complexity of the noun inflections, while considerable, need not necessarily be a problem to students who are learning only to read the language. Note that many of the inflections are ambiguous and overlapping; the student will often be obliged to rely on other signals, such as the form of the definite article or the form of the verb accompanying a noun form.

scip (ship, a neuter noun)

	singular	*plural*
nom.	scip	scipu
gen.	scipes	scipa
dat.	scipe	scipum
acc.	scip	scipu

bearn (child, a neuter noun)

	singular	*plural*
nom.	bearn	bearn
gen.	bearnes	bearna
dat.	bearne	bearnum
acc.	bearn	bearn

mearh (horse, a masculine noun)

	singular	*plural*
nom.	mearh	méaras
gen.	méares	méara
dat.	méare	méarum
acc.	mearh	méaras

wuldor (glory, a neuter noun)

	singular	*plural*
nom.	wuldor	wuldor
gen.	wuldres	wuldra
dat.	wuldre	wuldrum
acc.	wuldor	wuldor

ʒiefu (gift, a feminine noun)

	singular	*plural*
nom.	ʒiefu	ʒiefa/ʒiefe
gen.	ʒiefe	ʒiefa/ʒiefena
dat.	ʒiefe	ʒiefum
acc.	ʒiefe	ʒiefa/ʒiefe

láf (remainder, a feminine noun)

	singular	*plural*
nom.	láf	láfa/láfe
gen.	láfe	láfa
dat.	láfe	láfum
acc.	láfe	láfa/láfe

hand (hand, a feminine noun)

	singular	*plural*
nom.	hand	handa
gen.	handa	handa
dat.	handa	handum
acc.	hand	handa

mann (man, a masculine noun)

	singular	*plural*
nom.	mann	menn
gen.	mannes	manna
dat.	menn	mannum
acc.	mann	menn

dohtor (daughter, a feminine noun)

	singular	*plural*
nom.	dohtor	dohtor
gen.	dohtor	dohtra
dat.	dehter	dohtrum
acc.	dohtor	dohtor

fréond (friend, a masculine noun)

	singular	*plural*
nom.	fréond	fríend
gen.	fréondes	fréonda
dat.	fríend/fréonde	fréondum
acc.	fréond	fríend

lamb (lamb, a neuter noun)

	singular	*plural*
nom.	lamb	lambru
gen.	lambes	lambra
dat.	lambe	lambrum
acc.	lamb	lambru

PRETERITE-PRESENT VERBS

The preterite-present verbs belong to a small but important class of verbs. These verbs had formerly been ordinary strong verbs, but for some reason their old strong preterite forms came to be used with the force of the present tense. In other words, the form of their present tense is like the form of the preterite tense of ordinary strong verbs. (This may be compared to the Modern English "I have got it," which is present perfect tense in form, although it is present tense in meaning.) Having used up their old original preterite forms to express present tense, these verbs adopted new preterite forms on the model of the weak verbs. Thus, the present tense looks like a strong-verb preterite, and the preterite tense looks like a weak-verb preterite.

Note that the principal parts given for these verbs are not the same as those given for either the weak verbs or the ordinary strong verbs.

infinitive	pres. indic. 1st. and 3rd. pers. sg.	pres. indic. 2nd. pers. sg.	pres. indic. pl.	pret. sg.
ágan (possess)	áh	áhst	ágon	áhte
cunnan (know how to)	cann	cannst	cunnon	cúðe
dugan (avail)	déag	déaht	dugon	dohte
durran (dare)	dearr	dearrst	durron	dorste
magan (be able)	mæʒ	meaht	magon	meahte
mótan (be permitted)	mót	móst	móton	móste
munan (remember)	man	manst	munon	munde
nugan (suffice)	neah		nugon	nohte
sculan (must)	sceal	scealt	sculon	scolde
unnan (grant)	ann	annst	unnon	úðe
witan (know)	wát	wást	witon	wiste
þurfan (need)	þearf	þearft	þurfon	þorfte

The past participles of two of these verbs have become high-frequency adjectives:

cúþ (known)
ágen (own).

I-UMLAUT IN OLD ENGLISH

AN understanding of i-umlaut (or i-mutation) will help the student of Old English to recognize that certain words are semantically related to each other, although there may be a discrepancy in their vowels. For example, when a student learns that the adjective *beald* means "bold" or "courageous," it is to his advantage to be able to recognize that the verb *bieldan,* which means "embolden" or "encourage," is derived from the adjective. He will see at once that, although the consonants in the adjective and the verb are the same, the vowels are different. A knowledge of the rudiments of i-umlaut will make it all clear, thus aiding him to increase his reading vocabulary in Old English and incidentally explaining to him a good deal about Modern English.

In order to explain i-umlaut, it is necessary to begin with several earlier sound changes: because the i-umlaut changes were made *after* these earlier sound changes, the vowel that undergoes i-umlaut in these cases is different from the vowel that the student will encounter in the unumlauted forms of such words. In these examples, an asterisk (*) will be used to indicate a hypothetical form, i.e., one which we assume must have pre-existed, although we have not actually found it in the extant written records. (The symbol > means "becomes.") These earlier sound changes are as follows:

1. *a* > *æ* except when followed by *w* or a nasal (*m* or *n*) or by a single consonant followed by *a, o,* or *u.*

Example: **hwat* > *hwæt* but **hwatu* remains *hwatu.*

2. *æ* preceded by the palatal consonants (*č*, *ʒ*, and *sc*) > *ea*. Examples: **čæster* > *čeaster; ʒæf* > *ʒeaf; *scæl* > *sceal.*

3. The Old English short vowel *o* has often come from an earlier Germanic *u*.

Example: **guld* > *gold.*

I-umlaut, which is common to most of the Germanic languages, is the fronting of back vowels caused by anticipating an *i* sound in the following syllable. In the examples given below, the *i* that causes the vowel to umlaut is not shown; what the student chiefly needs to be clear about is which words in Old English are in umlaut relationship to each other, so that he will see the semantic relationship between two words even when one of them has had its vowel changed by i-umlaut.

The table of umlaut equivalents, with examples, follows (the symbol ⋝ means "becomes by i-umlaut"):

$$a \gtrless e \quad (mann \gtrless menn)$$
$$o \gtrless e \quad (ofst \gtrless efstan)$$
$$u \gtrless y \quad (full \gtrless fyllan)$$
$$ea \gtrless ie \quad (eald \gtrless ieldra)$$
$$eo \gtrless ie \quad (ʒeorn \gtrless ʒiernan)$$
$$á \gtrless ǽ \quad (lár \gtrless lǽran)$$
$$ó \gtrless é \quad (dóm \gtrless déma)$$
$$ú \gtrless ý \quad (tún \gtrless týnan)$$
$$éa \gtrless íe \quad (héan \gtrless híenan)$$
$$éo \gtrless íe \quad (stéor \gtrless stíeran)$$

In connection with i-umlaut, it ought to be pointed out that there was a much earlier sound change, the mutation of Primitive Germanic *e* to *i* when followed by an *i* in the next syllable. This Primitive Germanic mutation accounts for such forms as the second- and third-person singular present indicative forms of such verbs as *helpan* and *beran,* which are *hilpst, hilpþ, birst, birþ.* Thus, the student may think of *e* ⋝ *i* as one more item in the table of umlaut equivalents given

43

above, although this change actually precedes the rest of the i-umlaut changes by several centuries.

Umlauted forms occur in Old English when an inflectional or derivational suffix contained an *i* sound. The following are the commonest situations in which the student will encounter pairs of words in Old English that are in umlaut relationship to each other.

INFLECTION

Nouns: The nominative and accusative plural and the dative and instrumental singular of some nouns are umlauted.

Examples: mann — menn
dohtor — dehter
tóþ — téþ
fréond — fríend
burg — byriʒ

Adjectives: Comparatives and superlatives of some adjectives (and adverbs) are umlauted.

Examples: eald — ieldra, ieldest
lang — lenʒra, lenʒest
héah — híehra/híerra, híehst

Verbs: The second- and third-person singular present indicative forms of many verbs are umlauted.

Examples: gán — gǽst, gǽþ
weorpan — wierpst, wierpþ
standan — stent (*stendeþ > *stendþ > stent)

DERIVATION

Verbs derived from nouns:

Examples:

noun	*verb*
fóda	fédan
béacen	bíecnan
*guld (> OE gold)	gyldan

44

Verbs derived from adjectives:

Examples:

adjective	verb
full	fyllan
fús	fýsan
ȝearu	ȝierwan

Weak verbs derived from strong verbs (from the preterite singular):

Examples:

strong verb	weak verb
fór (pret. sg. of *faran*)	féran
*sat (formerly pret. sg. of *sittan*)	settan
*lag (formerly pret. sg. of *licgan*)	lecgan

Abstract nouns formed from adjectives by adding the suffix *-iþo:*

Example:

adjective	abstract noun
héan	híenþu

Feminine nouns formed from masculine nouns by adding the suffix *-in:*

Example:

masc. noun	fem. noun
*fux (> OE fox)	fyxen

Adjectives meaning "made of (something)" formed from nouns by adding the suffix *-in:*

Examples:

noun	adjective
stán	stǽnen
*hurn (> OE horn)	hyrnen

Adjectives derived from nouns by adding the suffix *-isc:*

Examples:

noun	adjective
mann	mennisc
Angel	Englisc

OLD ENGLISH METRICS

THE metrical system by which Old English poetry was composed is entirely different from that of any kind of Modern English poetry. Old English poetry is alliterative. Although Modern English poetry sometimes uses alliteration, it is only a decoration, whereas in Old English poetry it is a structural necessity.

In Old English alliterative poetry, the unit is the verse. The verses are arranged in alliterating pairs. A verse-pair is the same as a typographic line. A verse is often called a half-line. It is customary to refer to the first half-line as the on-verse and to call the second half-line the off-verse.

Each on-verse alliterates with its off-verse; that is, at least one stressed syllable in the on-verse begins with the same sound as one stressed syllable in the off-verse. For example:

ȝe-wát þá twelfa sum   torne ȝe-bolgen.

The on-verse usually has two alliterating syllables, although it may have only one. Double alliteration occurs only in the on-verse; the off-verse always has single alliteration. For example:

flód blóde wéoll   —folc tó sáwon—
hátan heolfre.   Horn stundum sang.

With a few exceptions, every sound alliterates with itself. Thus, a word beginning with b alliterates with another word beginning with b. For example:

46

*b*eorna *b*éag-ʒiefa   and his *b*róðor éac.

Any vowel is considered to alliterate with any other vowel. Thus, a word beginning with *ea* alliterates with a word beginning with *o* and with one beginning with *ie,* or with any other vowel or dipthong. For example :

*ea*ldres *o*r-wéna,   *ie*rringa slóg.

Impure *s* (*s* in a consonant cluster) is refined still further in this system : *sc* alliterates only with *sc ; st* alliterates only with *st ;* and *sp* (much rarer) alliterates only with *sp.* Other types of impure *s,* such as *sw* and *sl,* are treated the same as *s* plus a vowel. For example :

*sc*adu-helma ʒe-*sc*apu   *sc*ríðan cómon
*st*rǽt wæs *st*án-fág,   *st*íʒ wísode
*s*áwol-dréore,   *s*wát ýðum wéoll.

Palatalized *c* (pronounced like the *ch* in *church*) is considered to alliterate with unpalatalized *c* (pronounced like *k*). For example :

*c*úðe folme ;   *č*earu wæs ʒe-níewod.

Palatalized ʒ (pronounced like the *y* in *year*) is considered to alliterate with unpalatalized *g* (pronounced like the *g* in *good*). For example :

*g*ód-fremmendra   swelčum ʒifeðe biþ.

This slight artificiality has crept into Old English poetry because the Old Germanic poetic tradition was established long before these sounds palatalized. In dealing with *c* and *g,* then, the student may be guided by the appearance of the letters more than by their sound.

The words that alliterate in Old English poetry are usually nouns, adjectives, and adverbs, although other words such as

47

finite verbs and even pronouns and prepositions sometimes alliterate also.

THE FIVE TYPES OF VERSES

The basic system of scanning Old English poetry is known as the Sievers Five Types, named for the great German scholar, Eduard Sievers, who first analyzed the rhythmic types of Old Germanic poetry in his book, *Altgermanische Metrik* (Halle, 1893). The Sievers Five Types are A, B, C, D, and E, given these designations on the basis of frequency: A-verses are commonest, and E-verses are rarest.

All poetry is, of course, closely related to prose speech and takes its features from the nature of the language in which it is composed. For example, alliteration seems natural and even inevitable in the Germanic languages, which place a strong stress on the first syllable of most words. It seems clear that Old English was a three-stress language: that is, Old English had three levels of stress (or loudness) that were phonemic (responded to as signals by native speakers). We call these stress levels *primary, secondary,* and *weak* (in contrast to Modern English, which has four: primary, secondary, tertiary, and unstressed syllables). It is customary for structural linguists to indicate primary stress with a mark that is something like an acute accent, only larger, thus: ⁄. We shall use this symbol for primary stress in Old English poetry. Although a mark something like a circumflex, only larger, ⁀, is used to indicate secondary stress in Modern English, it seems on the whole best not to use it for Old English, because many editors now use such a mark for a special purpose in Old English poetic texts, which will be explained below (under the heading of Defective Formulas). We shall therefore indicate secondary stress by means of a mark that looks like a grave accent, only larger, ⟍. The weak-stressed syllables can be left unmarked, or a small X can be used. Our system, then, is:

$$\begin{array}{ll} \text{primary} & / \\ \text{secondary} & \backslash \\ \text{weak} & \times. \end{array}$$

Syllables that would receive a primary stress in a prose sentence usually receive it also in Old English poetry. For example, in the noun compound *word-hord,* the first element of the compound, *word,* gets primary stress, and *hord* gets secondary stress:

$$\overset{/\quad\backslash}{\text{word-hord.}}$$

A good way to begin scanning Old English poetry is to read it first just as if it were prose; the alliteration and the stresses usually become clear.

It is necessary now to explain the difference between a long syllable and a short syllable in Old English. A syllable is long if it has a long vowel (marked by the editor with a diacritic, such as the acute accent used in this book) or if it is a closed syllable. A closed syllable is one which has two consonants between the vowel of the syllable and the vowel of the next syllable; the second consonant is considered to be part of the next syllable, but the first one ends or closes the first syllable. Thus, the first syllable of *ende* is long, because it is closed by the *n*. We divide it into syllables thus: *en de.* In the word *hete,* both syllables are short. We divide it thus: *he te.* The short diphthongs, *ea, eo,* and *ie,* are just as short as the short monophthongs, *a, æ, e, i, o, u,* and *y.*

Each verse of Old English poetry is composed of two measures. In A-, D-, and E-verses, if there is double alliteration, there is one alliterating syllable in each measure; in B- and C-verses, if there is double alliteration, both alliterating syl-

49

lables are in the second measure. We shall indicate the boundary between measures by a vertical line:

wann under | wolcnum.

A-verses

In A-verses, the second measure is sharply limited, while the first measure can vary more. A normal A-verse (in the on-verse) usually has an alliterating stress at the beginning of each measure:

béaga | *b*ryttan.

The second measure of an A-verse can be primary-weak or primary-secondary:

$$\overset{/\quad\times}{\text{folc and}} \mid \overset{/\times}{\text{ríče}}$$

$$\overset{/\quad\times}{\text{strǽt wæs}} \mid \overset{/\quad\diagdown}{\text{stán-fág.}}$$

These are the only possibilities in the second measure of an A-verse, except for their resolved-stress equivalents (see the section on resolved stress, below) and a special kind of verse called the A4-verse, explained below.

The first measure of a normal A-verse begins with an alliterating stress, which may be followed by as little as (never less than) one weak-stressed syllable, but may be followed by a secondary stress *or* a secondary stress plus one or more weak stresses *or* by several weak stresses. The first measure of an A-verse, then, can vary considerably:

$$\overset{/\quad\times}{\text{mǽrne}} \mid \text{þéoden}$$

$$\overset{/\quad\times\ \times}{\text{wann under}} \mid \text{wolcnum}$$

$$\overset{/\quad\diagdown}{\text{frum-sceaft}} \mid \text{fíra}$$

Gúþ-láf and | Ós-láf

híerde ič þæt hé þone | heals-béag.

If an A-verse has double alliteration, each measure has an alliterating syllable:

beorhtre | bóte.

If a normal A-verse has single alliteration, the alliteration is only at the beginning of the first measure:

áne | hwíle.

Since all off-verses have only single alliteration, any A-verse in the off-verse always has its alliteration in the first measure.

Examples of A-Verses

With double alliteration:

dryhtnes | dóme

sund wiþ | sande

wicg ʒe-|wende

líexte se | léoma

bát under | beorge

eorla ofer | eorðan

wǽpnum ʒe-|weorðod

$$\overset{\diagup\quad\times\quad\diagup\quad\diagdown}{\text{féondes} \mid \text{fót-lást}}$$

$$\overset{\diagup\qquad\times\qquad\diagup\quad\diagdown}{\text{heard and} \mid \text{hring-mǽl}}$$

$$\overset{\diagup\times\quad\times\quad\diagup\quad\diagdown}{\text{ídel and} \mid \text{un-nytt}}$$

$$\overset{\diagup\quad\times\quad\times\quad\diagup\qquad\diagdown}{\text{helmas and} \mid \text{heard sweord.}}$$

With single alliteration:

$$\overset{\diagup\quad\times\quad\diagup\quad\times}{\text{gangan} \mid \text{cómon}}$$

$$\overset{\diagup\quad\times\qquad\diagup\quad\times}{\text{findan} \mid \text{meahte}}$$

$$\overset{\diagup\quad\times\quad\diagup\quad\times}{\text{wunden-}\vert\text{stefna}}$$

$$\overset{\diagup\quad\times\quad\times\quad\diagup\quad\times}{\text{ǽdre ʒe-}\vert\text{cýðan}}$$

$$\overset{\diagup\quad\times\quad\times\quad\diagup\quad\times}{\text{habban ne} \mid \text{meahte}}$$

$$\overset{\diagup\times\quad\diagup\quad\diagdown}{\text{léofa} \mid \text{Béo-wulf}}$$

$$\overset{\diagup\quad\times\quad\diagup\quad\diagdown}{\text{manna} \mid \text{ǽʒ-hwelč.}}$$

A3-VERSES

A distinct kind of A-verse, usually called the A3-verse, has the alliteration only in the second measure. The first measure is composed of at least two syllables. For example:

$$\text{lét se} \mid \text{\textit{h}earda.}$$

The first measure of an A3-verse is to be read as if the first syllable were an important syllable, giving it a primary stress, although it might be some ordinarily unimportant word such as *þá*. For example:

þá wæs ʒe-|síene.

A3-verses are found only in the on-verse.

Examples of A3-Verses

/ × × / ×
þá wæs on | sǽlum

/ × × / ×
cóm þá to | lande

/ × × / ×
þá wæs be | feaxe

/ × × / ×
æfter þǽm | wordum

/ × × / ×
swá hé ne | meahte

/ × × × / ×
bútan hit wæs | máre

/ × × × × / ×
þára-þe hé ʒe-|worhte

/ × × × / \
ǽr hé þone | grund-wang.

A4-VERSES

A very few A-verses have an exceptionally light second
measure consisting of only two short syllables. For example:

wæl-níþ | wera.

The traditional method of dealing with these exceptional A-
verses has been to distort the words and read the first syllable
of the second measure as if it were long. For a new suggestion
as to how to scan these verses, refer to the discussion of resolved stress, below.

Examples of A4-Verses

With double alliteration:

$$\acute{/} \quad \searrow \quad / \quad \times$$
wíd-cúþ | werum

$$/ \quad \searrow \quad / \quad \times$$
gúþ-horn | galan

$$/ \quad \searrow \quad / \quad \times$$
sorg-léas | swefan.

With single alliteration:

$$/ \quad \searrow \quad / \quad \times$$
frum-cynn | witan

$$/ \quad \searrow \quad / \quad \times$$
féa-sceaft | guma

$$/ \quad \times \quad / \quad \times$$
hwílum | dydon.

B-verses

B- and C-verses have a heavy second measure and a light first measure. If a B-verse has single alliteration, the alliterating stress comes at the beginning of the second measure. If a B-verse has double alliteration, both alliterating syllables are in the second measure.

The first measure of a B- or C-verse is the light measure and may contain from one to five unimportant syllables. Reading such a measure as if it were prose will usually show quite clearly which syllables are more important than the others. When B- and C-verse first measures contain three, four, or five syllables, the best practice is to do essentially what is done with the first measure of an A3-verse: stress the first syllable more strongly than the others. When the first measure of a B- or C-verse contains one or two syllables, it is customary to assume that there is an initial rest, which may have been a strum on the harp with which the poet accompanied himself.

We can indicate such an initial rest by a stress mark in parentheses, thus: $(/)$.

The second measure of a B-verse is either primary-weak-secondary or primary-weak-weak-secondary:

$$× (×)|/ × \textbackslash$$
$$× (×)|/ ×× \textbackslash.$$

For example:

$$× × / × \textbackslash$$
þǽr æt | hýðe stód

$$× / × \textbackslash$$
on | sídne sǽ

$$× × / × × \textbackslash$$
ac on | campe ȝe-crang

$$× × / × × \textbackslash$$
him be-|beorgan ne cann.

The system of scanning B- and C-verses outlined here was originated by John C. Pope in *The Rhythm of Beowulf* (New Haven, Conn., 1942). One may think of our system as the Sievers theorem plus the Pope corollary.

A prominent feature of the Pope system is that it is isochronic, that is, he assumes that every measure occupies the same length of time. It is evident that the theory of initial rests grows logically out of and is a necessary concomitant to the isochronic analysis of the poetry. Although the Pope system is favored by many, if not most, scholars today, it is not possible to prove that Old English poetry is isochronic or that the poets used any kind of initial rest. A student can learn to recognize the Five Types and scan Old English poetry, however, without reading it as isochronic or without in any way indicating initial rests. Indeed, there seems to be no good way to indicate such rests, short of tapping on a table while reading, surely best avoided. It is possible to urge caution regarding the two features of the Pope system that are perhaps difficult to prove, isochronism and the initial rest, while at the same time appreciating the very great contribution that the Pope system has made to the analysis of Old English poetry: Pope's perception that B- and C-verses are radically different from other types of verses in having all their alliteration, even when double, in the second measure. The Sievers system, and every other system until Pope's, failed to make poetic sense of the B- and C-verses. By moving the line between the first and second measures of B- and C-verses one syllable to the left of where Sievers drew it, Pope has solved the riddle of the music of Old English poetry.

Examples of B-Verses

With double alliteration:

$$\times \quad / \times \quad \backslash$$
þes | hearda héap

$$\times\times \quad / \quad \times \quad \backslash$$
ofer | mierčan mór

$$\times \quad \times \quad / \times \quad \backslash$$
wæs þæt | beorhte bold

$$\times \quad \times \quad \times \quad / \quad \times \quad \backslash$$
for-þǽm hé | manna mǽst

$$\times \times \times \times \quad / \quad \times \quad \backslash$$
þéah-þe hé his | bróðor bearn

$$\times \quad / \times \times \quad \backslash$$
þǽm | wífe þá word

$$\times\times \quad / \times \times \quad \backslash$$
ofer | borda ʒe-bræc

$$\times \quad \times \quad / \quad \times \times \quad \backslash$$
sé-þe his | worda ʒe-weald.

With single alliteration:

$$\times \quad / \quad \times \quad \backslash$$
ymb | brantne ford

$$\times \quad \times \quad / \times \quad \backslash$$
him þá | ellen-róf

56

$$\times \times \quad / \quad \times \quad \searrow$$
þá ič | furðum wéold

$$\times \quad / \quad \times \times \quad \searrow$$
on | féonda ʒe-weald

$$\times \quad \times \quad / \times \times \quad \searrow$$
þǽr mæʒ | nihta ʒe-hwǽm

$$\times \quad \times \times \quad / \times \times \quad \searrow$$
þéah-þe hé | dǽda ʒe-hwæs.

C-verses

The C-verse is very much like the B-verse. The first measure of a C-verse is exactly like the first measure of a B-verse: from one to five unimportant syllables.

Like the B-verse, if a C-verse has single alliteration, the alliterating syllable comes at the beginning of the second measure. If a C-verse has double alliteration, both alliterating syllables are in the second measure.

The second measure of a C-verse is primary-secondary-weak or primary-weak-weak:

$$\times \ (\times) \ | \ / \searrow \times$$
$$\times \ (\times) \ | \ / \times \times.$$

For example:

$$\times \quad / \quad \searrow \times$$
for | mann-cynne

$$\times \times \quad / \quad \searrow \times$$
ofer | hran-ráde

$$\times \quad \times \quad \times \times \quad / \quad \searrow \times$$
þæs-þe him ǽr | God sealde

$$\times \quad / \quad \times \times$$
on | bǽl-stede

$$\times \times \quad / \quad \times \times$$
ofer | wíd wæter

$$\times \quad \times \quad \times \quad / \quad \times \times$$
þæt him se | líč-hama.

Examples of C-Verses

With double alliteration:

of | brýd-búre

þæt hé | má móste

ʒeond | wíd-wegas

for-|grand gramum

on ʒe-|flit faran.

With single alliteration:

on | wæl-bedde

ac hé | mann-cynnes

þæs-þe him | ýþ-láde

on | béor-sele

þæt hé his | fréond wrece.

D-verses

A D-verse is like a B- or C-verse with an alliterating stress in the first measure. That is, the second measure of a D-verse is usually the equivalent of the second measure of a B- or C-verse:

hár | hilde-rinc

léof | land-fruma.

If a D-verse has double alliteration, there is an alliterating stress at the beginning of each measure. If a D-verse has single alliteration, it is always only in the first measure:

/   / × ×   \
*ea*ld | *e*nta ʒe-weorc

/   / ×   \
*s*wát | *ý*ðum wéoll

/   / × ×
*s*ecg | *w*ísode

/   /   \ ×
*f*éond | *m*ann-cynnes.

The first measure of a D-verse may be as little as one alliterating primary-stressed syllable, but it may be rather free and extended, much like the first measure of an A-verse. For example:

/
*þ*éod | eall-ʒearu

/   \
*sc*éotend | *S*cieldinga

/   × ×
*w*angas and | *w*ǐc-stede

/   × × ×
*s*org is mé to | secgenne.

Examples of D-Verses

With double alliteration:

/   /   \ ×
*w*earp | *w*æl-fýre

/   /   × ×
*sc*earp | *sc*ield-wiga

/   / ×   \
*f*ród | *f*olces weard

/   / × ×   \
*s*éon | *s*ibbe-ʒe-dryht

$$\acute{d}\text{réfan} \mid \acute{d}\text{éop wæter.}$$

With single alliteration:

$$\acute{t}\text{orn} \mid \text{un-lýtel}$$

$$\acute{h}\text{ord} \mid \text{scéawian}$$

$$\acute{b}\text{læd} \mid \text{wíde sprang}$$

$$w\acute{\text{i}}_{3} \mid \text{ealle for-nam}$$

$$\acute{o}\text{ftost} \mid \text{wísode.}$$

E-verses

An E-verse is something like a D-verse turned around:
the first measure of an E-verse is approximately the equivalent of the second measure of a C-verse, that is, primary-
secondary-weak, while the second measure is very short. The
second measure of an E-verse is sharply limited: it can be
only one primary stress (or its resolved-stress equivalent,
which see below in the section on resolved stress). For example:

$$\acute{m}\text{urnende} \mid \acute{m}\text{ód}$$

$$W\text{ælsinges 3e-}|\acute{w}\text{inn.}$$

If an E-verse has double alliteration, there is an alliterating
syllable in each measure. If an E-verse has single alliteration,
the alliterating syllable is at the beginning of the first measure.
For example:

$$\text{sorg-fullne} \mid \text{síþ}$$

$$n\text{iht-langne} \mid \text{first.}$$

Although the E-verse is heavily weighted on the first measure, the Pope system holds that some balance is maintained by assuming that a final rest comes at the end of the second measure. For example:

/ ＼× / (＼)
wæččendne | wer .

Examples of E-Verses

With double alliteration:

/ ＼× /
blǽd-fæstne | beorn

/ ＼ × /
bán-hús ʒe-|bræc

/＼× × /
Wélandes ʒe-|weorc.

With single alliteration:

/ ＼ × /
feorh-bennum | séoc

/ ＼× × /
folc-rihta ʒe-|hwelč

/ ＼ × /
word-hord on-|léac.

ANACRUSIS

Some verses have one or two unimportant syllables, often a weak-stressed prefix such as ʒe-, which seem to come *before* the first measure. It is as if the syllable (or syllables) has to be run in quickly, like a grace note, before launching into the measure itself. Anacrusis usually consists of a single syllable, but disyllabic anacrusis is also found. More than two syllables of anacrusis is rare. For example:

ʒe-|wát þá ofer | wǽʒ-holm
ofer |wearp þá | wériʒ-mód
ne ʒe-|wéox hé him to | willan.

RESOLVED STRESS

In all the examples cited thus far, the stressed syllables have
been long syllables. A possible variation is called resolved
stress, in which two short syllables combine to make the
equivalent of one long syllable. If the verb *hogode,* for example, is in a verse where it receives the important stress,
the first two syllables would be resolved into the equivalent
of one long syllable, thus:

$$\overset{\diagup}{\underset{\smile}{\text{x x}}}\ \text{x}$$

(It may illustrate the principle involved to imagine the result
if the second *o* in *hogode* disappeared by syncopation, as
indeed this verb often occurs: *hogde.* It would then be two
syllables, the first one closed and thus long: *hogde,* the exact
metrical equivalent of resolving the stress of the first two syllables of the unsyncopated form of the word.)

In cases of resolved stress, the first of the two syllables is
always short: it must have a short vowel (or diphthong) and
be open; that is, only one consonant comes between it and the
next vowel. The second syllable in resolved stress is somewhat
freer: it may be a closed syllable, but it may never have a
long vowel. For example:

weorolde $\overset{\diagup}{\underset{\smile}{\text{x x}}}\ \text{x}$

In many of the rhythmic types, resolved stress can fill the
role of a long syllable. For example, it can always receive the
primary stress at the beginning of an A-, D-, or E-verse:

(A-verse)	*s*igora Wealdend	$\overset{\diagup}{\underset{\smile}{\text{x x}}}\ \text{x} \mid \diagup \text{x}$
(D-verse)	*m*agu Ecg-láfes	$\overset{\diagup}{\underset{\smile}{\text{x x}}} \mid \diagup \diagdown \text{x}$
(E-verse)	*w*lite-beorhtne *w*ang	$\overset{\diagup}{\underset{\smile}{\text{x x}}} \diagdown \text{x} \mid \diagup$

62

Resolved stress can also receive the primary stress in the second measure of all five types of verses:

(A-verse)	*fús æt faroðe*	/ × | x́x ×
(B-verse)	*ofer fealone flód*	× × | x́x × \
(C-verse)	*hú þá æðelingas*	× × | x́x \ ×
(D-verse)	*wlanc Wedera léod*	/ | x́x × \
(E-verse)	*wynn-léasne wudu*	/ \ × | x́x

The two most rigidly restricted kinds of second measures, the second measure of an A-verse and the second measure of an E-verse, thus have one more possible variant. The second measure of a normal A-verse can ordinarily be only primary-secondary or primary-weak, but the primary stress of both these subtypes can be resolved stress:

$$\textit{mǽʒ and magu-þegn} \qquad / \times \mid \text{x́x} \; \setminus$$

$$\textit{hord-burg hæleða} \qquad / \setminus \mid \text{x́x} \; \times$$

The second measure of an E-verse is even more restricted. Leaving resolved stress aside, the only possibility is one primary stress. For example:

$$\textit{swíþ-ferhþes síþ} \qquad / \setminus \times \mid /$$

Resolved stress adds one more possible variant. For example:

$$\textit{sǽ-manna searu} \qquad / \setminus \times \mid \text{x́x}$$

In B-verses, the secondary stress at the end of the second measure may also be resolved stress. For example:

æfter *b*illes *b*ite   × × | ╱ × ×͜×

ofer *f*lóda ʒe-nipu   × × | ╱ × × ×͜×

In C-verses, the secondary stress in the second measure may also be resolved stress. For example:

hé on *we*ʒ losode   × × | ╱ ×͜× ×

and on *m*ere starodon   × × | ×͜× ×͜× ×

Caution: resolved stress can never come at the end of the second measure of an A-verse or a C-verse.

It has recently been suggested* that a combination of resolved stress and a final rest, as at the end of an E-verse, might allow a smoother scansion of the A4-verses, in which the second measure seems to be deficient, containing only two short syllables. For example:

bord-weall clufon.

The two short syllables of the second measure may be resolved into one primary stress and the measure is then finished off with a final rest:

bord-weall clufon   ╱ ╲ | ×͜× (╲)

EXPANDED VERSES

In addition to the Five Types of normal verses, a type of long line is occasionally found in Old English poetry. These expanded or hypermetric verses are very much rarer than the normal types of verses. They are usually found in groups of five or six lines, which seem to be scattered here and there in

* Robert P. Creed, "A New Approach to the Rhythm of *Beowulf*," *PMLA*, LXXXI (March 1966), 27.

poems otherwise composed of normal verses. It used to be assumed that the expanded verses were used to achieve an effect of solemnity or importance, but there seems to be no stylistic common denominator to the various patches of expanded verses found throughout Old English poetry. Some poems, such as *Judith* and *The Dream of the Rood,* contain a great many expanded verses. Other poems have none at all. *Beowulf* has three short patches of expanded verses, twenty-two verses in all, out of a total of over 6,000 verses.

Upon analysis, expanded verses seem to contain not the usual two measures, but three. Perhaps the simplest way to scan these verses is to assume that the second measure is the equivalent of a whole normal A-, D-, or E-verse. That is, each expanded verse may be said to have the equivalent of a whole normal A-, D-, or E-verse embedded in it. For example:

sigor and **sóþne ȝe-léafan,**   þæt ič mid þýs **sweorde móte**
éades and **ellen-dǽde.**   Hogodon þá **eorlas a-weččan.**

(The portions in boldface type would be normal A-verses if they stood alone.)

In the on-verse, the first measures of an expanded verse is usually the equivalent of the first measure of an A-verse. For example:

／   ✕ ✕✕
*wu*rpon hira | *wǽ*pen of dúne.

In the off-verse, the first measure of an expanded verse is usually the equivalent of the first measure of a B- or C-verse, one or more unimportant syllables. For example:

✕ ✕
hét þá | *ni*ða ȝe-blanden.

Expanded verses, like normal verses, usually have double alliteration in the on-verse and single alliteration in the off-verse.

The usual practice with the expanded verses is to read them slowly, at about half the speed of the normal verses.

DEFECTIVE FORMULAS

Where a traditional poetic formula persists in the extant Old English poetry, even though sound-changes have altered it in such a way that it no longer scans properly, some editors have adopted the practice of indicating that such a verse is not defective by using a special diacritic mark over one syllable. For example, the verse *héan húses* contains only three syllables, not enough, of course, for a correct verse. The problem here is that the adjective *héan* is now a monosyllable, although when the formula came into being it was disyllabic, **héahan*. It seems clear that the Anglo-Saxon poets preferred to keep these formulas and assigned to them the metrical weight that they had before the phonological developments that shortened them. While it is unthinkable to restore such archaic forms as **héahan,* an editor can indicate that the word is to be read as if it were still two syllables in order to keep the meter intact: he places a circumflex over the syllable. For example:

> nêan bídan
> feorh-séoc flêon
> déaþ-wíč sêon
> on flett gǽþ.

(This practice of using a diacritic like a circumflex is the reason alluded to earlier for not adopting the circumflex as the mark to indicate secondary stress, as is usually done in phonemic transcription of Modern English.)

A FEW POINTS TO KEEP IN MIND ABOUT SCANSION

1. Always look for the alliteration in a line first. The rhythmic pattern will usually fall into place around it.

2. Disregard weak-stressed prefixes, such as *ȝe-* and *ofer-*, when looking for alliteration. For examples, although the noun *be-gang* begins with a *b*, it alliterates on *g*.

3. No verse can ever have fewer than four syllables. If it has fewer than four, it is defective. It may, of course, have *more* than four.

4. Although an unimportant syllable, such as the prefix *ȝe-*, may be anacrusis at the beginning of an A-, D-, or E-verse, it may be the entire first measure of a B- or C-verse.

5. Resolved stress can never come at the very end of an A- or C-verse.

6. A3-verses occur only in the on-verse.

A SELECTIVE LIST OF
HELPFUL WORKS

Grammars
Campbell, A. *Old English Grammar*. Oxford, 1959.
Quirk, Randolph, and C. L. Wrenn. *An Old English Grammar*. London, 1958.

Dictionaries
Bessinger, J. B. *A Short Dictionary of Anglo-Saxon Poetry*. Toronto, 1960.
Bosworth, Joseph, and T. N. Toller. *An Anglo-Saxon Dictionary*. Oxford, 1898. *Supplement* (by Toller alone), Oxford, 1921.
Hall, John R. Clark. *A Concise Anglo-Saxon Dictionary*. Cambridge, 1931.
Holthausen, F. *Altenglisches Etymologisches Wörterbuch*. Heidelberg, 1934.
Sweet, Henry. *The Student's Dictionary of Anglo-Saxon*. Oxford, 1896.

Definitive Edition of the Entire Corpus of Old English Poetry
Krapp, George Philip, and Elliott Van Kirk Dobbie, eds. *The Anglo-Saxon Poetic Records, a collective edition*. New York, 1931–53.
    I. *The Junius Manuscript*
    II. *The Vercelli Book*

III. *The Exeter Book*
IV. *Beowulf* and *Judith*
 V. *The Paris Psalter* and *The Meters of Boethius*
VI. *The Anglo-Saxon Minor Poems*

Meter

Pope, John Collins. *The Rhythm of Beowulf*. New Haven, Conn., 1942.
Sievers, Eduard. *Altgermanische Metrik*. Halle, 1893.

Critical Discussions of Old English Literature

Anderson, George K. *The Literature of the Anglo-Saxons*. Princeton, N.J., 1949.
Greenfield, Stanley B. *A Critical History of Old English Literature*. New York, 1965.
Wrenn, C. L. *A Study of Old English Literature*. New York, 1967.

PROSE

The Voyages of Óht-here and Wulf-stán
in Scandinavia and the Baltic

Óht-here sæʒde his hláforde, Ælf-rǽde cyninge, þæt hé eallra
Norþ-manna norþ-mǽst búde. Hé cwæþ þæt hé búde on þǽm
lande norþ-weardum wiþ þá West-sǽ. Hé sæʒde þéah þæt
þæt land síe swíðe lang norþ þanan, ac hit is eall wéste, bútan
5 on féawum stówum styčče-mǽlum wíciaþ Finnas, on huntoðe
on wintre and on sumore on fiscoðe be þǽre sǽ.
Hé sæʒde þæt hé æt sumum čierre wolde fandian hú lange
þæt land norþ-rihte láge, oþþe hwæðer ǽniʒ mann be norðan
þǽm wéstene búde. Þá fór hé norþ-rihte be þǽm lande: lét
10 him eallne weʒ þæt wéste land on þæt stéor-bord and þá
wíd-sǽ on þæt bæc-bord þríe dagas. Þá wæs hé swá feorr
norþ swá hwæl-huntan fierrest faraþ. Þá fór hé þá-ʒíet norþ-
rihte swá feorr swá hé meahte on þǽm óðrum þrim dagum
ʒe-siʒlan. Þá béag þæt land þǽr éast-rihte, oþþe séo sǽ inn
15 on þæt land—hé niste hwæðer—bútan hé wiste þæt hé þǽr
bád westan-windes and hwón norðan, and siʒlde þá éast be
lande swá swá hé meahte on féower dagum ʒe-siʒlan. Þá
scolde hé þǽr bídan riht-norðan-windes, for-þǽm þæt land
béag þǽr súþ-rihte, oþþe séo sǽ inn on þæt land—hé niste
20 hwæðer.
Þá siʒlde hé þanan súþ-rihte be lande swá swá hé meahte
on fíf dagum ʒe-siʒlan. Þá læʒ þǽr án mičel éa upp inn on

The Voyages of Ohthere and Wulfstan
(*Translation*)

Ohthere told his lord, King Alfred, that he lived farthest north of all Norsemen. He said that he lived in the northern land (i.e., northern part of the country) along the West Sea (i.e., the North Atlantic). He said, however, that the land extends (lit. is) very far north from there, but it is all uninhabited, except (that) Lapps dwell in a few places here and there, (engaged) in hunting in winter and in fishing in the sea in summer.

He said that he once (lit. at a certain time) wanted to find out how far the land might extend due north, or whether any man was living north of the uninhabited (part). Then he traveled due north along the land : the whole way he kept (lit. left) the uninhabited land on his starboard and the open sea on his port for three days. Then he was as far north as the farthest that the whale-hunters go. Then he still kept going due north as far as he could sail in the second three days. Then the land curved due east there, or the sea (ran) inland —he did not know which—but he knew that he waited there for a wind from the west and a little north, and he sailed east then along the land as (far) as he was able to sail in four days. Then he had to wait there for a wind from due north, because the land curved due south there, or the sea inland— he did not know which.

Then he sailed due south from there along the land as (far) as he was able to sail in five days. Then at that point a large

þæt land. Þá čierdon híe upp inn on þá éa, for-þǽm híe ne
dorston forþ be þǽre éa siʒlan for un-friðe, for-þǽm þæt
land wæs eall ʒe-bún on óðre healfe þǽre éa. Ne métte hé ǽr
nán ʒe-bún land siþþan hé fram his ágnum háme fór; ac him
5 wæs eallne weʒ wéste land on þæt stéor-bord, bútan fiscerum
and fugolerum and huntum, and þæt wǽron eall Finnas. And
him wæs á wíd-sǽ on þæt bæc-bord.

Þá Beormas hæfdon swíðe wel ʒe-búd hira land, ac híe ne
dorston þǽr-on cuman. Ac þára Ter-Finna land wæs eall
10 wéste, bútan þǽr huntan ʒe-wícodon, oþþe fisceras, oþþe
fugoleras.

Fela spella him sæʒdon þá Beormas ǽʒðer ʒe of hira ágnum
lande ʒe of þǽm landum þe ymb híe útan wǽron, ac hé niste
hwæt þæs sóðes wæs, for-þǽm hé hit self ne ʒe-seah. Þá
15 Finnas, him þúhte, and þá Beormas sprǽcon néah án ʒe-
þéode.

Swíðost hé fór þider, to éacan þæs landes scéawunge, for
þǽm hors-hwalum, for-þǽm híe habbaþ swíðe æðele bán on
hira tóðum. Þá téþ híe bróhton sume þǽm cyninge. And hira
20 hýd biþ swíðe gód to scip-rápum. Sé hwæl biþ mičele lǽssa
þonne óðre hwalas: ne biþ hé lenʒra þonne seofon elna lang.
Ac on his ágnum lande is se betsta hwæl-huntoþ: þá béoþ
eahta and féowertiʒes elna lange, and þá mǽstan fíftiʒes elna
lange; þára hé sæʒde þæt hé siexa sum of-slóge siextiʒ on
25 twǽm dagum.

Hé wæs swíðe spédiʒ mann on þǽm ǽhtum þe hira spéda
on béoþ, þæt is, on wildrum. Hé hæfde þá-ʒíet, þá hé þone
cyning sóhte, tamra déora un-be-bohtra siex hund. Þá déor
híe hátaþ hránas. Þára wǽron siex stǽl-hránas; þá béoþ
30 swíðe díere mid Finnum, for-þǽm híe fóþ þá wildan hránas
mid. Hé wæs mid þǽm fyrstum mannum on þǽm lande.
Nǽfde hé þéah má þonne twéntiʒ hríðera, and twéntiʒ scéapa,
and twéntiʒ swína. And þæt lýtle þæt hé erede, hé erede mid
horsan.

river extended up inland. Then they turned up into the river, because they did not dare sail past the river for (fear of) hostility (of the natives), because the country was all inhabited on the other side of the river. He had not encountered any (lit. no) inhabited land before (this) since he had left his own home; for (lit. but) the uninhabited land had been on his starboard the whole way, except for fishermen and fowlers and hunters, and they were all Lapps. And the open sea was always on his port.

The Permians had cultivated their land very well, but they did not dare to go in there. But the land of the Terfinns was all uninhabited, except where hunters camped, or fishermen, or fowlers.

The Permians told him many stories both of their own country and of the countries that lay around them, but he did not know how much of it was true (lit. what was of the truth), because he did not see it himself. The Lapps, it seemed to him, and the Permians spoke nearly the same (lit. one) language.

He went there chiefly, in addition to exploring the country, for the walruses, because they have very fine ivory in their teeth. They brought some (of) these teeth to the king. And their hide is very good for ship-ropes. This whale (i.e. walrus: in O.E., lit. horse-whale) is much smaller than other whales: it will not be more (lit. longer) than seven ells long. But the best whaling is in his own country: those (whales) are forty-eight ells long, and the largest fifty ells long; he said that he and five others (lit. he as one of six) killed sixty of those in two days.

He was a very prosperous man in those possessions in which their wealth consists (lit. is), that is, in wild animals. He still had, when he visited the king, six hundred unsold tame animals. They call these animals reindeer. Of these, six were decoy-reindeer; those are very valuable among the Lapps, because they catch the wild reindeer with (them). He was among the foremost men in the country. He did not have more than twenty cattle, however, and twenty sheep, and twenty pigs. And the little that he plowed, he plowed with horses.

Ac hira ár is mǽst on þǽm gafole þe þá Finnas him ȝieldaþ. Þæt gafol biþ on déora fellum, and on fugola feðerum, and hwæles báne, and on þǽm scip-rápum þe béoþ of hwæles hýde ȝe-worht and of séoles. Æȝ-hwelč ȝielt be his ȝe-byrdum.

5 Se byrdesta sceal ȝieldan fíftíene mearðes fell, and fíf hránes, and án biren fell, and tíen ambra feðra, and birenne cyrtel oþþe yterenne, and twéȝen scip-rápas; ǽȝðer síe siextiȝ elna lang, óðer síe of hwæles hýde ȝe-worht, óðer of séoles.

Hé sæȝde þæt Norþ-manna land wǽre swíðe lang and
10 swíðe smæl. Eall þæt his man ǽȝðer oþþe ettan oþþe erian mæȝ, þæt liȝeþ wiþ þá sǽ, and þæt is þéah on sumum stówum swíðe clúdiȝ. And licgaþ wilde móras wiþ éastan and wiþ upp on efen-lange þǽm býnum lande. On þǽm mórum eardiaþ Finnas. And þæt býne land is éaste-weard brádost, and simble
15 swá norðor swá smælre. Éaste-weard hit mæȝ béon siextiȝ míla brád, oþþe hwéne brádra; and midde-weard þrítiȝ oþþe brádra; and norðe-weard, hé cwæþ, þǽr hit smalost wǽre, þæt hit meahte béon þréora míla brád to þǽm móre, and se mór siþþan, on sumum stówum, swá brád swá man mæȝ on
20 siex dagum ofer-féran.

Þonne is to-efenes þǽm lande súðe-weardum, on óðre healfe þæs móres, Swéo-land, oþ þæt land norðe-weard; and to-efenes þǽm lande norðe-weardum, Cwéna land. Þá Cwénas hergiaþ hwílum on þá Norþ-menn ofer þone mór, hwílum þá
25 Norþ-menn on híe. And þǽr sint swíðe mičele meras fersce ȝeond þá móras; and beraþ þá Cwénas hira scipu ofer land on þá meras and þanan hergiaþ on þá Norþ-menn. Híe habbaþ swíðe lýtle scipu and swíðe léohte.

Óht-here sæȝde þæt séo scír hátte Hálgo-land, þe hé on
30 búde. Hé cwæþ þæt nán mann ne búde be norðan him. Þonne is án port on súðe-weardum þǽm lande, þone man hát Sciringes-héal. Þider hé cwæþ þæt man ne meahte ȝe-seȝlian on ánum mónðe, ȝief man on niht wícode and ǽlče dæȝe hæfde ambyrne wind; and ealle þá hwíle hé sceal seȝlian be lande.

But their income (lit. property) is mostly in the tribute that the Lapps pay them. This tribute is in hides of animals, and in feathers of birds, and whalebone, and in the ship-ropes that are made of the hide of the walrus and the seal. Each pays according to his rank. The highest ranking has to pay fifteen marten skins, and five reindeer (skins), and one bear skin, and ten measures of feathers, and a bear-skin or otter-skin coat, and two ship-ropes; each (may be) sixty ells long, one (may be) made of walrus hide, one of seal skin.

He said that the land of the Norsemen was very long and very narrow. All of it that one can either graze or plow lies along the sea, and it is, however, very rocky in some places. And wild mountains lie to the east and up parallel to the inhabited land. In these mountains dwell the Lapps. And the inhabited land is broadest to the east (south?) and ever the farther north the narrower. To the east (south?) it may be sixty miles broad or a little broader; and in the middle thirty or broader; and to the north, he said, where it is narrowest, that it might be three miles broad to the upland, and the upland after that in some places as broad as one can cross in six days.

Then parallel to the southern (part of the) country, on the other side of the mountains, is Sweden as far as the northern (part of the) country; and parallel to the northern (part of the) country, the land of the (Suomi) Finns. The Finns sometimes raid the Norsemen over the mountains, sometimes the Norsemen (raid) them. And there are very large fresh-water lakes there throughout the mountains; and the Finns carry their boats overland to the lakes and from there raid the Norsemen. They have very small and very light boats.

Ohthere said that the district that he lived in was called Helgeland. He said that no man lived north of him. Then there is a trading center in the southern (part of the) country which is called (lit. one calls) Skirings-salr. He said that one would not be able to sail there in one month, if one camped at night and had a favorable wind every day; and all the while he must sail along the land. And on his starboard will be first

And on þæt stéor-bord him biþ ǽrest Íra-land and þonne þá
ieȝ-land þe sint be-tweox Íra-land and þissum lande. Þonne
is þis land, oþ hé cymþ to Sciringes-héale, and eallne weȝ on
þæt bæc-bord Norþ-weȝ. Wiþ súðan þone Sciringes-héal
5 fielþ swiðe micel sǽ upp inn on þæt land; séo is brádre þonne
ǽniȝ mann ofer séon mæȝe. And is Got-land on óðre healfe
on-ȝeȝn, and siþþan Sillende. Séo sǽ liȝeþ maniȝ hund míla
upp inn on þæt land.

And of Sciringes-héale hé cwæþ þæt hé seȝlode on fíf dagan
10 to þǽm porte þe man hát æt-Hǽðum, sé stent be-tweox
Winedum, and Seaxum, and Angle, and híerþ inn on Dene.
Þá hé þider-weard seȝlode fram Sciringes-héale, þá wæs him
on þæt bæc-bord Dena-mearc and on þæt stéor-bord wíd-sǽ
þríe dagas. And þá, twéȝen dagas ǽr hé to Hǽðum cóme, him
15 wæs on þæt stéor-bord Got-land and Sillende and ieȝ-landa
fela. On þǽm landum eardodon Engle, ǽr híe hider on land
cómon. And him wæs þá twéȝen dagas on þæt bæc-bord þá
ieȝ-land þe inn to Dene-mearce híeraþ.

Wulf-stán sæȝde þæt hé ȝe-fóre of Hǽðum, þæt hé wǽre
20 on Trúsó on seofon dagum and nihtum, þæt þæt scip was
eallne weȝ iernende under seȝle. Weonod-land him wæs on
stéor-bord, and on bæc-bord him wæs Langa-land, and Lǽ-
land, and Falster, and Scónéȝ; and þás land eall híeraþ to
Dene-mearcan. And þonne Burgenda-land wæs ús on bæc-
25 bord, and þá habbaþ him selfe cyning. Þonne æfter Burgenda-
land wǽron ús þás land, þá sint hátene ǽrest Blécinga-ég, and
Méore, and Éow-land, and Got-land on bæc-bord; and þás
land híeraþ to Swéom.

Weonod-land wæs ús eallne weȝ on stéor-bord oþ Wísle-
30 múðan. Séo Wísle is swiðe micel éa, and héo to-liȝeþ Wít-land
and Weonod-land; and þæt Wít-land be-limpeþ to Estum.
And séo Wísle liȝeþ út of Weonod-lande and liȝeþ on Est-
mere; and se Est-mere is húru fíftíene míla brád. Þonne
cymeþ Ilfing éastan on Est-mere of þǽm mere þe Trúsó

76

Ireland (Iceland?) and then the islands that are between Ireland (?) and this country (i.e., Norway). Then (i.e., next) is this country, until he gets to Skirings-salr, and the whole way Norway (will be) on the port (side). South of that (city of) Skirings-salr a large sea (i.e., the Baltic) runs up inland; it is broader than any man can see over. And Jutland is opposite on the other side, and then Zealand. That sea extends many hundred miles inland.

And from Skirings-salr he said that he sailed in five days to the trading center that is called (lit. one calls) Haddeby, which is (lit. stands) between the Wends, and the Saxons, and the Angles, and belongs to the Danes. When he sailed there from Skirings-salr, then Denmark was on his port (side) and the open sea on (his) starboard for three days. And then, two days before he got to Haddeby, Jutland and Zealand and many islands were (lit. was) on his starboard. In those lands dwelt the English, before they came here to (this) country. And then for two days the islands that belong to Denmark were (lit. was) on his port (side).

Wulfstan said that he journeyed from Haddeby so that he got to (lit. was in) Truso in seven days and nights, (and) that the ship was running under sail the whole way. Wendland was on his starboard, and on his port were (lit. was) Langland, and Laaland, and Falster, and Skaane; and all these lands belong to Denmark. And then Bornholm was on our port (side), and those (people) have their own king. Then, after Bornholm, those lands that are called, first, Blekinge, and (then) Möre, and (then) Öland, were on our port (side) ; and these lands belong to the Swedes.

Wendland was on our starboard the whole way up to the mouth of the Vistula. The Vistula is a very large river, and it divides Witland (Latvia?) and Wendland; and Witland belongs to the Esthonians. And the Vistula runs out of Wendland and runs into the Frisches Haff ; and the Frisches Haff is at least fifteen miles broad. Then the Elbing comes from the east into the Frisches Haff from the lake on the shore of which Truso stands (i.e., Drausensee) ; and they flow (lit.

standeþ on stæðe; and cumaþ út samod on Est-mere, Ilfing
éastan of Est-lande, and Wísle súðan of Weonod-lande. And
þonne be-nimþ Wísle Ilfing hire naman and liзeþ of þǽm
mere west and norþ on sǽ; for-þý hit man hát Wísle-múða.

5   Þæt Est-land is swiðe micel, and þǽr biþ swíðe maniз
burg, and on ǽlĉre byriз biþ cyning. And þǽr biþ swíðe micel
huneз, and fiscoþ. And se cyning and þá ríĉostan menn
drincaþ míeran meoluc, and þá un-spédiзan and þá þéowan
drincaþ medu. Þǽr biþ swíðe micel зe-winn be-twéonan him.

10 And ne biþ þǽr nǽniз ealu зe-browen mid Estum, ac þǽr
biþ medu зe-nóg.

And þǽr is mid Estum þéaw, þonne þǽr biþ mann déad, þæt
hé liзeþ inne un-for-bærned mid his mágum and fréondum
mónaþ, зe hwílum twéзen, and þá cyningas and þá óðre héah-
15 þungene menn swá miĉele lenз swá híe máran spéda habbaþ,
hwílum healf зéar þæt híe béoþ un-for-bærned and licgaþ
bufan eorðan on hira húsum. And ealle þá hwíle þe þæt lic
biþ inne, þǽr sceal béon зe-drynĉ and plega, oþ þone dæз þe
híe hine for-bærnaþ. Þonne þý ilcan dæзe [þe] híe hine to
20 þǽm áde beran willaþ, þonne to-dǽlaþ híe his feoh, þæt þǽr
to láfe biþ æfter þǽm зe-drynĉe and þǽm plegan, on fíf
oþþe siex, hwílum on má, swá swá féos and-efen biþ.
A-lecgaþ hit þonne for-hwega on ánre míle þone mǽstan dǽl
fram þǽm túne, þonne óðerne, þonne þone þriddan, oþ-þe
25 hit eall a-leзd biþ on þǽre ánre míle; and sceal béon se lǽsta
dǽl níehst þǽm túne þe se déada mann on liзeþ. Þonne sculon
béon зe-samnode ealle þá menn þe swiftoste hors habbaþ on
þǽm lande, for-hwega on fíf mílum oþþe on siex mílum fram
þǽm féo. Þonne iernaþ híe ealle tó-weard þǽm féo. Þonne
30 cymeþ se mann sé þæt swiftoste hors hafaþ to þǽm ǽrestan
dǽle and to þǽm mǽstan, and swá ǽlĉ æfter óðrum, oþ hit
biþ eall зe-numen; and sé nimþ þone lǽstan dǽl sé níehst
þǽm túne þæt feoh зe-ierneþ. And þonne rídeþ ǽlĉ his weзes
mid þǽm féo, and hit móton habban eall. And for-þý þǽr

come) out together into the Frisches Haff, the Elbing from
the east out of Esthonia, and the Vistula from the south out
of Wendland. And then the Vistula deprives the Elbing of its
name and runs out of the lake (i.e., the Frisches Haff) west
and north to the sea; therefore it is called the mouth of the
Vistula.

Esthonia is very large, and there are very many towns
there, and in each town there is a king. And there is very
much honey, and fishing. And the king and the richest men
drink mares' milk, and the poor and the slaves drink mead.
There is very much warfare among them. And there is no ale
brewed among the Esthonians, but there is mead enough.

And there is a custom among the Esthonians, when a man
dies (lit. is dead) there, that he lies inside uncremated among
his kinsmen and friends for a month, and sometimes two, and
the kings and the other men of high rank as much longer as
they have greater wealth, sometimes half a year that they are
uncremated and lie above ground in their houses. And all the
while that the body is inside, there is to be drinking and
festivity, until the day that they cremate him. Then on the
same day that they are about to take him to the pyre, then they
divide up his property, that is left there after the drinking and
the festivity, in five or six, sometimes in more, according to
the amount of property (lit. as the amount of the property is).
Then they lay it out within about a mile from the village,
(first) the largest portion, then the second, then the third,
until it is all laid out within that one mile; and the smallest
portion must be nearest to the village in which the dead man
is lying. Then all the men who have the swiftest horses in the
countryside are supposed to be assembled within about five
or six miles from the property. Then they all gallop (lit. run)
toward the property. Then the man who has the swiftest horse
comes to the first portion and the largest, and so each after
the other, until it is all taken; and the one who wins (lit. gets
by racing) the property nearest to the village gets the smallest
portion. And then each goes (lit. rides) his way with the
property, and they may keep it all. And for this reason swift

béoþ þá swiftan hors un-ʒe-fóge díere. And þonne his ʒe-
stréon béoþ þus eall a-spended, þonne birþ man hine út and
for-bærnaþ mid his wǽpnum and hræʒle. And swíðost ealle
his spéda híe for-spendaþ mid þǽm langan leʒere þæs déadan
5   mannes inne, and þæs-þe híe be þǽm wegum a-lecgaþ, þe þá
fremdan tó iernaþ and nimaþ.

And þæt is mid Estum þéaw þæt þǽr sceal ǽlčes ʒe-þéodes
mann béon for-bærned. And ʒief man án bán findeþ un-for-
bærned, híe hit sculon mičelum ʒe-bétan.

10   And þǽr is mid Estum án mǽʒþ þæt híe magon čiele ʒe-
wyrčan; and þý þǽr licgaþ þá déadan menn swá lange and
ne fúliaþ, þæt híe wyrčaþ þone čiele him on. And þéah man
a-sette twéʒen fǽtels full ealuþ oþþe wæteres, híe ʒe-dóþ þæt
óðer biþ ofer-froren, sam hit síe sumor sam winter.

horses are exceedingly valuable there. And when his treasures are thus all consumed, then he is carried out and cremated (lit. one carries him out and cremates) with his weapons and clothing. But (lit. and) mostly they squander all his wealth with the long funeral wake of the dead man inside, and with (lit. of) that which they lay out along the roads, which the strangers race to and take.

And it is a custom among the Esthonians that there (any) man of any tribe must be cremated. And if one finds (even) one bone uncremated, they are obliged to make great amends for it.

And there is among the Esthonians one tribe that can produce cold; and by means of this, (that is) that they produce this cold in them, the dead men lie there so long and do not putrefy. And though one should set two vessels full of ale or water, they bring it about that both (lit. one) is frozen, the same (whether) it be summer or winter.

The Story of King Cyne-wulf of Wessex
from *The Anglo-Saxon Chronicle*
for the years 755 and 786

755. Hér Cyne-wulf be-nam Siȝe-beorht his ríces and West-Seaxna witan for un-rihtum dǽdum bútan Hám-tún-scíre; and hé hæfde þá oþ hé of-slóg þone ealdor-mann þe him lenȝest wunode. And hine þá Cyne-wulf on Andred a-drǽfde, and hé þǽr wunode oþ-þæt hine án swán of-stang æt Pryfetes-flódan—and hé wræc þone ealdor-mann Cumbran. And sé Cyne-wulf oft miċelum ȝe-feohtum feaht wiþ Bret-Wéalum.

And ymb xxxi wintra þæs-þe hé ríċe hæfde, hé wolde a-drǽfan ánne æðeling, sé wæs Cyne-heard háten; and sé Cyne-heard wæs þæs Siȝe-beorhtes bróðor.

And þá ȝe-áscode hé þone cyning lýtle weorode on wíf-cýþþe on Meran-túne and hine þǽr be-rád and þone búr be-éode, ǽr hine þá menn on-fundon þe mid þǽm cyninge wǽron. And þá on-ȝeat se cyning þæt, and hé on þá duru éode, and þá un-héan-líċe hine werede oþ hé on þone æðeling lócode, and þá út rǽsde on hine and hine miċelum ȝe-wundode; and híe ealle on þone cyning wǽron feohtende oþ-þæt híe hine of-slæȝenne hæfdon. And þá on þæs wífes ȝe-bǽrum on-fundon þæs cyninges þeȝnas þá un-still-nesse and þá þider urnon, swá-hwelċ-swá þonne ȝearu wearþ and hrædost.

And hira se æðeling ȝe-hwelċum feoh and feorh ȝe-béad, and hira nǽniȝ hit ȝe-þicgan nolde, ac híe simble feohtende wǽron oþ híe ealle lágon bútan ánum Brittiscum ȝísle, and

The Story of King Cynewulf of Wessex
(*Translation*)

755. In this year (lit. here) Cynewulf and the councillors of the West Saxons deprived Sigeberht of his kingdom except Hampshire because of (his) unjust acts; and he kept that until he killed the ealdorman who had remained (with) him the longest. And then Cynewulf drove him away into the Weald, and he remained there until a certain peasant stabbed him to death by the stream near Privett—and he was avenging Ealdorman Cumbra. And this Cynewulf often fought in great battles against the Celts.

And thirty-one years from the (time) when he ruled (i.e., began ruling), he was about to exile a certain prince, who was called Cyneheard; and this Cyneheard was the brother of that (same) Sigeberht.

And then he (Cyneheard) found out (that) the king (was) visiting a woman (lit. in woman-intercourse) with a small troop at Merton and surrounded him (on horseback) and surrounded the cottage (on foot), before the men who were with the king discovered him. And then the king perceived it, and he went to the door, and then defended himself creditably until he caught sight of the prince (Cyneheard), and then (the king) rushed out at him and wounded him severely; and they all kept fighting against the king until they had killed him. And then from the screams of the woman the king's retainers became aware of the disturbance and came running (lit. ran thither), whoever was ready and quickest.

And the prince (Cyneheard) offered each of them (i.e., the slain King Cynewulf's retainers) money and life, and none of them was willing to accept it, but they kept fighting until they all lay dead except one British (i.e., Celtic) hostage, and he

83

sé swíðe ʒe-wundod wæs.

Þá on morgene ʒe-híerdon þæt þæs cyninges þeʒnas þe
him be-æftan wǽron, þæt se cyning of-slæʒen wæs. Þá ridon
híe þider, and his ealdor-mann Ós-ríč, and Wíʒ-ferhþ his
5 þeʒn, and þá menn þe hé be-æftan lǽfde ǽr.

And þone æðeling on þǽre byriʒ métton, þǽr se cyning
of-slæʒen læʒ—and þá ʒeatu him tó be-locen hæfdon—and
þǽr-tó éodon. And þá ʒe-béad hé him hira ágenne dóm féos
and landes, ʒief híe him þæs ríčes úðon, and him cýðde þæt
10 hira mágas him mid wǽron, þá-þe him fram noldon. And þá
cwǽdon híe þæt him nǽniʒ mǽʒ léofra nǽre þonne hira
hláford and híe nǽfre his banan folgian noldon. And þá budon
híe hira mágum þæt híe ʒe-sunde fram éodon; and híe
cwǽdon þæt þæt ilce hira ʒe-férum ʒe-boden wǽre þe ǽr mid
15 þǽm cyninge wǽron. Þá cwǽdon híe þæt híe þæs ne on-
mundon "þon má þe éowre ʒe-féran þe mid þǽm cyninge
of-slæʒene wǽron."

And híe þá ymb þá ʒeatu feohtende wǽron oþ-þæt híe þǽr-
inne fulgon and þone æðeling of-slógon and þá menn þe him
20 mid wǽron, ealle bútan ánum. Sé wæs þæs ealdor-mannes
god-sunu, and hé his feorh ʒe-nerede, and þéah hé wæs oft
ʒe-wundod.

And sé Cyne-wulf rícsode xxxi wintra, and his líč liʒeþ
æt Wintan-čeastre, and þæs æðelinges æt Axan-mynster; and
25 hira riht-fæderen-cynn gǽþ to Čerdiče.

was severely wounded.

Then in the morning the king's retainers who had been left (lit. were) behind him heard that, (that is) that the king had been slain. Then they rode up (lit. thither)—his ealdorman Osric and his thane Wigferth and the men that he (i.e., the slain king) had formerly left behind him.

And they came upon the prince (Cyneheard) in the stronghold where the king lay slain—and they had locked the gates —and they (i.e., the late arrivals) went up to them (i.e., the gates). And then he (i.e., Cyneheard) offered them money and land on their own terms (lit. offered them their own judgment of money and land), if they would grant him the kingdom (i.e., acknowledge his rule), and informed them that kinsmen of theirs were with him who had no intention of leaving him (lit. did not wish from him). And then they said that no kinsman could be dearer to them than their lord and they would never follow (i.e., become followers of) his slayer. And then they offered to their kinsmen that they (might) walk (out) unharmed; and they (i.e., the kinsmen inside the stronghold) said that the same thing had been offered to their companions who had been with the king before. Then they said that they did not consider themselves worthy of it "any more than your comrades (did) who were slain with the king."

And they kept fighting around the gates until they got inside there and killed the prince and the men who were with him, all except one. That one was the ealdorman's godson, and he saved his life, and even so he was often wounded.

And Cynewulf had reigned thirty-one years, and his body lies at Winchester, and the prince's (body) at Axminster; and their direct paternal ancestry goes (back) to Cerdic.

The Wars of King Alfred against the Vikings
from *The Anglo-Saxon Chronicle*
for the years 871–872 and 892–901

871. Hér cóm se here to Réadingum on West-Seaxe, and þæs
ymb iii niht ridon ii eorlas upp. Þá ȝe-métte híe Æðel-wulf
ealdor-mann on Engla-felda, and him þǽr wiþ ȝe-feaht, and
siȝe nam. Þæs ymb iiii niht Æðel-rǽd cyning and Ælf-rǽd
5   his bróðor þǽr miċele fierd to Réadingum ȝe-lǽddon and wiþ
þone here ȝe-fuhton; and þǽr wæs miċel wæl ȝe-slæȝen on
ȝe-hwæðere hand, and Æðel-wulf ealdor-mann wearþ of-
slæȝen; and þá Deniscan áhton wæl-stówe ȝe-weald.
   And þæs ymb iiii niht ȝe-feaht Æðel-rǽd cyning and Ælf-
10 rǽd his bróðor wiþ eallne þone here on Æsces-dúne; and híe
wǽron on twǽm ȝe-fylċum: on óðrum wæs Bac-secg and
Healf-Dene, þá hǽðnan cyningas, and on óðrum wǽron þá
eorlas. And þá ȝe-feaht se cyning Æðel-rǽd wiþ þára cyninga
ȝe-truman, and þǽr wearþ se cyning Bac-secg of-slæȝen; and
15 Ælf-rǽd his bróðor wiþ þára eorla ȝe-truman, and þǽr wearþ
Síd-roc eorl of-slæȝen se ealda, and Síd-roc eorl se ȝeonga,
and Ós-bearn eorl, and Frǽna eorl, and Harald eorl; and þá
herȝas béȝen ȝe-fliemde, and fela þúsenda of-slæȝenra, and
on-feohtende wǽron oþ niht.
20   And þæs ymb xiiii niht ȝe-feaht Æðel-rǽd cyning and
Ælf-rǽd his bróðor wiþ þone here æt Basingum, and þǽr
þá Deniscan siȝe námon.
   And þæs ymb ii mónaþ ȝe-feaht Æðel-rǽd cyning and
Ælf-rǽd his bróðor wiþ þone here æt Mere-túne, and híe

The Wars of King Alfred
(*Translation*)

871. In this year (lit. here) the (Scandinavian) army came to Reading in Wessex, and three days later two jarls rode inland. Then Ealdorman Ethelwulf met them at Englefield, and fought against them there and was victorious (lit. took victory). Four days later King Ethelred and his brother Alfred led a large (English) army to Reading and fought against the (Scandinavian) army; and there was great slaughter (lit. was great slaughter struck) on either side, and Ealdorman Ethelwulf was killed; and the Danes had control of the battlefield.

And four days later King Ethelred and his brother Alfred fought against the whole (Scandinavian) army at Ashdown; and they (i.e., the Scandinavians) were in two divisions: in one were (lit. was) Bacsecg and Halfdane, the heathen kings, and in the other were the jarls. And then King Ethelred fought against the troop of the kings, and King Bacsecg was killed there; and his brother Alfred (fought) against the troop of the jarls, and Jarl Sidroc the Old was slain there, and Jarl Sidroc the Young, and Jarl Osbearn, and Jarl Fræna, and Jarl Harald; and both the (Scandinavian) armies (were) put to flight, and (there were) many thousands of slain, and they kept fighting until night.

And a fortnight later King Ethelred and his brother Alfred fought against the (Scandinavian) army at Basing, and the Danes were victorious (lit. took victory) there.

And two months later King Ethelred and his brother Alfred fought against the (Scandinavian) army at Merton, and

wǽron on twǽm ȝe-fylčum, and híe bú-tú ȝe-flíemdon and lange on dæȝ siȝe áhton. And þǽr wearþ mičel wæl-slieht on ȝe-hwæðere hand, and þá Deniscan áhton wæl-stówe ȝe-weald. And þǽr wearþ Héah-mund biscop of-slæȝen, and
5 fela gódra manna. And æfter þissum ȝe-feohte cóm mičel sumor-lida to Réadingum.

And þæs, æfter Éastran, ȝe-fór Æðel-rǽd cyning; and hé rícsode v ȝéar; and his líč liȝeþ æt Win-burnan.

Þá féng Ælf-rǽd Æðel-wulfing his bróðor to West-
10 Seaxna ríče.

And þæs ymb ánne mónaþ ȝe-feaht Ælf-rǽd cyning wiþ eallne þone here lýtle weorode æt Wil-túne and hine lange on dæȝ ȝe-flíemde, and þá Deniscan áhton wæl-stówe ȝe-weald.

And þæs ȝéares wurdon viiii folc-ȝe-feoht ȝe-fohten wiþ
15 þone here on þý cyne-ríče be súðan Temese, bútan þǽm-þe him Ælf-rǽd þæs cyninges bróðor and án-líepiȝ ealdor-mann and cyninges þeȝnas oft ráde on-ridon þe man ná ne rímde. And þæs ȝéares wǽron of-slæȝene viiii eorlas and án cyning. And þý ȝéare námon West-Seaxe friþ wiþ þone here.
20 872. Hér fór se here to Lunden-byriȝ fram Réadingum and þǽr winter-setl nam; and þá námon Mierče friþ wiþ þone here.

*   *   *   *   *   *   *   *   *   *   *

25 892. Hér on þissum ȝéare fór se mičela here, þe wé ȝe-fyrn ymb sprǽcon, eft of þǽm Éast-ríče west-weard to Bunnan and þǽr wurdon ȝe-scipode swá þæt híe a-setton him on ánne síp ofer mid horsum mid ealle, and þá cóm upp on Limene múðan mid ccl hunde scipa. Sé múða is on éaste-
30 weardre Cent, æt þæs mičelan wuda éast-ende þe wé Andred hátaþ. Sé wudu is éast-lang and west-lang hund-twelftiȝes míla lang, oþþe lenȝra, and þrítiȝes míla brád. Séo éa, þe wé ǽr ymb sprǽcon, liȝeþ út of þǽm wealda. On þá éa híe tugon upp hira scipu oþ þone weald, iiii míla fram þǽm múðan

88

they were in two divisions, and they put both to flight and were victorious (lit. had victory) late in the day. And there was great slaughter on either side, and the Danes had control of the battlefield. And Bishop Heahmund was killed there, and many good men. And after this battle a great summer fleet came to Reading.

And later, after Easter, King Ethelred died; and he had reigned five years; and his body lies at Wimborne.

Then his brother Alfred, son of Ethelwulf, succeeded to the throne of the West Saxons.

And one month later King Alfred, with a small force, fought against the entire (Scandinavian) army at Wilton and put it to flight late in the day, and the Danes had control of the battlefield.

And during that year nine major battles were fought against the (Scandinavian) army in the kingdom south of the Thames, except those (in) which the king's brother Alfred and an individual ealdorman and retainers of the king often rode out on an expedition, which were not counted (lit. which one did not count at all). And in that year nine jarls and one king were killed. And in that year the West Saxons made peace with the (Scandinavian) army.

872. In this year the (Scandinavian) army went from Reading to London and took up winter quarters there; and then the Mercians made peace with the (Scandinavian) army.

*   *   *   *   *   *   *   *   *   *   *

892. In this year the great (Scandinavian) army, which we have spoken about before, went back from the Eastern Kingdom to Boulogne and there were provided with ships so that they crossed (lit. set themselves over) in one trip with horses and everything, and then came up into the Lympne estuary with 250 ships. That estuary is in eastern Kent, at the east end of the large forest that we call Andred (i.e., the Weald). That forest is 120 miles long from east to west, or longer, and thirty miles wide. The river, which we spoke about before, runs out of that forest. They pulled (rowed? towed?) their ships up the river as far as the forest, four miles from the outer estuary, and there destroyed a fortifica-

úte-weardum, and þǽr a-brǽcon án ʒe-weorc. Inne on þǽm
fæstene sǽton féawa čierlisc menn on, and wæs sám-worht.
Þá sóna æfter þǽm cóm Hǽsten mid lxxx scipa upp on
Temese múðan and worhte him ʒe-weorc æt Middel-túne, and
5 se óðer here æt Apuldre.

893. On þýs ʒéare, þæt wæs ymb twelf mónaþ þæs-þe híe
on þǽm Éast-ríče ʒe-weorc ʒe-worht hæfdon, Norþ-Hymbre
and Éast-Engle hæfdon Ælf-rǽde cyninge áðas ʒe-seald, and
Éast-Engle fore-ʒísla vi. And þéah, ofer þá tréowa, swá oft
10 swá þá óðre herʒas mid ealle herʒe út fóron, þonne fóron híe,
oþþe mid oþþe on hira healfe. Þá ʒe-gadrode Ælf-rǽd cyning
his fierd and fór þæt hé ʒe-wícode be-tweox þǽm twǽm her-
ʒum, þǽr þǽr hé níehst rýmet hæfde for wudu-fæstene and
for wæter-fæstene, swá þæt hé meahte ǽʒðerne ʒe-rǽčan,
15 ʒief híe ǽniʒne feld séčan wolden. Þá fóron híe siþþan æfter
þǽm wealda hlóðum and flocc-rádum, be swá-hwæðerre efes
swá hit þonne fierd-léas wæs. And him man éac mid óðrum
floccum sóhte mǽstra daga ǽlče, oþþe on dæʒ oþþe on niht,
ʒe of þǽre fierde ʒe éac of þǽm burgum. Hæfde se cyning his
20 fierd on tú to-numen, swá þæt híe wǽron simble healfe æt
hám, healfe úte, bútan þǽm mannum þe þá burga healdan
scolden. Ne cóm se here oftor eall úte of þǽm setum þonne
tuwa: óðre síðe þá híe ǽrest to lande cómon, ǽr séo fierd
ʒe-samnod wǽre; óðre síðe þá híe of þǽm setum faran wold-
25 on. Þá híe ʒe-féngon mičele here-húþ and þá woldon ferian
norþ-weardes ofer Temese inn on Éast-Seaxe on-ʒeʒn þá
scipu. Þá for-rád séo fierd híe foran, and him wiþ ʒe-feaht
æt Fearn-háme and þone here ʒe-flíemde and þá here-húða
a-hreddon; and híe flugon ofer Temese bútan ǽlčum forda,
30 þá upp be Colne on ánne íegoþ. Þá be-sæt séo fierd híe útan
þá-hwíle-þe híe þǽr lenʒest mete hæfdon; ac híe hæfdon
þá hira stefn ʒe-setenne and hira mete ʒe-nyttodne; and wæs
se cyning þá þider-weardes on fare, mid þǽre scíre þe mid
him fierdodon. Þá hé þá wæs þider-weardes, and séo óðru

90

tion. Inside that stronghold there were (lit. sat) a few peasants, and (it) was (only) half-built.

Then immediately after that Hæsten came with eighty ships up into the Thames estuary and built himself a fortification at Milton, and the other (Scandinavian) army (did likewise) at Appledore.

893. In this year, that was twelve months after they had built a fortification in the Eastern Kingdom, the Northumbrians and East Anglians (i.e., Scandinavians settled in Northumbria and East Anglia) had given pledges to King Alfred, and the East Anglians (had given) six preliminary hostages. And nevertheless, contrary to the pledges, as often as the other (Scandinavian) armies went out in full force, then they went either with (them) or on their (own) behalf. Then King Alfred assembled his army and moved so that he encamped between the two (Scandinavian) armies, where he was at the most convenient distance (lit. had the nearest space) from (lit. for) the stronghold in the forest and the stronghold by the water, so that he would be able to reach either (army), if they should wish to make for any open country. Then after that they went along the forest in bands and mounted detachments, by whichever edge (of the forest) was then undefended by the English army (lit. army-less). And they were sought (lit. one sought them) also with other bands, both from the (English) army and from the towns almost every day (lit. each of most days), either by day or by night. The king had divided his army in two, so that they were always half at home and half out (in the field), except for the men who were supposed to guard the towns. The (Scandinavian) army did not all come out of those camps oftener than twice: once when they first came to (this) country (i.e., England), before the (English) army had been assembled; once when they wished to leave (lit. go from) those camps. Then they seized much booty and wished to carry it north across the Thames into Essex to meet the ships. Then the (English) army intercepted them on horseback (lit. forerode them) and fought against them at Farnham and put the (Scandinavian) army to flight and recovered the booty; and they fled across the Thames without (even using) any ford, then up the Colne to a certain island. Then the (English) army besieged them there (from outside) as long as (lit. while they longest) they (i.e., the English) had food; but they had finished their term of service and used up their food; and the king was then on the way there, with the division that was serving with him. When he was on the way there, and the

fierd wæs hám-weardes, and þá Deniscan sǽton þǽr be-hindan, for-þǽm hira cyning wæs ʒe-wundod on þǽm ʒe-feohte,
þæt híe hine ne meahton ferian, þá ʒe-gadrodon þá-þe on
Norþ-Hymbrum búiaþ and on Éast-Englum sum hund scipa
5   and fóron súþ ymb-útan, and sum féowertiʒ scipa norþ ymb-
útan, and ymb-sǽton án ʒe-weorc on Defna-scíre be þǽre
Norþ-sǽ; and þá-þe súþ ymb-útan fóron ymb-sǽton Exan-
čeaster.

   Þá se cyning þæt híerde, þá wende hé hine west wiþ Exan-
10 čeastres mid eallre þǽre fierde, bútan swíðe ʒe-wealdenum
dǽle éast-weardes þæs folces.

   Þá fóron forþ oþ-þe híe cómon to Lunden-byriʒ, and
þá, mid þǽm burg-warum and þǽm fultume þe him westan
cóm, fóron éast to Béam-fléote. Wæs Hǽsten þá þǽr cumen
15 mid his herʒe þe ǽr æt Middel-túne sæt, and éac se mičela
here wæs þá þǽr-tó cumen þe ǽr on Limene múðan sæt æt
Apuldre. Hæfde Hǽsten ǽr ʒe-worht þæt ʒe-weorc æt Béam-
fléote, and wæs þá út a-faren on herʒaþ, and wæs se mičela
here æt hám. Þá fóron híe tó and ʒe-flíemdon þone here and
20 þæt ʒe-weorc a-brǽcon and ʒe-námon eall þæt þǽr binnan
wæs, ʒe on féo, ʒe on wífum, ʒe éac on bearnum, and bróhton
eall inn to Lunden-byriʒ; and þá scipu eall oþþe to-brǽcon,
oþþe for-bærndon, oþþe to Lunden-byriʒ bróhton, oþþe to
Hrofes-čeastre; and Hǽstenes wíf and his suna twéʒen man
25 bróhte to þǽm cyninge, and hé híe him eft a-ʒeaf, for-þǽm-
þe hira wæs óðer his god-sunu, óðer Æðel-rǽdes ealdor-
mannes. Hæfdon híe hira on-fangen ǽr Hǽsten to Béam-
fléote cóme, and hé him hæfde ʒe-seald ʒíslas and áðas; and
se cyning him éac wel feoh sealde, and éac swá þá hé þone
30 cniht a-ʒeaf and þæt wíf. Ac sóna swá híe to Béam-fléote
cómon, and þæt ʒe-weorc ʒe-worht wæs, swá hergode hé on
his ríče, þone ilcan ende þe Æðel-rǽd, his cumpæder, healdan scolde; and eft óðre síðe hé wæs on herʒaþ ʒe-lend on
þæt ilce ríče, þá þá man his ʒe-weorc a-bræc.

92

other (English) army was on the way home, and the Danes were staying behind there, because their king had been wounded in the battle, so that they could not move him, then those (Scandinavians) who were living (lit. are living) in Northumbria and East Anglia collected some hundred ships and went south around the coast (lit. south out around), and some forty ships (went) north around the coast (lit. north out (around), and besieged a certain fortification on the north coast of Devonshire (lit. in Devonshire by the North Sea, i.e., the Bristol Channel) ; and those who had gone around the south coast besieged Exeter.

When the king heard that, he turned west toward Exeter with the entire army, except for a very inconsiderable portion of the eastern folk (i.e., people from the eastern part of the country).

Then they kept going until they came to London, and then, with the townspeople and the reinforcements (lit. help) that came to them from the west, they went east to Benfleet. Hæsten had then gone there with his army which had formerly been at Milton, and the large (Scandinavian) army that had formerly been at Appledore in the Lympne estuary had gone there also. Hæsten had previously built that fortification at Benfleet, and (he) had then gone out on a raid, and the large (Scandinavian) army was at home. Then they (i.e., the English) went there and put the army to flight and destroyed the fortification and seized everything that was inside there, both property and women, and also children, and brought everything to London; and they either broke up or burned up all the ships, or brought them to London or to Rochester ; and Hæsten's wife and his two sons were brought (lit. one brought) to the king, and he (i.e., King Alfred) gave them back to him, because one of them was his godson, the other (was) Ealdorman Ethelred's (godson). They had stood sponsor for them before Hæsten went to Benfleet, and he had given him (i.e., King Alfred) hostages and pledges; and the king had also given him generous gifts of money (lit. well gave him money), and also (did) so when he gave back the boys (lit. the boy) and the woman. But as soon as they came to Benfleet, and the fortification had been built, he (i.e., Hæsten) raided his (i.e., Alfred's) kingdom, that very district which Ethelred, his son's godfather, was supposed to be guarding; and again on a second occasion he had gone on a raid in that same kingdom (i.e., that same part of the kingdom), when his fortification was destroyed (lit. one destroyed his fortification).

Þá se cyning hine þá west wende mid þǽre fierde wiþ
Exan-čeastres, swá ič ǽr sægde, and se here þá burg be-seten
hæfde, þá hé þǽr-tó ʒe-faren wæs, þá éodon híe to hira scipum. Þá hé þá wiþ þone here þǽr west a-bisgod wæs, and
5 þá herʒas wǽron þá ʒe-gadrode béʒen to Scéo-byriʒ on Éast-
Seaxum, and þǽr ʒe-weorc worhton, fóron béʒen æt-gædre
upp be Temese. And him cóm mičel éaca tó ǽʒðer ʒe of Éast-
Englum ʒe of Norþ-Hymbrum. Fóron þá upp be Temese
oþ-þæt híe ʒe-dydon æt Sæferne, þá upp be Sæferne. Þá
10 ʒe-gadrode Æðel-rǽd ealdor-mann, and Æðel-helm ealdor-
mann, and Æðel-nóþ ealdor-mann, and þá cyninges þeʒnas
þe þá æt hám æt þǽm ʒe-weorcum wǽron, of ǽlčre byriʒ
be éastan Pedredan, ʒe be westan Seal-wuda ʒe be éastan,
ʒe éac be norðan Temese, and be westan Sæfern, ʒe éac sum
15 dǽl þæs Norþ-Wéal-cynnes. Þá híe þá ealle ʒe-gadrode wǽron, þá of-fóron híe þone here hindan æt Butting-túne, on
Sæferne stæðe, and hine þǽr útan be-sǽton on ǽlče healfe,
on ánum fæstene. Þá híe þá fela wucena sǽton on twá healfa
þǽre éa, and se cyning wæs west on Defnum wiþ þone scip-
20 here, þá wǽron híe mid mete-líeste ʒe-wǽʒde, and hæfdon
mičelne dǽl þára horsa freten, and þá óðre wǽron hungre
a-cwolen. Þá éodon híe út to þǽm mannum þe on éast-healfe
þǽre éa wícodon and him wiþ ʒe-fuhton, and þá Crístnan hæfdon siʒe. And þǽr wearþ Ord-héah cyninges þeʒn of-
25 slæʒen, and éac maniʒe óðre cyninges þeʒnas; and þára Den-
iscra þǽr wearþ swíðe mičel wæl ʒe-slæʒen, and se dǽl þe
þǽr on-weʒ cóm wurdon on fléame ʒe-nerede.

Þá híe on Éast-Seaxe cómon to hira ʒe-weorce and to hira
scipum, þá ʒe-gadrode séo láf eft of Éast-Englum and of
30 Norþ-Hymbrum mičelne here on-foran winter, and be-fæston
hira wíf and hira scipu and hira feoh on Éast-Englum, and
fóron án-strečes dæʒes and nihtes, þæt híe ʒe-dydon on ánre
wéstre čeastre on Wír-héalum, séo is Léga-čeaster ʒe-háten.
Þá ne meahte séo fierd híe ná hindan of-faran, ǽr híe wǽron

When the king had turned west with the (English) army towards Exeter, as I said before, and the (Scandinavian) army had besieged the town, they went to their ships when he got there. Then, when he was occupied against the (Scandinavian) army there in the west, and both the (other) armies were assembled at Shoebury in Essex and had built a fortification there, both (of them) went up the Thames together. And a great reinforcement came to them from East Anglia and from Northumbria. Then they went up along the Thames until they got to the Severn, then up along the Severn. Then Ealdorman Ethelred and Ealdorman Ethelhelm and Ealdorman Ethelnoth and the retainers of the king who were then at home at the fortifications assembled (an army) from every town east of the Parret (river) and both west and east of Selwood (Forest) and also north of the Thames and west of the Severn, and also a certain portion of the Welsh people. Then when they were all assembled, they overtook the (Scandinavian) army from behind at Buttington on the bank of the Severn and besieged it on every side in a certain stronghold. Then, when they had stayed on the two sides of the river for many weeks, and the king was in the west in Devon (fighting) against the (viking) fleet, then they (i.e., the Scandinavians who were under siege) were afflicted by lack of food and had eaten up a large number of the horses, and the others had died of starvation. Then they went out to the men who were encamped on the east side of the river and fought against them, and the Christians were victorious (lit. had victory). And there Ordheah, the king's retainer, was killed, and also many other retainers of the king; and there was a very great slaughter of the Danes, and the part that got away were saved by flight.

When they got to Essex to their fortification and to their ships, then the survivors again collected a large army from East Anglia and Northumbria before winter, and put their women and ships and their property in safekeeping in East Anglia, and went day and night without stopping until they reached a certain deserted city in the Wirral, which is called Chester. Then the (English) army was not able to overtake them from behind before they got (lit. were) inside the

inne on þǽm ʒe-weorce. Be-sǽton þéah þæt ʒe-weorc útan
sume twéʒen dagas and ʒe-námon čéapes eall þæt þǽr bútan
wæs and þá menn of-slógon þe híe foran for-rídan meahton
bútan ʒe-weorce, and þæt corn eall for-bærndon, and mid hira
5 horsum fretton on ǽlčre efen-níehþe. And þæt wæs ymb twelf
mónaþ þæs-þe híe hider ofer sǽ cómon.

    894. And þá sóna æfter þǽm, on þýs ʒéare, fór se here of
Wír-héale inn on Norþ-Wéalas, for-þǽm híe þǽr sittan ne
meahton. Þæt wæs for-þý-þe híe wǽron be-numene ǽʒðer
10 ʒe þæs čéapes ʒe þæs cornes þe híe ʒe-hergod hæfdon. Þá
híe þá eft út of Norþ-Wéalum wendon mid þǽre here-húðe þe
híe þǽr ʒe-numen hæfdon, þá fóron híe ofer Norþ-Hymbra
land and Éast-Engla, swá swá séo fierd híe ʒe-rǽčan ne
meahte, oþ-þæt híe cómon on Éast-Seaxna land éaste-weard
15 on án íeʒ-land þæt is úte on þǽre sǽ, þæt is Meres-íeʒ háten.

    And þá se here eft hám-weard wende þe Exan-čeaster
be-seten hæfde, þá hergodon híe upp on Súþ-Seaxum néah
Čisse-čeastre, and þá burg-ware híe ʒe-flíemdon and hira
maniʒ hund of-slógon and hira scipu sumu ʒe-námon.

20   Þá þý ilcan ʒéare on fore-weardne winter þá Deniscan þe
on Meres-íeʒe sǽton tugon hira scipu upp on Temese and þá
upp on Lýʒan. Þæt wæs ymb twá ʒéar þæs-þe híe hider ofer
sǽ cómon.

    895. And þý ilcan ʒéare worhte se fore-sprecena here ʒe-
25 weorc be Lýʒan, xx míla bufan Lunden-byriʒ. Þá þæs on
sumora fóron mičel dǽl þára burg-wara, and éac swá óðres
folces, þæt híe ʒe-dydon æt þára Deniscena ʒe-weorce and
þǽr wurdon ʒe-flíemde, and sume féower cyninges þeʒnas
of-slæʒene. Þá þæs on hærfeste þá wícode se cyning on néa-
30 wiste þǽre byriʒ þá-hwile-þe híe hira corn ʒe-ripon, þæt þá
Deniscan him ne meahton þæs ripes for-wiernan. Þá sume
dæʒe rád se cyning upp be þǽre éa and ʒe-háwode hwǽr man
meahte þá éa for-wyrčan, þæt híe ne meahton þá scipu út
brenʒan. And híe þá swá dydon: worhton þá tú ʒe-weorc

fortification. They besieged the fortification for some two days, however, and seized all of the cattle that was outside and killed the men whom they had been able to cut off outside the fortification, and burned up all the grain and grazed their horses in the whole vicinity. And that was twelve months after they had come here (from) across the sea.

894. And then immediately after that, in this year, the (Scandinavian) army went out of the Wirral into Wales, because they could not stay there. That was because they had been deprived both of the cattle and of the grain which they (i.e., the English) had laid waste. Then, when they turned back out of Wales with the booty that they had taken there, they went across Northumbria and East Anglia, so that the (English) army could not get at them, until they got to eastern Essex to an island that is out in the sea, which is called Mersea.

And when the (Scandinavian) army which had been besieging Exeter was turning homeward again, then they made a raid up in Sussex near Chichester, and the townspeople put them to flight and killed many hundreds of them and captured some (of) their ships.

Then in that same year in early winter the Danes who were stationed on Mersea pulled their ships up the Thames and then up the Lea. That was two years after they had come here across the sea.

895. And in the same year the aforesaid (Scandinavian) army built a fortification on the Lea, twenty miles above London. Then afterwards in the summer a great part of the townspeople and also of other folk marched until (lit. so that) they got to the fortification of the Danes and there were put to flight, and some four (of the) king's retainers (were) killed. Then later, in the autumn, the king encamped in the vicinity of the city while they were reaping their grain, so that the Danes could not prevent them from harvesting (lit. hinder to them of the harvest). Then one day the king rode up along the river and surveyed where one might be able to block the river so that they could not bring their ships out. And then they did so: (they) built two fortifications on the two sides

on twá healfa þǽre éa. Þá híe þá þæt ȝe-weorc furðum on-
gunnen hæfdon and þǽr-tó ȝe-wícod hæfdon, þá on-ȝeat se
here þæt híe ne meahton þá scipu út brenȝan. Þá for-léton híe
híe and éodon ofer land þæt híe ȝe-dydon æt Brycge be Sæfern
5   and þǽr ȝe-weorc worhton. Þá rád séo fierd west æfter þǽm
herȝe, and þá menn of Lunden-byriȝ ȝe-fetodon þá scipu,
and þá ealle þe híe a-lǽdan ne meahton to-brǽcon, and þá-
þe þǽr stæl-weorðe wǽron binnan Lunden-byriȝ ȝe-bróhton.
And þá Deniscan hæfdon hira wíf be-fæst innan Éast-Engle,
10   ǽr híe út of þǽm ȝe-weorce fóron. Þá sǽton híe þone winter
æt Brycge. Þæt wæs ymb þréo ȝéar þæs-þe híe on Limene
múðan cómon hider ofer sǽ.

896. Þá þæs on sumora on þissum ȝéare to-fór se here,
sum on Éast-Engle, sum on Norþ-Hymbre. And þá-þe feoh-
15   léase wǽron him þǽr scipu be-ȝéaton and súþ ofer sǽ fóron
to Síȝene.

Næfde se here, Godes þances, Angel-cynn ealles for-swíðe
ȝe-brocod; ac híe wǽron miċele swíðor ȝe-brocode on þǽm
þrim ȝéarum mid ċéapes cwielde and manna, ealles swíðost
20   mid þǽm þæt maniȝe þára sélestena cyninges þeȝna þe þǽr
on lande wǽron forþ-férdon on þǽm þrim ȝéarum. Þára wæs
sum Swíþ-wulf biscop on Hrofes-ċeastre, and Ċéol-mund
ealdor-mann on Cent, and Beorht-wulf ealdor-mann on Éast-
Seaxum, and Wulf-rǽd ealdor-mann on Hám-tún-scíre, and
25   Ealh-heard biscop æt Dorce-ċeastre, and Éad-wulf cyninges
þeȝn on Súþ-Seaxum, and Beorn-wulf wíċ-ȝe-féra on Win-
tan-ċeastre, and Ecg-wulf cyninges hors-þeȝn, and maniȝe
éac him, þéah iċ þá ȝe-þungenestan nemde.

Þý ilcan ȝéare dreahton þá herȝas on Éast-Englum and
30   on Norþ-Hymbrum West-Seaxna land swíðe be þǽm súþ-
stæðe mid stæl-herȝum, eallra swíðost mid þǽm æscum þe
híe fela ȝéara ǽr timbredon. Þá hét Ælf-rǽd cyning timbran
lang-scipu on-ȝeȝn þá æscas. Þá wǽron full néah tú swá lange
swá þá óðru: sume hæfdon lx ára, sume má. Þá wǽron ǽȝðer

of the river. When they had just begun the work and had made camp for that purpose, then the (Scandinavian) army perceived that they could not bring the ships out. Then they abandoned them and went overland until they got to Bridgnorth on the Severn and built a fortification there. Then the (English) army rode west after the (Scandinavian) army, and the men from London fetched the ships, and broke up all of them that they were not able to take away, and took those that were serviceable to (lit. inside) London. And the Danes had put their women in safekeeping in East Anglia, before they left the fortification. Then they stayed the winter at Bridgnorth. That was three years after they had come here across the sea into the Lympne estuary.

896. Then afterwards in the summer in this year the (Scandinavian) army split up, one (part going) into East Anglia, one into Northumbria. And those that were without money got ships for themselves and went south across the sea to the Seine.

The (Scandinavian) army, by the grace of God, had not afflicted the English people so very much; but they were much more severely afflicted in those three years by a pestilence of cattle and men, and most of all by the fact that many of the best retainers of the king that there were in the country died in those three years. One of these was Swithwulf, bishop of Rochester, and Ceolmund, ealdorman of Kent, and Berhtwulf, ealdorman of Essex, and Wulfred, ealdorman of Hampshire, and Ealhheard, bishop of Dorchester, and Eadwulf, a royal officer in Sussex, and Beornwulf, bailiff of Winchester, and Ecgwulf, the royal marshal, and many besides them, though I have named the most distinguished.

In the same year the (Scandinavian) armies in East Anglia and Northumbria sorely harassed Wessex along the south coast with marauding bands, most of all with the viking ships which they had built many years before. Then King Alfred ordered warships built to oppose (lit. against) the viking ships. These were very nearly twice as long as the others (i.e., the viking ships) : some had sixty oars, some more. They were

ȝe swiftran, ȝe un-wealtran, ȝe éac híerran þonne þá óðru. Næron næȝðer né on Frésisc ȝe-scæpene né on Denisc, búte swá him selfum þúhte þæt hit nytt-weorðoste béon meahten.

5 Þá æt sumum čierre þæs ilcan ȝéares cómon þǽr siex scipu to Wiht and þǽr mičel yfel ȝe-dydon, ǽȝðer ȝe on Defnum ȝe wel-hwǽr be þǽm sǽ-riman. Þá hét se cyning faran mid nigunum tó þára níewena scipa, and for-fóron him þone múðan foran on úter-mere. Þá fóron híe mid þrim scipum út on-ȝeȝn híe, and þréo stódon æt ufe-weardum þǽm múðan

10 on dryȝum. Wǽron þá menn uppe on lande of a-gáne. Þá ȝe-féngon híe þára þréora scipa tú æt þǽm múðan úte-weardum and þá menn of-slógon, and þæt án oþ-wand. On þǽm wǽron éac þá menn of-slæȝene bútan fífum. Þá cómon for-þý on-weȝ þe þára óðerra scipu a-sǽton. Þá wurdon éac

15 swíðe un-íeðe-líče a-seten: þréo a-sǽton on þá healfe þæs déopes þe þá Deniscan scipu a-seten wǽron, and þá óðru eall on óðre healfe, þæt hira ne meahte nán to óðrum. Ac þá þæt wæter wæs a-ebbod fela fur-langa fram þǽm scipum, þá éodon þá Deniscan fram þǽm þrim scipum to þǽm óðrum

20 þrim þe on hira healfe be-ebbode wǽron, and híe þá þǽr ȝe-fuhton. Þǽr wearþ of-slæȝen Lucuman cyninges ȝe-réfa, and Wulf-heard Frésa, and Ǽbbe Frésa, and Ǽðel-here Frésa, and Ǽðel-ferhþ cyninges ȝe-néat, and eallra manna, Frésiscra and Engliscra, lxii, and þára Deniscena cxx. Þá cóm þǽm

25 Deniscum scipum þéah ǽr flód tó, ǽr þá Crístnan meahten hira út a-scúfan, and híe for-þý út oþ-réowon. Þá wǽron híe to þǽm ȝe-sárgode þæt híe ne meahton Súþ-Seaxna land útan be-rówan, ac hira þǽr tú sǽ on land wearp, and þá menn man lǽdde to Wintan-čeastre to þǽm cyninge, and hé híe þǽr

30 a-hón hét. And þá menn cómon on Éast-Engle þe on þǽm ánum scipe wǽron swíðe for-wundode.

Þý ilcan sumora for-wearþ ná lǽs þonne xx scipa mid mannum mid ealle be þǽm súþ-riman. Þý ilcan ȝéare forþ-férde Wulf-ríč cyninges hors-þeȝn, sé wæs éac Wealh-ȝe-

both swifter and steadier and also higher than the others (i.e., the viking ships). They were built neither on the Frisian (design) nor on the Danish, but as it seemed to him (i.e., the king) himself that they (lit. it) might be most serviceable.

Then at a certain time in the same year six (viking) ships came to (the Isle of) Wight and did great damage there, both in Devon and everywhere along the (south) coast. Then the king ordered (a detachment) to proceed there with nine of the new ships, and they blocked to them the estuary from the outside (lit. from in front in the outer bay). Then they (i.e., the vikings) went out against them with three ships, and three were on dry land in the upper (part of the) estuary. The men (i.e., from the three beached ships) had gone up inland. Then they (i.e., the English) captured two of those three ships in the outer (part of the) estuary and killed the men, and one (ship) escaped. In it also (all) the men except five were killed. Those got away because the ships of the others (i.e., the English) were aground. They were, furthermore, very awkwardly stranded: three were aground on that side of the channel where the Danish ships were stranded, and all the others (were) on the other side, so that none of them could (get) to the others. But when the water had ebbed many furlongs from the ships, then the Danes from those three ships went to the other three (English ships) that were stranded on their side (of the channel), and then they fought there. Lucuman, the royal reeve, was killed there, and Wulfheard the Frisian, and Æbba the Frisian, and Ethelhere the Frisian, and Ethelferth, a royal officer (lit. king's companion, i.e., a member of the king's household), and of all men, Frisian and English, sixty-two, and 120 of the Danes. The tide reached the Danish ships sooner, however, before the Christians could launch theirs, and on account of this they rowed away. They were then so wounded that they were not able to row past Sussex, but the sea cast two of them ashore, and the men were taken (lit. one led the men) to Winchester to the king, and he ordered them hanged there. And the men who were in that one ship reached East Anglia severely wounded.

That same summer no fewer than twenty ships, with men and all, were lost along the south coast. That same year died

réfa.

898. Hér on þissum ʒéare ʒe-fór Æðel-helm Wil-tún-scíre ealdor-mann, nigun nihtum ǽr middum sumora. And hér forþ-férde Héah-stán, sé wæs on Lundene biscop.

5   901. Hér ʒe-fór Ælf-rǽd Æðel-wulfing, siex nihtum ǽr eallra háliʒra mæssan. Sé wæs cyning ofer eall Angel-cynn bútan þǽm dǽle þe under Dena an-wealde wæs. And hé héold þæt ríče óðrum healfum lǽs þe xxx wintra. And þá féng Éad-weard his sunu to ríče.

Wulfric, the royal marshal, who was also Welsh-reeve.

898. In this year, nine days before midsummer, died Ethelhelm, ealdorman of Wiltshire. And in this year died Heahstan, who was bishop of London.

901. In this year Alfred son of Ethelwulf died, six days before All Saints' day (lit. mass of all saints). He had been king over the English people except for that part which was under the rule of the Danes. And he had ruled (lit. held the kingdom) for twenty-eight and a half years (lit. one and a half less than thirty). And then his son Edward succeeded to the throne.

King Alfred's Preface to
Pope Gregory's *Pastoral Care*

Ælf-rǽd cyning háteþ grétan Wǽr-ferhþ biscop his wordum
luf-líče and fréond-líče.

And [ič] þé cýðan háte þæt mé cóm swíðe oft on ʒe-mynd
hwelče witan ʒéo wǽron ʒeond Angel-cynn, ǽʒðer ʒe god-
5   cundra háda ʒe weorold-cundra, and hú ʒe-sǽliʒ-líča tída þá
wǽron ʒeond Angel-cynn, and hú þá cyningas þe þone an-
weald hæfdon þæs folces on þǽm dagum Gode and his ǽrend-
racum híer-sumodon, and hú híe ǽʒðer ʒe hira sibbe ʒe hira
sidu ʒe hira an-weald innan-bordes ʒe-héoldon, and éac út
10 hira éðel ʒe-rýmdon. And hú him þá spéow ǽʒðer ʒe mid
wíʒe ʒe mid wís-dóme, and éac þá god-cundan hádas hú
ʒeorne híe wǽron ǽʒðer ʒe ymb láre ʒe ymb leornunga ʒe
ymb ealle þá þéowot-dómas þe híe Gode dón scoldon. And hú
man útan-bordes wís-dóm and láre hider on land sóhte, and
15 hú híe nú scoldon úte be-ʒietan, ʒief wé híe habban scoldon.
Swá clǽne héo wæs oþ-feallenu on Angel-cynne þæt swíðe
féawa wǽron be-heonan Humbre þe hira þeʒnunga cúðen
under-standan on Englisc oþþe furðum án ǽrend-ʒe-writ of
Lǽdene on Englisc a-reččan, and ič wéne þætte náht maniʒe
20 be-ʒeondan Humbre nǽren. Swá féawa hira wǽron þæt ič
furðum ánne án-líepne ne mæʒ ʒe-þenčan be súðan Temese,
þá þá ič to ríče féng. Gode eall-mihtiʒum síe þanc þætte wé
nú ǽniʒne an-steall habbaþ láreowa.

And for-þon ič be-béode þæt þú dó swá ič ʒe-líefe þæt
25 þú wille, þæt þú þeč þissa weorold-þinga to þǽm ʒe-ǽmettiʒe,

Preface to *Pastoral Care*
(Translation)

King Alfred bids Bishop Wærferth be greeted with his words affectionately and in friendship.

And I bid made known to you that it has very often come to my mind what learned men there were formerly throughout England, in (lit. of) both sacred and secular offices, and what happy times there were then throughout England, and how the kings who had the authority over (lit. of) the people in those days obeyed God and his representatives, and how they maintained their peace and their morality and their authority at home and also extended their domain abroad. And how they prospered (lit. it prospered to them) both in war and in learning, and also how zealous the sacred orders were about teaching and learning and all the services that they were supposed to perform for God. And how abroad one looked to this country for learning and instruction, and how we should now have to get it from abroad, if we were to have it. So completely had it lapsed in England that there were very few on this side of the Humber who could understand their mass-books in English or translate even one written message from Latin into English, and I believe that there were by no means many beyond the Humber. There were so few of them that I cannot think of even a single one south of the Thames, when I succeeded to the throne. Thanks be to God almighty that we now have any supply of teachers.

And therefore I command you that you do that which I believe that you will, that you turn your attention from (lit. empty yourself of) these worldly affairs, as often as you can

swá swá þú oftost mæȝe, þæt þú þone wís-dóm þe þé God
sealde þǽr þǽr þú hine be-fæstan mæȝe, be-fæste. ȝe-þenč
hwelč wítu ús þá be-cómon for þisse weorolde, þá þá wé hit
ná-hwæðer né selfe ne lufodon, né éac óðrum mannum ne
30 líefdon: þone naman ánne wé lufodon þætte wé Crístne
wǽren, and swíðe féawa þá þéawas.

Þá ič þis eall ȝe-munde, þá ȝe-munde ič hú ič ȝe-seah,
ǽr-þǽm-þe hit eall for-hergod wǽre and for-bærned, hú þá
čiričan ȝeond eall Angel-cynn stódon máðma and bóca ȝe-
10 fylde, and éac mičel meniȝu Godes þéowa, and þá swíðe lýtle
feorme þára bóca wiston, for-þǽm-þe híe hira nán-wiht on-
ȝietan ne meahton, for-þǽm-þe híe nǽron on hira ágen
ȝe-þéode a-writene. Swelče híe cwǽden: "Úre ieldran, þá-þe
þás stówa héoldon, híe lufodon wís-dóm and þurh þone híe
15 be-ȝéaton welan and ús lǽfdon. Hér man mæȝ ȝíet ȝe-séon
hira swæþ, ac wé him ne cunnon æfter spyrian, and for-þǽm
wé habbaþ nú ǽȝðer for-lǽten ȝe þone welan ȝe þone wís-
dóm, for-þǽm-þe wé noldon to þǽm spore mid úre móde on-
lútan."

20 Þá ič þá þis eall ȝe-munde, þá wundrode ič swíðe swíðe
þára gódena witena þe ȝéo wǽron ȝeond Angel-cynn and þá
béč ealla be fullan ȝe-leornod hæfdon, þæt hira þá nánne dǽl
noldon on hira ágen ȝe-þéode wendan. Ac ič þá sóna eft mé
selfum and-wyrde and cwæþ: "Híe ne wéndon þætte ǽfre
25 menn scoldon swá réče-léase weorðan and séo lár swá oþ-
feallan. For þǽre wilnunga híe hit for-léton, and woldon þæt
hér þý mára wís-dóm on lande wǽre þý wé má ȝe-þéoda
cúðon."

Þá ȝe-munde ič hú séo ǽ wæs ǽrest on Ebreisc ȝe-þéode
30 funden, and eft, þá híe Crécas ȝe-leornodon, þá wendon híe
híe on hira ágen ȝe-þéode ealle, and éac ealle óðre béč. And
eft Lǽden-ware swá same, siþþan híe híe ȝe-leornodon, híe
híe wendon ealla þurh wíse wealh-stódas on hira ágen ȝe-
þéode. And éac ealla óðra Crístna þéoda sumne dǽl hira on

(lit. as you most often can), to this, that you may implant the learning that God has given you wherever (lit. where) you can implant it. Think what troubles befell us on account of this world, when we neither loved it (i.e., learning) ourselves nor moreover allowed it to other men: we loved the name alone of being (lit. that we were) Christians and very few of the virtues.

When I recalled all this, then I remembered how I had seen, before it had all been devastated and burned, how the churches throughout England were (lit. stood) filled with treasures and books, and also a great multitude of God's servants (i.e., monks), and they got (lit. knew) very little benefit from (lit. of) those books, for they could not understand any (lit. nothing) of them, because they were not written in their own language. (It was) as if they had said: "Our forebears, who formerly occupied these positions, they loved learning and through it they acquired riches and left (them) to us. Here one can still see their track, but we do not know how to follow after them, for we have given up both the riches and the learning, because we were not willing to incline our minds to that course."

When I recalled all this, then I marveled very greatly at those excellent learned men who formerly were throughout England and had fully studied all those books, (and I marveled) that they had not wished to translate any (lit. no) portion of them into their own language. But I then immediately in turn answered myself and said: "They did not think that men would ever become so careless and teaching (would) lapse so. They neglected (lit. left) it (i.e., the work of translation) for that reason (lit. desire), and they wished that the more languages we knew the greater might learning be in this country."

Then I recalled how the law was first found in the Hebrew language, and in turn, when the Greeks learned it, then they translated it all into their own language, and also all other books. And likewise in turn the Latin-speaking people, when they learned it, they translated them all (i.e., the books of the Bible) through learned interpreters into their own language. And also all the other Christian peoples translated some por-

hira ágen ʒe-þéode wendon. For-þý mé þynčeþ betere, ʒief
éow swá þynčeþ, þæt wé éac suma béč, þá-þe níed-be-þearf-
osta síen eallum mannum to witenne, þæt wé þá on þæt
ʒe-þéode wenden þe wé ealle ʒe-cnáwan mæʒen, and ʒe-dón,
5 swá wé swíðe éaðe magon mid Godes fultume, ʒief wé þá
still-ness habbaþ, þætte eall séo ʒeoguþ þe nú is on Angel-
cynne fréora manna, þára-þe spéda hæbben þæt híe þǽm
be-féolan mæʒen, síen to leornunga oþ-fæste, þá-hwíle-þe híe
to nánre óðerre note ne mæʒen, oþ þone first þe híe wel
10 cunnen Englisc ʒe-writ a-rǽdan. Lǽre man siþþan furðor on
Læden-ʒe-þéode þá-þe man furðor lǽran wille and to híerran
háde dón wille. Þá ič ʒe-munde hú séo lár Læden-ʒe-þéodes
ǽr þissum a-feallen wæs ʒeond Angel-cynn—and þéah maniʒe
cúðon Englisc ʒe-writ a-rǽdan—þá on-gann ič on-ʒe-mang
15 óðrum mis-líčum and maniʒ-fealdum bisgum þisses cyne-ríčes
þá bóc wendan on Englisc þe is ʒe-nemned on Læden 'Pastoralis,' and on Englisc 'Hierde-bóc,' hwílum word be worde,
hwílum and-ʒiet of and-ʒiete, swá swá ič híe ʒe-leornode æt
Pleg-munde, mínum ærče-biscope, and æt Assere, mínum
20 biscope, and æt Grimm-bealde, mínum mæsse-préoste, and æt
Ióhanne, mínum mæsse-préoste. Siþþan ič híe þá ʒe-leornod
hæfde, swá swá ič híe for-stód, and swá ič híe and-ʒiet-ful-
líčost a-reččan meahte, ič híe on Englisc a-wende, and to
ǽlčum biscop-stóle on mínum ríče wille áne on-sendan; and
25 on ǽlčre biþ án æstel sé biþ on fíftiʒum mancussa. And ič
be-béode on Godes naman þæt nán man þone æstel fram þǽre
béč ne dó né þá bóc fram þǽm mynstre. Un-cúþ hú lange
þǽr swá ʒe-lǽrde biscopas síen, swá swá nú, Gode þanc, wel-
hwǽr sindon. For-þý ič wolde þætte híe ealneʒ æt þǽre stówe
30 wǽren, bútan se biscop híe mid him habban wille oþþe héo
hwǽr to lǽne síe oþþe hwá óðre bí wríte.

tion of them into their own language. Therefore it seems
better to me, if it seems so to you, that we also (translate)
certain books, which may be most necessary for all men to
know, that we translate them into the language that we can
all understand, and (that we) bring it about, as we very easily
can with God's help, if we have peace, that young people (of
the class) of freemen who are now in England who have the
means (lit. wealth) so that they may be able to devote themselves to it, be set to studying, as long as (lit. while) they
cannot (be set) to any (lit. no) other employment, until the
time when they know how to read English writing well. One
may then further instruct in the Latin language those whom
one may wish to instruct further and may wish to place in a
higher office. When I recalled how instruction in the Latin
language had fallen off before this throughout England—and
yet many knew how to read English writing—then among the
other various and manifold preoccupations of this kingdom I
began to translate into English this book which is called in
Latin 'Pastoralis,' and in English 'Pastor's Book,' sometimes
word for word, sometimes meaning for meaning, as I learned
it from Plegmund, my archbishop, and from Asser, my bishop,
and from Grimbold, my mass-priest, and from John, my mass-
priest. When I had learned it then, so that I understood it and
was able to expound it most sensibly, I translated it into
English, and I wish to send one (copy) to each diocese in my
kingdom; and in each there will be a book-mark worth (lit.
in) fifty mancuses. And in God's name I command that no
one take the book-mark from the book nor the book from the
cathedral. No one knows (lit. unknown) how long there may
be such learned bishops there, as now, thanks to God, there
are everywhere (i.e., in all dioceses). For that reason I should
wish that they might always be in that place, unless the bishop
may wish to take (lit. have) them with him or it may be on
loan somewhere or some one may be making a copy (lit.
writing another) from (it).

POETRY

Cædmon's Hymn

Nú wé sculon herian   heofon-ríčes Weard,
Meotodes meahte   and his mód-ʒe-þanc,
weorc Wuldor-Fæder,   swá hé wundra ʒe-hwæs,
éče Dryhten,   ór on-stealde.
5   Hé ǽrest scóp   ielda bearnum
     heofon to hrófe,   háliʒ Scieppend;
     þá middan-ʒeard   mann-cynnes Weard,
     éče Dryhten,   æfter téode,
     fírum foldan,   Fréa eall-mihtiʒ.

Cædmon's Hymn
(*Translation*)

Now we must praise the Guardian of the kingdom of heaven,
the might of the Creator and his purpose of mind, the work of
the Father of glory, as he, the eternal Lord, established the
beginning of every wonder. (5) He, the holy Creator, first
created heaven as a roof for the sons of men; then the
Guardian of mankind, the eternal Lord, the Lord almighty,
afterwards prepared the world, the earth for men.

The Battle of Brúnan-burg

Hér Æðel-stán cyning,   eorla dryhten,
beorna béag-ӡiefa,   and his bróðor éac,
Éad-mund æðeling,   ealdor-langne tír
ӡe-slógon æt sæcče   sweorda ecgum
5 ymbe Brúnan-burg.   Bord-weall clufon,
héowon heaðu-linda   hamora láfum
eaforan Éad-weardes,   swá him ӡe-æðele wæs
fram cnéo-mágum   þæt híe æt campe oft
wiþ láðra ӡe-hwone   land ealgodon,
10 hord and hámas.   Hettend crungon,
Scotta léode   and scip-flotan,
fǽӡe féollon.   Feld dennode
secga swáte,   siþþan sunne upp
on morgen-tíd,   mǽre tungol,
15 glád ofer grundas,   Godes candel beorht,
éčes Dryhtnes,   oþ séo æðele ӡe-sceaft
ság to setle.   Þǽr læӡ secg maniӡ
gárum a-ӡíeted,   guma Norðerna
ofer scield scoten,   swelče Scyttisc éac,
20 wériӡ, wíӡes sæd.   West-Seaxe forþ
and-langne dæӡ   éorod-cystum
on lást leӡdon   láðum þéodum,

The Battle of Brunanburg
(Translation)

Here King Athelstan, lord of nobles, ring-giver of men, and
his brother also, Prince Edmund, won in battle life-long glory
with the edges of their swords at Brunanburg. (5b) The sons
of Edward split the shield-wall, hewed the linden-wood battle-
shields with the leavings of hammers (i.e., swords), as was
fitting to them from their ancestors that they should often
defend in battle their land, treasure, and homes against every
enemy. (10b) Enemies fell, people of the Scots and seamen
(i.e., Scandinavian invaders), fell doomed to die. (12b) The
field flowed with the blood of warriors, after the sun, splendid
star, bright candle of God, the eternal Lord, in the morning
glided up over the plains, until that noble creation sank to its
resting place (i.e., set). (17b) Many a warrior lay dead there,
killed by spears, (many a) Norseman (lit. man of the North-
erners) shot over his shield, likewise (many a) Scot also,
weary, sated with battle. (20b) The West Saxons kept
pursuing the enemies (lit. hostile peoples) with their elite
troops the entire day, hacked the fugitives severely from be-

héowon here-flíeman   hindan þearle
méčum mylen-scearpum.   Mierče ne wierndon
25 heardes hand-plegan   hæleða nánum
þára-þe mid An-láfe   ofer éar-ʒe-bland
on lides bósme   land ʒe-sóhton,
fǽʒe to ʒe-feohte.   Fífe lágon
on þǽm camp-stede   cyningas ʒeonge,
30 sweordum a-swefede,   swelče seofone éac
eorlas An-láfes,   un-rím herʒes,
flotena and Scotta.   Þǽr ʒe-flíemed wearþ
Norþ-manna bregu,   níede ʒe-bǽded,
to lides stefne   lýtle weorode ;
35 créad cnearr on flot,   cyning út ʒe-wát
on fealone flód,   feorh ʒe-nerede.
Swelče þǽr éac se fróda   mid fléame cóm
on his cýþþe norþ,   Constantínus,
hár hilde-rínc.   Hréman ne þorfte
40 méča ʒe-mánan ;   hé wæs his mága sceard,
fréonda ʒe-fielled   on folc-stede,
be-slæʒen æt sæčče,   and his sunu for-lét
on wæl-stówe   wundum for-grunden,
ʒeongne æt gúðe.   ðielpan ne þorfte
45 beorn blanden-feax   bill-ʒe-sliehtes,
eald inwidda,   né An-láf þý má ;
mid hira here-láfum   hliehhan ne þorfton
þæt híe beadu-weorca   beteran wurdon
on camp-stede   cumbol-ʒe-hnástes,
50 gár-mittinge,   gumena ʒe-mótes,
wǽpen-ʒe-wrixles,   þæs híe on wæl-felda
wiþ Éad-weardes   eaforan plegodon.
ʒe-witon him þá Norþ-menn   næʒled-cnearrum,
dréoriʒ daroða láf,   on Dinges mere
55 ofer déop wæter   Dyflin séčan,
eft Íra-land,   ǽwisc-móde.

hind with grindstone-sharpened swords. (24b) The Mercians did not refuse fierce hand-to-hand fighting to any (lit. none) of the men who had come to the country (i.e., England) with Olaf over the turbulence of the sea in the bosom of a ship, doomed to die in battle. (28b) Five young kings lay dead on the battlefield, put to sleep by swords, likewise also seven jarls of Olaf, a countless number of the army, of sailors and Scots. (32b) The ruler of the Norsemen was put to flight there, forced by necessity, to the prow of a ship with a small company; the ship hastened to sea, the king went out on the dark flood, saved his life. (37) Likewise there also the old (man) went in flight north to his native land, Constantine, the hoary warrior. (39b) He had no need to boast of the sword-play (lit. intercourse of swords); he was bereft of his kinsmen, deprived (by killing) of friends on the battlefield, struck down in battle, and he left his son on the battlefield destroyed by wounds, the young (man), in battle. (44b) The gray-haired (lit. blent-haired) man had no need to boast of the sword-slaughter, the wicked old (man), nor Olaf the more; with the remnants of their army they had no need to rejoice (lit. laugh) that they were better in warlike deeds, in the clash of banners on the battlefield, the spear-conflict, the meeting of men, the weapon-exchange, (to boast of the fact) that they had fought against the sons of Edward on the battle-field. (53) The Norsemen departed then in their nailed ships, wretched survivors (lit. remainder) of spears, to Dingesmere (?), over the deep water to go to Dublin, Ireland again,

    Swelče þá ȝe-bróðor   béȝen æt-samne,
    cyning and æðeling,   cýþþe sóhton,
    West-Seaxna land,   wíȝes hrémiȝe.
60 Léton him be-hindan   hrǽw bryttian
    salwiȝ-pádan,   þone sweartan hræfn,
    hyrned-nebban,   and þone hasu-pádan,
    earn æftan hwít,   æses brúcan,
    grǽdiȝne gúþ-hafoc   and þæt grǽȝe déor,
65 wulf on wealda.   Ne wearþ wæl máre
    on þýs íeȝ-lande   ǽfre ȝieta
    folces ȝe-fielled   be-foran þissum
    sweordes ecgum,   þæs-þe ús secgaþ béč,
    ealde úþ-witan,   siþþan éastan hider
70 Engle and Seaxe   upp be-cómon,
    ofer brád brimu   Breotone sóhton,
    wlance wíȝ-smiðas,   Wéalas ofer-cómon,
    eorlas ár-hwæte   eard be-ȝéaton.

abashed in spirit. (57) Likewise the brothers, both together, king and prince, went to their home, the land of the West Saxons, exultant over the battle. (60) They left behind them to divide the corpses the dark-coated (one), the black raven, horny-beaked, and the dusky-coated eagle with white tail (lit. white from behind), to enjoy the carrion,—the greedy war-hawk, and the gray beast, the wolf in the forest. (65b) Never (lit. not ever) yet before this had there been a greater slaughter on this island of an armed force laid low by the edges of the sword, according to what (lit. of that which) books tell us, old scholars, since the Angles and Saxons came ashore here from the east, came over the broad seas to Britain, proud warriors (lit. war-smiths), overcame the Celts, glorious heroes seized a country.

The Battle of Maldon

  * * * * brocen wurde.
Hét þá hyssa hwone hors for-lǽtan,
feorr a-fýsan and forþ gangan,
hycgan to handum and to hyʒe gódum.
5 Þá þæt Offan mǽʒ ǽrest on-funde,
þæt se eorl nolde ierʒþu ʒe-þolian,
hé lét him þá of handum léofne fléogan
hafoc wiþ þæs holtes, and to þǽre hilde stóp;
be þǽm man meahte on-cnáwan þæt se cniht nolde
10 wácian æt þǽm wíʒe þá hé to wǽpnum féng.
Éac him wolde Éad-ríč his ealdre ʒe-lǽstan,
fréan to ʒe-feohte; on-gann þá forþ beran
gár to gúðe. Hé hæfde gód ʒe-þanc
þá-hwíle-þe hé mid handum healdan meahte
15 bord and brád sweord; béot hé ʒe-lǽste
þá hé æt-foran his fréan feohtan scolde.
  Þá þǽr Beorht-nóþ on-gann beornas trymian,
rád and rǽdde, rincum tǽhte
hú híe scoldon standan and þone stede healdan,
20 and bæd þæt hira randas rihte héolden
fæste mid folmum and ne forhtoden ná.
Þá hé hæfde þæt folc fæʒere ʒe-trymed,

The Battle of Maldon
(*Translation*)

. . . was broken. Then he commanded each (lit. some one) of the young men to leave (his) horse, to drive (it) away (lit. far) and to keep going on foot, to give thought to hands (i.e., hand-to-hand fighting) and (to be) of good courage. (5) When the kinsman of Offa first discovered this, that the earl would not tolerate slackness, he let his beloved falcon fly from his hands toward the wood, and he advanced to the battle; by this one could perceive that the young man would not grow weak in the combat when he took up arms. (11) In addition to him (i.e., Offa's kinsman), Eadric wished to stand by his chief, his lord in battle; he began then to carry his spear forward to battle. (13b) He had a good purpose as long as he was able to hold with his hands shield and broad sword; he fulfilled his vow when he was supposed to fight before his lord.

(17) Then Byrhtnoth began to arrange the warriors there, he rode and instructed, he directed the men how they had to stand and hold that position, and he ordered that they should hold their shields correctly, firmly with their hands, and that they should not become frightened at all. (22) When he had

hé líehte þá mid léodum   þǽr him léofost wæs,
þǽr hé his heorþ-weorod   holdost wiste.

25   Þá stód on stæðe,   stíþ-líče clipode
wíčinga ár,   wordum mǽlde,
sé on béot a-béad   brim-líðendra
ǽrende to þǽm eorle   þǽr hé on ófre stód:
"Mé sendon to þé   sǽ-menn snelle,

30   héton þé secgan   þæt þú móst sendan hræðe
béagas wiþ ȝe-beorge;   and éow betere is
þæt ȝé þisne gár-rǽs   mid gafole for-ȝielden
þonne wé swá hearde   hilde dǽlen.
Ne þurfe wé ús spillan   ȝief ȝé spédaþ to þǽm;

35   wé willaþ wiþ þǽm golde   griþ fæstnian.
ȝief þú þæt ȝe-rǽdest,   þe hér ríčost eart,
þæt þú þíne léode   líesan wille,
sellan sǽ-mannum   on hira selfra dóm
feoh wiþ fréode   and niman friþ æt ús,

40   wé willaþ mid þǽm sceattum   ús to scipe gangan,
on flot féran,   and éow friðes healdan."
    Beorht-nóþ maðelode,   bord hafenode,
wand wácne æsc,   wordum mǽlde
ierre and án-rǽd,   a-ȝeaf him and-sware:

45   "ȝe-híerest þú, sǽ-lida,   hwæt þis folc sæȝeþ?
Híe willaþ éow to gafole   gáras sellan,
ǽtrenne ord   and ealde sweord,
þá here-ȝeatwe   þe éow æt hilde ne déag.
Brim-manna boda,   a-béod eft on-ȝeȝn,

50   sæȝe þínum léodum   mičele láðre spell,
þæt hér stent un-for-cúþ   eorl mid his weorode,
þe wile ȝe-ealgian   éðel þisne,
Æðel-rǽdes eard,   ealdres mínes,
folc and foldan.   Feallan sculon

55   hǽðne æt hilde.   Tó héan-líč mé þynčeþ
þæt ȝé mid úrum sceattum   to scipe gangen

arranged the army properly, he dismounted then among people where it was most pleasing to him (to be), where he knew his band of household retainers (to be) most loyal.

(25) Then a messenger of the vikings stood on the shore, called out sternly, spoke with words, who threateningly announced the message of the seafarers to the earl where he was standing on the river-bank:

(29) "Bold seamen have sent me to you, have commanded (me) to say to you that you must (lit. may) quickly send rings (i.e., treasure) for protection; and it is better for you that you should buy off this onslaught of spears with tribute than (that) we should take part in such cruel combat. (34) We need not kill each other if you are that wealthy; we are willing to make (lit. secure) peace for the gold. (36) If you who are most powerful (i.e., in command) here decide that you wish to redeem your people, to hand over to the seamen on their own terms money in return for peace and to accept peace from us, we are willing to go aboard ship with the coins, to go to sea, and to keep peace with you."

(42) Byrhtnoth discoursed, held up his shield, brandished his slender ash-wood spear, spoke with words, angry and resolute, gave him answer:

(45) "Do you hear, seafarer, what this people says? They are willing to give you (only) spears as tribute, deadly (lit. poisonous) spear-point and ancient swords, that battle-gear that will not be good for you in battle. (49) Messenger of the seamen, announce again in reply, tell your people a much more hostile message, that here stands a dauntless warrior with his troop, who is about to defend this homeland, land of Ethelred, my lord, people and ground. (54b) Heathens are destined to fall in battle. It seems to me too ignominious

un-be-fohtene,   nú ʒé þus feorr hider
on úrne eard   inn be-cómon.
    Ne scule ʒé swá sófte   sinc ʒe-gangan ;
60   ús sceal ord and ecg   ǽr ʒe-séman,
    grimm gúþ-plega,   ǽr wé gafol sellen."
    Hét þá bord beran,   beornas gangan
þæt híe on þǽm éa-stæðe   ealle stódon.
    Ne meahte þǽr for wætere   weorod to þǽm óðrum ;
65   þǽr cóm flówende   flód æfter ebban,
    lucon lagu-stréamas.   Tó lang hit him þúhte
    hwonne híe to-gædre   gáras bǽren.
    Híe þǽr Pantan stréam   mid prasse be-stódon,
    Éast-Seaxna ord   and se æsc-here.
70   Ne meahte hira ǽniʒ   óðrum derian,
    bútan hwá þurh flánes flyht   fiell ʒe-náme.
    Se flód út ʒe-wát.   Þá flotan stódon ʒearwe,
    wičinga fela,   wíʒes ʒeorne.
    Hét þá hæleða hléow   healdan þá brycge
75   wigan wíʒ-heardne,   sé wæs háten Wulf-stán,
    cáfne mid his cynne ;   þæt wæs Čéolan sunu,
    þe þone forman mann   mid his francan of-scéat
    þe þǽr beald-líčost   on þá brycge stóp.
    Þǽr stódon mid Wulf-stáne   wigan un-forhte,
80   Ælf-here and Maccus,   módʒe twéʒen ;
    þá noldon æt þǽm forda   fléam ʒe-wyrčan,
    ac híe fæst-líče   wiþ þá fíend weredon
    þá-hwíle-þe híe wǽpna   wealdan móston.
    Þá híe þæt on-ʒéaton   and ʒeorne ʒe-sáwon
85   þæt híe þǽr brycg-weardas   bitere fundon,
    on-gunnon lytiʒian þá   láðe ʒiestas,
    bǽdon þæt híe upp-gang   ágan mósten,
    ofer þone ford faran,   féðan lǽdan.
    Þá se eorl on-gann   for his ofer-móde

that you should go aboard ship with our coins, unopposed, now that you have come in thus far into our country. (59) You shall not so easily obtain treasure; sooner shall spear-point and sword, fierce battle-play, reconcile us, before we pay tribute."

(62) Then he commanded shields to be borne, warriors to go until they all stood on the river-bank. (64) On account of the water (one) army could not (get) to the other; the tide came flowing there after the ebb, the tidal currents joined. (66b) It seemed to them too long until they might bear spears together. They stood on both sides of the Pante stream in proud array, the battle-line of the East Saxons and the (men of the) viking fleet. (70) None (lit. not any) of them could harm the others, unless someone might get (his) death through the flight of an arrow.

(72) The tide went out. The pirates stood ready, many vikings, eager for battle. (74) Then the protector of warriors (i.e., Byrhtnoth) commanded a warrior brave in battle, who was called Wulfstan, bold among his race, to hold the causeway; it was the son of Ceola who with his spear shot down the first man who advanced most boldly there onto the causeway. (79) Fearless warriors stood there with Wulfstan, Ælfhere and Maccus, a courageous pair; they did not wish to take flight at the ford, but (on the contrary) they steadily defended themselves against the enemies as long as they might wield weapons.

(84) When they realized that and clearly perceived that they had encountered there fierce guardians of the causeway, the hostile strangers then began to become guileful, asked that they might have passage onto land, go over the ford, lead their troop.

(89) Then the earl on account of his overconfidence began

90 a-líefan landes tó fela láðre þéode.

On-gann čeallian þá ofer čeald wæter
Beorht-helmes bearn— beornas ʒe-hlyston—:
"Nú éow is ʒe-rýmed, gáþ recene to ús,
guman to gúðe. God ána wát

95 hwá þǽre wæl-stówe wealdan móte."

Wódon þá wæl-wulfas— for wætere ne murnon—,
wíčinga weorod, west ofer Pantan,
ofer scír wæter scieldas wǽgon,
lid-menn to lande linda bǽron.

100 Þǽr on-ʒeʒn gramum ʒearwe stódon
Beorht-nóþ mid beornum; hé mid bordum hét
wyrčan þone wíʒ-hagan and þæt weorod healdan
fæste wiþ féondum. Þá wæs feohte néah,
tír æt ʒe-tohte. Wæs séo tíd cumen

105 þæt þǽr fǽʒe menn feallan scoldon.
Þǽr wearþ hréam a-hafen, hræfnas wundon,
earn ǽses ʒeorn. Wæs on eorðan čierm.

Híe léton þá of folman féol-hearde speru,
ʒe-grundene gáras fléogan.

110 Bogan wǽron bisiʒe, bord ord on-féng.
Biter wæs se beadu-rǽs, beornas féollon
on ʒe-hwæðere hand, hyssas lágon.
Wund wearþ Wulf-mǽr, wæl-reste ʒe-čéas,
Beorht-nóðes mǽʒ; hé mid billum wearþ,

115 his sweostor sunu, swíðe for-héawen.
Þǽr wearþ wíčingum wiðer-léan a-ʒiefen.
ʒe-híerde ič þæt Éad-weard ánne slóge
swíðe mid his sweorde, swenʒes ne wiernde,
þæt him æt fótum féoll fǽʒe cempa;

120 þæs him his þéoden þance ʒe-sæʒde,
þǽm búr-þeʒne, þá hé byre hæfde.

Swá stefnetton stíþ-hycgende
hyssas æt hilde, hogodon ʒeorne

to give too much ground to the hostile people. (91) The son of Byrhthelm began then to shout across the cold water—the men listened—:

(93) "Now that way is made for you, come quickly to us, men to battle. God alone knows who may be permitted to control this battlefield."

(96) The slaughter-wolves (i.e., vikings) advanced—they did not care about the water—, the band of vikings, west over the Pante, carried their shields over the glistening water, the seamen bore their linden-wood shields ashore. (100) There opposite the fierce (men) Bryhtnoth with his men stood ready; he commanded the shield-wall (lit. battle-hedge) to be made with shields and (commanded) the troop to hold fast against the enemies. (103b) Then battle was near, glory in combat. The time had come when doomed men were destined to fall there. (106) The alarm was raised there, ravens wheeled, the eagle eager for carrion. There was noise on earth.

(108) Then they let fly from hand file-hard (i.e., as hard as a file?) spears, sharpened (lit. ground) spears. (110) Bows were busy, shield received spear-point. The onslaught (lit. battle-rush) was fierce, warriors fell on either hand, young men lay dead. (113) Wulfmær was wounded, Byrhtnoth's kinsman was laid low (lit. chose a bed of slaughter); he, the son of his (i.e., Byrhtnoth's) sister, was fiercely hacked to pieces with swords. (116) Requital was given to the vikings there. I heard that Edward struck one fiercely with his sword, did not withhold the blow, so that the doomed warrior fell at his feet; for this his chieftain said thanks to him, to the chamberlain, when he had an opportunity.

(122) So the resolute young warriors stood fast in battle, eagerly considered who there with spear-point first might be

hwá þǽr mid orde   ǽrest meahte
125 on fǽȝan menn   feorh ȝe-winnan,
wigan mid wǽpnum;   wæl féoll on eorðan.
Stódon stede-fæste;   stihte híe Beorht-nóþ,
bæd þæt hyssa ȝe-hwelč   hogode to wíȝe,
þe on Denum wolde   dóm ȝe-feohtan.
130   Wód þá wíȝes heard,   wǽpen upp a-hóf,
bord to ȝe-beorge,   and wiþ þæs beornes stóp.
Éode swá án-rǽd   eorl to þǽm čeorle;
ǽȝðer hira óðrum   yfeles hogode.
Sende þá se sǽ-rinc   súðerne gár,
135 þæt ȝe-wundod wearþ   wiȝena hláford.
Hé scéaf þá mid þǽm scielde,   þæt se sceaft to-bærst
and þæt spere sprenȝde,   þæt hit sprang on-ȝeȝn.
Ȝe-gremed wearþ se gúþ-rinc;   hé mid gáre stang
wlancne wíčing   þe him þá wunde for-ȝeaf.
140 Fród wæs se fierd-rinc;   hé lét his francan wadan
þurh þæs hysses heals,   hand wísode
þæt hé on þǽm fǽr-scaðan   feorh ȝe-rǽhte.
Þá hé óðerne   ofost-líče scéat,
þæt séo byrne to-bærst;   hé wæs on bréostum wund
145 þurh þá hring-locan,   him æt heortan stód
ǽterne ord.   Se eorl wæs þý blíðra,
hlóg þá módiȝ mann,   sæȝde Meotode þanc
þæs dæȝ-weorces   þe him Dryhten for-ȝeaf.
For-lét þá drenga sum   daroþ of handa,
150 fléogan of folman,   þæt sé tó forþ ȝe-wát
þurh þone æðelan   Æðel-rǽdes þeȝn.
Him be healfe stód   hyse un-weaxen,
cniht on ȝe-campe,   sé full cáf-líče
bræȝd of þǽm beorne   blódiȝne gár,
155 Wulf-stánes bearn,   Wulf-mǽr se ȝeonga,
for-lét for-heardne   faran eft on-ȝeȝn;
ord inn ȝe-wód,   þæt sé on eorðan læȝ

able to wrest the life from a doomed man, a warrior with (his) weapons; the slain (lit. slaughter) fell to the earth. (127) They stood steadfast; Byrhtnoth directed them, ordered that each of the young men, who wished to win glorious reputation by fighting against the Danes, should concentrate on battle.

(130) Then (a viking) brave in battle advanced, raised his weapon, his shield as a protection, and advanced toward the warrior (i.e., Bryhtnoth). (132) Equally resolute the earl went to the man; each of them intended harm to the other.

(134) Then the seafarer sent a southern (i.e., Frankish) spear, in such a way that the lord of warriors was wounded. (136) He thrust then with the shield, so that the shaft was shattered and the spear shivered, so that it sprang back. (138) The battle-warrior became enraged; with a spear he stabbed the proud viking who had given him the wound. (140) The English warrior was experienced; he let his spear go through the young man's neck, his hand guided (it) so that he fatally wounded (lit. hit the life of) the sudden enemy. (143) Then he hastily shot another, so that the byrnie shattered; he was wounded in the breast through the coat of chain-mail, the deadly spear-point stopped in his heart. (146b) The earl was the happier, the courageous man laughed, said thanks to the Creator for the day's work that the Lord had granted him.

(149) Then one of the warriors let go a javelin from his hand, (let it) fly from his hand, in such a way that it went forward through the noble retainer of Ethelred. (152) By his side stood a young warrior not fully grown, a boy in battle, who very boldly pulled the bloody spear out of the warrior, Wulfstan's son, Wulfmær the young(er), let the very hard (spear) go back again; the point went in, so that he who had

þe his þéoden ǽr   þearle ʒe-rǽhte.
    Éode þá ʒe-sierwed   secg to þǽm eorle;
160   hé wolde þæs beornes   béagas ʒe-feččan,
réaf and hringas   and ʒe-reʒnod sweord.
Þá Beorht-nóþ bræʒd   bill of scéaðe,
brád and brún-ecg,   and on þá byrnan slóg.
Tó raðe hine ʒe-lette   lid-manna sum,
165   þá hé þæs eorles   earm a-mierde.
Féoll þá to foldan   fealu-hilte sweord,
ne meahte hé ʒe-healdan   heardne méče,
wǽpnes wealdan.   Þá-ʒiet þæt word ʒe-cwæþ
hár hilde-rinc,   hyssas bielde,
170   bæd gangan forþ   góde ʒe-féran.
Ne meahte þá on fótum lenʒ   fæste ʒe-standan.
Hé to heofonum wlát:
    "Ič ʒe-þancie þé,   þéoda Wealdend,
eallra þára wynna   þe ič on weorolde ʒe-bád.
175   Nú ič áh, milde Meotod,   mǽste þearfe
þæt þú mínum gáste   gódes ʒe-unne,
þæt mín sáwol to þé   síðian móte
on þín ʒe-weald,   Þéoden enʒla,
mid friðe ferian.   Ič eom frymdiʒ to þé
180   þæt híe hell-scaðan   híenan ne móten."
    Þá hine héowon   hǽðne scealcas,
and béʒen þá beornas   þe him bí stódon,
Ælf-nóþ and Wulf-mǽr   béʒen lágon,
þá on-efen hira fréan   feorh ʒe-sealdon.
185   Híe bugon þá fram beadwe   þe þǽr béon noldon.
Þǽr wearþ Oddan bearn   ǽrest on fléame,
God-ríč fram gúðe,   and þone gódan for-lét
þe him maniʒne oft   mearh ʒe-sealde;
hé ʒe-hléop þone eoh   þe áhte his hláford,
190   on þǽm ʒe-rǽdum   þe hit riht ne wæs,
and his bróðru mid him   béʒen ærndon,

grievously hit his chieftain before lay dead on the ground. (159) Then an armed warrior went to the earl; he was about to seize the warrior's valuables, armor and rings and ornamented sword. (162) Then Byrhtnoth drew his sword from its sheath, broad and bright-edged, and struck on the byrnie of the viking. (164) Too quickly one of the seafarers hindered him, and (lit. when) he wounded the earl's arm. (166) Then the golden-hilted sword fell to the ground, he could not hold the hard sword, wield the weapon. (168b) Still the hoary battle-warrior spoke these words (lit. this word), encouraged the young men, bade the good comrades to go forward. (171) Then he was no longer able to stand firm on his feet. He looked to heaven:

(173) "I thank thee, Lord of hosts, for all the joys that I have experienced in the world. (175) Now, merciful Creator, I have the greatest need that thou grant grace to my spirit, so that my soul may journey to thee, into thy keeping, Prince of angels, (may) depart in peace. (179b) I beseech thee (lit. am desirous from thee) that the devils of hell be not permitted to humiliate it."

(181) Then the heathen men cut him down, and both the warriors that had been standing by him, Ælfnoth and Wulfmær both lay dead, who gave up their life beside their lord.

(185) They who did not wish to be there retreated then from battle. The son of Odda was first in flight there, Godric from the battle, and abandoned the good (man) who had often given him many a steed; he mounted the horse that his lord had owned, in those trappings which it was not right (for him to take), and both his brothers galloped away with him, Godwin and Godwig, they did not care about the battle,

God-wine and God-wíȝ,   gúðe ne ȝíemdon,
ac wendon fram þǽm wíȝe   and þone wudu sóhton,
flugon on þæt fæsten   and hira feore burgon,
195 and manna má   þonne hit ǽniȝ mǽþ wǽre,
ȝief híe þá ȝe-earnunga   ealle ȝe-mundon
þe hé him to duguðe   ȝe-dón hæfde.
Swá him Offa on dæȝ   ǽr a-sæȝde
on þǽm mæðel-stede,   þá hé ȝe-mót hæfde,
200 þæt þǽr módiȝ-líče   maniȝe sprǽcon
þe eft æt þearfe   þolian noldon.
Þá wearþ a-feallen   þæs folces ealdor,
Æðel-rǽdes eorl;   ealle ȝe-sáwon
heorþ-ȝe-néatas   þæt hira hearra læȝ.
205 Þá þǽr wendon forþ   wlance þeȝnas,
un-earge menn   efston ȝeorne;
híe woldon þá ealle   óðer twéȝa:
líf for-lǽtan   oþþe léofne ȝe-wrecan.
Swá híe bielde forþ   bearn Ælf-ríčes,
210 wiga wintrum ȝeong,   wordum mǽlde,
Ælf-wine þá cwæþ,   hé on ellen spræc:
"ȝe-munaþ þá mǽla   þe wé oft æt medu sprǽcon,
þonne wé on benče   béot a-hófon,
hæleþ on healle,   ymbe heard ȝe-winn;
215 nú mæȝ cunnian   hwá céne síe.
Ič wille míne æðelu   eallum ȝe-cýðan,
þæt ič wæs on Mierčum   mičeles cynnes;
wæs mín ealda fæder   Ealh-helm háten,
wís ealdor-mann   weorold-ȝe-sǽliȝ.
220 Ne sculon mé on þǽre þéode   þeȝnas æt-wítan
þæt ič of þisse fierde   féran wille,
eard ȝe-séčan,   nú mín ealdor liȝeþ
for-héawen æt hilde.   Mé is þæt hearma mǽst;
hé wæs ǽðȝer mín mæȝ   and mín hláford."
225 Þá hé forþ éode,   fǽhþe ȝe-munde,

but turned from the combat and made for the forest, fled into that safe retreat and saved their lives, and more men than was at all fitting (lit. than it was any fitness), if they had remembered all the favors that he (i.e., Byrhtnoth) had done for their benefit. (198) So Offa had formerly said to him once (lit. on a day) in the meeting-place, when he was holding a council, that many were talking boldly there who later would not hold out at need.

(202) Then the chieftain of the army, Ethelred's earl, was laid low; all the hearth-companions (i.e., his closest retainers) saw that their lord lay dead. (205) Then proud retainers went forward, undaunted men hastened eagerly; they all desired then one (lit. the second) of two (things): to give up their life or to avenge their dear (leader). (209) Thus the son of Ælfric urged them on, a warrior young in years, spoke with words, Ælfwine then said, he spoke courageously:

(212) "Remember the times when we often spoke at mead (-drinking), when (seated) on the bench we, warriors in the hall, made (lit. raised up) our vow about hard battle; now whoever may be bold will be able to put it to the test. (216) I wish to make known my lineage to all, that I was of a great family among the Mercians; my grandfather was called Ealhhelm, a wise ealdorman prosperous in wordly goods. (220) Retainers among that people shall not reproach me for wishing (lit. that I wish) to leave (lit. go from) this army, make for home, now that my lord lies dead, cut down in battle. (223b) It is the greatest of griefs to me: he was both my kinsman and my lord."

(225) Then he went forward, gave his attention to (lit.

131

þæt hé mid orde   ánne ʒe-réhte
flotan on þǽm folce,   þæt sé on foldan læʒ
for-weʒen mid his wǽpne.   On-gann þá winas man-
    ian,
fríend and ʒe-féran,   þæt híe forþ éoden.

230   Offa ʒe-mǽlde,   æsc-holt a-scóc:
"Hwæt, þú, Ælf-wine,   hafast ealle ʒe-manode
þeʒnas to þearfe.   Nú úre þéoden liʒeþ,
eorl on eorðan,   ús is eallum þearf
þæt úre ǽʒ-hwelč   óðerne bielde

235   wigan to wíʒe,   þá-hwíle-þe hé wǽpen mæʒe
habban and healdan,   heardne méče,
gár and gód sweord.   Ús God-ríč hæfþ,
earg Oddan bearn,   ealle be-swicene.
Wénde þæs for-maniʒ mann,   þá hé on méare rád,

240   on wlancan þǽm wicge,   þæt wǽre hit úre hláford.
For-þon wearþ hér on felda   folc to-twǽmed,
scield-burg to-brocen.   A-bréoðe his an-ʒinn,
þæt hé hér swá maniʒne   mann a-flíemde!"
    Léof-sunu ʒe-mǽlde   and his linde a-hóf,

245   bord to ʒe-beorge;   hé þǽm beorne on-cwæþ:
"Ič þæt ʒe-háte,   þæt ič heonan nylle
fléon fótes trem   ac wille furðor gán,
wrecan on ʒe-winne   mínne wine-dryhten.
Ne þurfon mé ymbe Stúr-mere   stede-fæste hæleþ

250   wordum æt-wítan,   nú mín wine ʒe-crang,
þæt ič hláford-léas   hám síðie,
wende fram wíʒe,   ac mé sceal wǽpen niman,
ord and íren."   Hé full ierre wód,
feaht fæst-líče,   fléam hé for-hogode.

255   Dunnere þá cwæþ,   daroþ a-cweahte,
un-orne čeorl,   ofer eall clipode,
bæd þæt beorna ʒe-hwelč   Beorht-nóþ wrǽce:
"Ne mæʒ ná wandian   sé-þe wrecan þenče

132

remembered) revenge, in such a way that he hit one viking in the host with his spear-point, so that he lay dead on the ground, slain by his weapon. (228b) Then he began to exhort (his) comrades, friends and companions, that they should go forward.

(230) Offa spoke, brandished his ash-wood (spear) : "Lo, you, Ælfwine, have exhorted all the retainers as is needed (lit. at need). (232b) Now that our chieftain lies dead, the earl on the earth, we all have need (lit. there is need for us all) that each of us should encourage the other warrior to battle, as long as he may be able to hold and keep a weapon, a hard sword, spear and good sword. (237b) Godric, the cowardly son of Odda, has betrayed us all. (239) Very many a man believed this, when he rode off on the horse, on that proud steed, that it was our lord. (241) For that reason here on the field the army was divided, the shield-wall (lit. shield-fortress) broken apart. May his action (lit. beginning) fail, causing (lit. that he caused) so many a man here to flee !"

(244) Leofsunu spoke and raised his linden-wood (shield), his shield as a protection ; he replied to the warrior : "I promise this, that I will not flee from here the space of (even) a foot but will go farther, avenge my friendly lord in battle. (249) Steadfast warriors about Sturmer will not need to reproach me with words, now that my friendly lord has fallen, (reproach me) that I journey home lordless, (that I) turn from the battle, but (rather) a weapon shall kill (lit. take) me, spear-point and iron (sword)." (253b) He advanced, very angry, fought stoutly, he scorned flight.

(255) Dunnere spoke then, brandished his javelin, an honest fellow, called out over all, bade that each of the warriors avenge Byrhtnoth : "He who intends to avenge his lord in the

fréan on folce,   né for feore murnan."

260 Þá híe forþ éodon,   feores híe ne róhton;
on-gunnon þá híred-menn   heard-líče feohtan,
grame gár-berend,   and God bǽdon
þæt híe mósten ȝe-wrecan   hira wine-dryhten
and on hira féondum   fiell ȝe-wyrčan.

265 Him se ȝísl on-gann   ȝeorn-líče fylstan;
hé wæs on Norþ-Hymbrum   heardes cynnes,
Ecg-láfes bearn;   him wæs Æsc-ferhþ nama.
Hé ne wandode ná   æt þǽm wíȝ-plegan,
ac hé fýsde forþ   flán ȝe-neahhe;

270 hwílum hé on bord scéat,   hwílum tǽsde,
ǽfre ymbe stunde   hé sealde sume wunde,
þá-hwíle-þe hé wǽpna   wealdan móste.
Þá-ȝíet on orde stód   Éad-weard se langa,
ȝearu and ȝeorn-full,   ȝielp-wordum spræc

275 þæt hé nolde fléogan   fót-mǽl landes,
ofer bæc búgan,   þá his betera lǽȝ.
Hé bræc þone bord-weall   and wiþ þá beornas feaht,
oþ-þæt hé his sinc-ȝiefan   on þǽm sǽ-mannum
weorþ-líče wræc,   ǽr hé on wæle láge.

280 Swá dyde Æðel-ríč,   æðele ȝe-féra,
fús and forþ-ȝeorn   feaht eornoste.
Siȝe-beorhtes bróðor   and swíðe maniȝ óðer
clufon cellod bord,   céne híe weredon;
bærst bordes lǽriȝ,   and séo byrne sang

285 gryre-léoða sum.   Þá æt gúðe slóg
Offa þone sǽ-lidan,   þæt hé on eorðan féoll,
and þǽr Gaddes mǽȝ   grund ȝe-sóhte.
Raðe wearþ æt hilde   Offa for-héawen;
hé hæfde þéah ȝe-forðod   þæt hé his fréan ȝe-hét,

290 swá hé béotode ǽr   wiþ his béag-ȝiefan,
þæt híe scoldon béȝen   on burg rídan,
hále to háme,   oþþe on here cringan,

army can not hesitate at all nor care about (losing his) life."

(260) Then they went forward, they did not care about (losing) life; then the household retainers began to fight bravely, fierce spearsmen (lit. spear-bearers), and prayed God that they might avenge their friendly lord and inflict (lit. work) death on their enemies.

(265) The hostage began to help them zealously; he was of a brave family in Northumbria, the son of Ecglaf; his name was Æscferth. (268) He did not hesitate at all in the combat, but he often sent forth an arrow; at times he shot at a shield, at times wounded (someone), ever and again he gave a wound, as long as he was able to wield weapons.

(273) Edward the tall still stood in the front rank, ready and eager, declared with proud words that he would not flee a foot of ground, turn back, since his superior lay dead. (277) He broke the shield-wall and fought against the warriors, until he had creditably avenged his treasure-giver on the seamen, before he lay dead in the slaughter.

(280) Likewise did Ætheric, a noble companion, striving forward and eager to advance, (he) fought earnestly. (282) Sigbyrht's brother and very many another split the hollow (?) shields, defended themselves fiercely; shield-edge burst, and the byrnie sang a song of terror. (285) Then in battle Offa struck a (lit. the) viking, so that he fell to the earth, and there a kinsman of Gadd fell to (lit. sought) the ground. (288) Quickly Offa was cut down in combat; he had, however, carried out what he had promised his lord, as he had vowed formerly to his ring-giver, that they must both ride into the fortress, unharmed to (their) home, or fall among the

135

on wæl-stówe   wundum sweltan;
hé læ3 þe3n-líče   þéodne 3e-hende.

295   Þá wearþ borda 3e-bræc.   Brim-menn wódon,
gúðe 3e-gremede;   gár oft þurh-wód
fǽ3es feorh-hús.   Forþ þá éode Wí3-stán,
Þur-stánes sunu,   wiþ þás secgas feaht;
hé wæs on 3e-þrange   hira þréora bana,

300   ǽr him Wí3-helmes bearn   on þǽm wæle láge.
Þǽr wæs stíþ 3e-mót;   stódon fæste
wigan on 3e-winne,   wí3end crungon
wundum wéri3e.   Wæl féoll on eorðan.
Ós-weald and Éad-weald   ealle hwíle,

305   bé3en þá 3e-bróðru,   beornas trymedon,
hira wine-mágas   wordum bǽdon
þæt híe þǽr æt þearfe   þolian scoldon,
un-wác-líče   wǽpna néotan.

     Beorht-weald   maðelode,   bord hafenode—

310   sé wæs eald 3e-néat—   æsc a-cweahte;
hé full beald-líče   beornas lǽrde:
"Hy3e sceal þý heardra,   heorte þý cénre,
mód sceal þý máre   þý úre mæ3en lýtlaþ.
Hér li3eþ úre ealdor   eall for-héawen,

315   gód on gréote.   Á mæ3 gnornian
sé-þe nú fram þis wí3-plegan   wendan þenčeþ.
Ič eom fród feores;   fram ič ne wille,
ac ič mé be healfe   mínum hláforde,
be swá léofan menn,   licgan þenče."

320   Swá híe Æðel-gáres bearn   ealle bielde,
God-ríč to gúðe.   Oft hé gár for-lét,
wæl-spere windan   on þá wičingas,
swá hé on þǽm folce   fyrmest éode,
héow and híende,   oþ-þæt hé on hilde 3e-crang.

325   Næs þæt ná sé God-ríč   þe þá gúðe for-béag * * *

host, die of wounds on the battlefield; he lay dead near his chieftain as a loyal retainer ought to do (lit. "thanely").

(295) Then there was a crash of shields. The seamen advanced, enraged by the fight; a spear often pierced the body (lit. life-house) of a doomed (man). (297b) Then Wigstan went forward, the son of Thurstan, fought against the warriors; he was the slayer of three of them in the throng, before the son of Wighelm lay dead in the slaughter. (301) There was a fierce encounter there; warriors stood fast in the struggle, warriors fell, weary with wounds. (303b) The slain (lit. slaughter) fell to the earth. Oswald and Eadwald, both the brothers, all the while exhorted the warriors, with words ordered their beloved kinsmen that they had to hold out there at need, make use of their weapons without weakening (lit. unweakly).

(309) Byrhtwald discoursed, raised his shield—he was an old retainer—brandished his ash-wood spear; he very boldly instructed the warriors: (312) "Courage must be the stronger, heart the bolder, courage must (be) the greater, as our strength diminishes. (314) Here lies our lord all cut to pieces, good (man) in the dust. He who thinks now to turn from this battle-play will always be able to regret (it). (317) I am old (lit. old of life); I will not (go) away, but I intend to lie beside my lord, by so beloved a man."

(320) Likewise the son of Æthelgar, Godric, exhorted them all to battle. Often he let a spear, a deadly spear, fly into the vikings, as he went foremost in the host, hacked and brought down (enemies), until he fell in battle. (325) It was not that Godric who fled the battle.

The Dream of the Rood

    Hwæt, ič swefna cyst   secgan wille,
hwæt mé ʒe-mǽtte   to midre nihte,
siþþan reord-berend   reste wunodon.
Þúhte mé þæt ič ʒe-sáwe   seld-líčre tréo
5   on lyft lǽdan,   léohte be-wunden,
béama beorhtost.   Eall þæt béacen wæs
be-goten mid golde.   Ȝimmas stódon
fæʒere æt foldan scéatum,   swelče þǽr fífe wǽron
uppe on þǽm eaxl-ʒe-spanne.   Be-héoldon þǽr enʒlas Dryhtnes,
10   fæʒere þurh forþ-ʒe-sceaft.   Ne wæs þǽr húru fracuðes ʒealga,
ac hine þǽr be-héoldon   háliʒe gástas,
menn ofer moldan,   and eall þéos mǽre ʒe-sceaft.
Seld-líč wæs se siʒe-béam,   and ič synnum fág,
for-wundod mid wammum.   Ȝe-seah ič wuldres tréo,
15   wǽdum ʒe-weorðod,   wynnum scínan,
ʒe-ʒiered mid golde;   ʒimmas hæfdon
be-wriʒen weorþ-líče   Wealdendes tréo.
Hwæðere ič þurh þæt gold   on-ʒietan meahte
earmra ǽr-ʒe-winn,   þæt hit ǽrest on-gann
20 swǽtan on þá swiðran healfe.   Eall ič wæs mid sorgum ʒe-dréfed.
Forht ič wæs for þǽre fæʒeran ʒe-sihþe.   Ȝe-seah ič þæt fúse
béacen

The Dream of the Rood
(*Translation*)

Lo, I wish to tell the best of dreams, what I dreamed in the middle of the night, when humans (lit. speech-bearers) were at rest. (4) It seemed to me that I saw a wonderful cross borne aloft enveloped in light, the brightest of trees. (6b) That entire apparition (lit. beacon) was gilded (lit. overpoured with gold). Beautiful gems lay (lit. stood) on the surface of the ground, likewise there were five (gems) up on the intersection of the beams. (9b) Angels of the Lord looked on there, beautiful by creation. There was certainly not the gallows of a criminal, but holy spirits beheld it there, (and) men on earth, and all this splendid creation. (13) Wonderful was the tree of victory, and I (was) stained with sins, severely wounded with stains. I saw the cross of glory, adorned with robes, shine beautifully, decked with gold; gems had splendidly covered the Lord's cross. (18) Nevertheless I was able to make out through the gold the former struggle of wretched (men), (make out) that it first began to bleed on the right side. (20b) I was utterly afflicted with sorrows. I was fearful before the beautiful vision. I saw the shifting (lit. eager,

wendan wǽdum and bleôm;   hwílum hit wæs mid wǽtan be-
stíemed,
be-swiled mid swátes gange,   hwílum mid since ȝe-ȝierwed.
    Hwæðere ič þǽr licgende   lange hwíle
      25   be-héold hréow-čeariȝ   Hǽlendes tréo,
      oþ-þæt ič ȝe-híerde   þæt hit hléoðrode;
      on-gann þá word sprecan   wudu sélesta :
      "Þæt wæs ȝéara ȝéo—   ič þæt ȝíeta ȝe-man—
      þæt ič wæs a-héawen   holtes on ende,
30   a-styred of stefne mínum.   Ȝe-námon mé þǽr strange féondas,
ȝe-worhton him þǽr to wǽfer-síene,   héton mé hira weargas
hebban.
Bǽron mé þǽr beornas on eaxlum,   oþ-þæt híe mé on beorg
a-setton;
ȝe-fæstnodon mé þǽr féondas ȝe-nóge.   Ȝe-seah ič þá Fréan
mann-cynnes
efstan ellne mičele   þæt hé mé wolde on ȝe-stígan.
      35   Þǽr ič ne dorste   ofer Dryhtnes word
      búgan oþþe berstan,   þá ič bifian ȝe-seah
      eorðan scéatas.   Ealle ič meahte
      féondas ȝe-fiellan;   hwæðere ič fæste stód.
On-ȝierede hine þá ȝeong Hæleþ—   þæt wæs God eall-mihtiȝ—
      40   strang and stíþ-mód.   Ȝe-stág hé on ȝealgan héanne,
módiȝ on maniȝra ȝe-sihþe,   þá hé wolde mann-cynn líesan.
Bifode ič þá mé se Beorn ymb-clypte;   ne dorste ič hwæðere
búgan to eorðan,
feallan to foldan scéatum,   ac ič scolde fæste standan.
      Ród wæs ič a-rǽred;   a-hóf ič ríčne Cyning,
      45   heofona Hláford;   hieldan mé ne dorste.
Þurh-drifon híe mé mid deorcum næȝlum;   on mé sindon þá dolg
ȝe-síene,
opene inwitt-hlemmas;   ne dorste ič hira ǽniȝum scieþþan.
Bismerodon híe unc bú-tu æt-gædre.   Eall ič wæs mid blóde be-
stíemed,

hastening) vision change its robes and colors: at times it was moistened with blood (lit. fluid), drenched with the flow of blood, at times decked with treasure.

(24) Nevertheless, lying there for a long time, sorrowful, I beheld the Savior's cross, until I heard that it spoke; the excellent tree (lit. wood) began to speak these words:

(28) "It was years ago—I still remember it—that I was cut down by a forest side, removed from my trunk. Strong enemies seized me there, made (me) a spectacle for themselves there, commanded me to lift up their criminals. (32) Men carried me there on their shoulders, until they put me on a hill; many foes made me fast there. I saw then the Lord of mankind hasten with great zeal because he wished to climb up on me.

(35) There I dared not bend or break contrary to the Lord's word, when I saw the surface of the earth tremble. I could have felled all the enemies, yet I stood firm. (39) Then the young Hero undressed himself—it was God almighty—, strong and resolute. He climbed on the high gallows, courageous in the sight of many, when he was about to redeem mankind. (42) I trembled when the Hero embraced me; yet I did not dare to bend down to the earth, to fall to the surface of the earth, but I had to stand firm. (44) As a cross I was raised up; I lifted up the powerful King, the Lord of heaven; I did not dare to bend. (46) They pierced me with dark nails; the wounds are visible on me, gaping (lit. open), malicious wounds; I did not dare harm any of them. (48) They mocked

be-goten of þæs Guman sídan,   siþþan hé hæfde his gást on-
sended.
50   Fela ič on þǽm beorge   ʒe-biden hæbbe
     wráðra wyrda.   ʒe-seah ič weoroda God
     þearle þenian.   Þíestru hæfdon
     be-wriʒen mid wolcnum   Wealdendes hrǽw,
     scírne scíman ;   scadu forþ-éode
55   wann under wolcnum.   Wéop eall ʒe-sceaft,
     cwíðdon Cyninges fiell.   Críst wæs on róde.
     Hwæðere þǽr fúse   feorran cómon
     to þǽm Æðelinge.   Ič þæt eall be-héold.
Sáre ič wæs mid sorgum ʒe-dréfed ;   hnág ič hwæðere þǽm
     secgum to handa,
60 éaþ-mód, ellne mičele.   ʒe-námon híe þǽr eall-mihtiʒne God,
a-hófon hine of þǽm hefiʒan wíte.   For-léton mé þá hilde-rincas
standan stéame be-drifenne ;   eall ič wæs mid strǽlum for-wundod.
A-leʒdon híe þǽr lim-wériʒne ;   ʒe-stódon him æt his líčes
     héafdum ;
be-héoldon híe þǽr heofones Dryhten,   and hé hine þǽr hwíle
     reste,
65 méðe æfter þǽm mičelan ʒe-winne.   On-gunnon him þá mold-
     ærn wyrčan
beornas on banan ʒe-sihþe ;   curfon híe þæt of beorhtan stáne ;
ʒe-setton híe þǽr-on sigora Wealdend.   On-gunnon him þá sorg-
     léoþ galan
earme on þá ǽfen-tíde,   þá híe woldon eft síðian,
méðe fram þǽm mǽran Þéodne.   Reste hé þǽr mǽte weorode.
70   Hwæðere wé þǽr gréotende   góde hwíle
     stódon on staðole,   siþþan stefn upp ʒe-wát
     hilde-rinca.   Hrǽw cólode,
     fǽʒer feorh-bold.   Þá ús man fiellan on-gann
     ealle to eorðan.   Þæt wæs eʒes-líč wyrd !
75 Be-dealf ús man on déopan séaðe.   Hwæðere mé þǽr Dryhtnes
     þeʒnas,

us two both together. I was all moistened with blood, poured from the side of the Man, after he had sent forth his spirit.

(50) I have endured many cruel fates on the hill. I saw the God of hosts painfully (lit. severely) stretched out. Darkness had covered with clouds the Lord's corpse, the shining splendor; a shadow went forth, dark under the clouds. (55b) All creation wept, lamented the death of the King. Christ was on the cross.

(57) Yet (certain ones) came there hastening from afar to the Prince. I saw it all. I was grievously afflicted with sorrows; yet I bowed to the hands (lit. hand) of the men, humble, with great zeal. (60b) There they took almighty God, lifted him from the severe torment. The warriors left me standing covered with blood; I was all wounded with arrows. (63) They laid the limb-weary (one) there; they stood at the head of his corpse; they beheld there the Lord of heaven, and he rested himself there for a time, tired after the great struggle. (65b) Then, in the sight of the slayer, men began to make him a tomb; they hewed it out of bright stone; they set therein the Lord of victories. (67b) They began then to sing him a dirge, wretched (people), in the evening, when they were about to travel back, weary, from the famous Prince. He rested there with a small company.

(70) Yet we stood there on our foundation weeping for a good while, after the voice of the warriors went up. The corpse grew cold, the fair body (lit. life-house). (73b) Then one began to fell us all to the ground. That was a fearful fate! One buried us in a deep pit. Yet the disciples and friends of the

fréondas ʒe-frugnon
and ʒieredon mé   golde and seolfre.

   Nú þú meaht ʒe-híeran,   hæleþ mín se léofa,
þæt ič bealu-wara weorc   ʒe-biden hæbbe,

80   sárra sorga.   Is nú sǽl cumen
þæt mé weorðiaþ   wíde and síde
menn ofer moldan   and eall þéos mǽre ʒe-sceaft,
ʒe-biddaþ him to þissum béacne.   On mé Bearn Godes
þrówode hwíle.   For-þon ič þrymm-fæst nú

85   hlífie under heofonum,   and ič hǽlan mæʒ
ǽʒ-hwelčne ánra,   þára-þe him biþ eʒesa to mé.
ðéo ič wæs ʒe-worden   wíta heardost,
léodum láðost,   ǽr-þon ič him lífes weʒ
rihtne ʒe-rýmde,   reord-berendum.

90   Hwæt, mé þá ʒe-weorðode   wuldres Ealdor
ofer holt-wudu,   heofon-ríčes Weard,
swelče swá hé his módor éac,   Márian selfe,
eall-mihtiʒ God,   for ealle menn
ʒe-weorðode   ofer eall wífa cynn.

95   Nú ič þé háte,   hæleþ mín se léofa,
þæt þú þás ʒe-sihþe   secge mannum;
on-wréoh wordum   þæt hit is wuldres béam,
sé-þe eall-mihtiʒ God   on þrówode

for mann-cynnes   maniʒum synnum
100   and Ádames   eald-ʒe-wyrhtum.
Déaþ hé þǽr bieriʒde;   hwæðere eft Dryhten a-rás
mid his mičelan meahte   mannum to helpe.
Hé þá on heofonas a-stág.   Hider eft fundaþ
on þisne middan-ʒeard   mann-cynn sécan

105   on Dóm-dæʒe   Dryhten selfa,
eall-mihtiʒ God   and his enʒlas mid,
þæt hé þonne wile déman,   sé áh dómes ʒe-weald,
ánra ʒe-hwelčum,   swá hé him ǽror hér
on þissum lǽnan   lífe ʒe-earnaþ.

Lord sought me out there and decked me with gold and silver.

(78) Now you can hear, my beloved man, that I have endured pain (inflicted by) evil-doers, (the pain) of grievous sorrows. (80b) Now a time has come when men honor me far and wide throughout the earth and all this glorious creation, pray to this sign. (83b) On me the Son of God suffered for a time. Therefore I now tower glorious under the heavens, and I can save every one of those who are in awe of me (lit. each of the ones to whom is awe toward me). (87) Long ago I had become the cruelest of torments, most hateful to men, before I opened up to them the true way of life, for humans (lit. speech-bearers). (90) Lo, the Lord of glory, the Guardian of the kingdom of heaven, honored me beyond the trees of the forest, just as he, almighty God, also honored his mother, Mary herself, before all men, beyond the whole race of women.

(95) Now I command you, my beloved man, that you relate this vision to men; reveal in words that it is the tree of glory, which almighty God suffered on for the many sins of mankind and Adam's ancient deeds. (101) He tasted death there; yet the Lord rose up again with his great power as a help to men. (103) He ascended then to heaven. The Lord himself will come here again to this earth to seek mankind on the Judgment Day, almighty God and his angels with (him), when he who has power of judgment will then judge each one, as he deserves (according to what he has done) formerly here (on

110   Ne mæʒ þǽr ǽniʒ   un-forht wesan
      for þǽm worde   þe se Wealdend cwiþ.
      Friʒneþ hé for þǽre meniʒe   hwǽr se mann síe,
      sé-þe for Dryhtnes naman   déaðes wolde
      biteres on-bierʒan,   swá hé ǽr on þǽm béame dyde.
115   Ac híe þonne forhtiaþ,   and féa þenčaþ
      hwæt híe to Críste   cweðan on-ʒinnen.
      Ne þearf þǽr ǽniʒ   un-forht wesan
      þe him ǽr on bréostum bereþ   béacna sélest,
      ac þurh þá róde sceal   ríče ʒe-séčan
120   of eorþ-weʒe   ǽʒ-hwelč sáwol,
      séo-þe mid Wealdende   wunian þenčeþ."
         Ʒe-bæd ič mé þá to þǽm béame   blíðe móde,
      ellne mičele,   þǽr ič ána wæs
      mǽte weorode.   Wæs mód-sefa
125   a-fýsed on forþ-weʒe,   fela eallra ʒe-bád
      langung-hwíla.   Is mé nú lífes hyht
      þæt ič þone siʒe-béam   séčan móte
      ána oftor   þonne ealle menn
      wel weorðian ;   mé is willa to þǽm
130   mičel on móde,   and mín mund-byrd is
      ʒe-riht to þǽre róde.   Náh ič ríčra fela
      fréonda on foldan,   ac híe forþ heonan
ʒe-witon of weorolde dréamum,   sóhton him wuldres Cyning,
      libbaþ nú on heofonum   mid Héah-Fædere,
135   wuniaþ on wuldre,   and ič wéne mé
      daga ʒe-hwelče   hwonne mé Dryhtnes ród,
      þe ič hér on eorðan   ǽr scéawode,
      on þissum lǽnan   lífe ʒe-fetie
      and mé þonne ʒe-bringe   þǽr is bliss mičel,
140   dréam on heofonum,   þǽr is Dryhtnes folc
      ʒe-seted to symble,   þǽr is sin-gál bliss,
      and mé þonne a-sette   þǽr ič siþþan mót

earth) in this transitory life. (110) No one (lit. not any) can be unafraid there before the word which the Lord says. He will ask before the multitude where the man is who would be willing to taste bitter death for the sake (lit. name) of the Lord, as he did formerly on the cross. (115) But they will be afraid then, and they will have no idea (lit. little think) what they may undertake to say to Christ. (117) No one need be frightened (lit. not any need be unafraid) there who bears in his breast the best of signs, but each soul that intends to dwell with the Lord must through the cross seek the kingdom (which is far) from earth (lit. earth-way)."

(122) Then with a glad heart I prayed to the cross with great zeal, where I was alone with a small company. (My) soul was urged to depart (lit. onto the way forth), I endured many times of longing. (126b) Now I have (lit. is to me) expectation of life, that I may be permitted to seek the triumphant cross, (I) alone oftener than all (other) men to honor (it) well; my desire for it is great in my mind, and my (hope of) protection is directed to the cross. (131b) I have not many powerful friends on earth, but they have gone away from here, from the joys of the world, they have sought the King of glory, they live now in heaven with the great Father, they dwell in glory, and every day I look forward to (a time) when the cross of the Lord, which I formerly beheld here on earth, will carry me off from this transitory life and then bring me where there is great bliss, joy in heaven, where the Lord's people are (lit. is) seated at the feast, where there is perpetual bliss, and will set me then where I may afterwards dwell in

wunian on wuldre, wel mid þǽm hálȝum
dréames brúcan. Síe mé Dryhten fréond,
145 sé-þe hér on eorðan ǽr þrówode
on þǽm ȝealg-tréowe for guman synnum.
Hé ús on-líesde and ús líf for-ȝeaf,
heofon-líčne hám. Hyht wæs ȝe-níewod
mid blǽdum and mid blisse þǽm-þe þǽr bryne
  þolodon.
150 Se Sunu wæs sigor-fæst on þǽm síþ-fæte,
mihtiȝ and spédiȝ, þá hé mid meniȝe cóm,
gásta weorode, on Godes ríče,
An-wealda eall-mihtiȝ, enȝlum to blisse
and eallum þǽm hálȝum þǽm-þe on heofonum ǽr
155 wunodon on wuldre, þá hira Wealdend cóm,
eall-mihtiȝ God, þǽr his éðel wæs.

glory, partake of joy abundantly with the saints. (144b) May the Lord be a friend to me, who suffered formerly here on earth on the cross (lit. gallows-tree) for the sins of man. (147) He redeemed us and gave us life, a heavenly home. Hope was renewed with glories and with bliss, for those who had endured the fire there (i.e., in hell). (150) The Son was victorious on that expedition (i.e., the harrowing of hell), mighty and successful, when he, the almighty Lord, came with the multitude, the host of spirits, into the kingdom of God, to the delight of the angels and all the saints who were dwelling before in heaven in glory, when their Lord, almighty God, came where his home was.

The Wanderer

Oft him án-haga   áre ʒe-bídeþ
Meotodes mildse,   þéah-þe hé mód-čeariʒ
ʒeond lagu-láde   lange scolde
hréran mid handum   hrím-čealde sǽ,
5   wadan wræc-lástas.   Wyrd biþ full án-rǽd!
    Swá cwæþ eard-stapa,   earfoða ʒe-myndiʒ,
wráðra wæl-sliehta,   wine-mága hryre:
Oft ič scolde ána   úhtna ʒe-hwelče
míne čeare cwíðan;   nis nú cwicra nán
10   þe ič him mód-sefan   mínne durre
sweotule a-secgan.   Ič to sóðe wát
þæt biþ on eorle   inn-dryhten þéaw
þæt hé his ferhþ-locan   fæste binde,
healde his hord-cofan,   hycge swá hé wille.
15   Ne mæʒ wériʒ-mód   wyrde wiþ-standan
né se hréo hyʒe   helpe ʒe-fremman;
for-þon dóm-ʒeorne   dréoriʒne oft
on hira bréost-cofan   bindaþ fæste.
Swá ič mód-sefan   mínne scolde,
20   oft earm-čeariʒ,   éðle be-dǽled,
fréo-mágum feorr,   feterum sǽlan,
siþþan ʒéara ʒéo   gold-wine mínne

The Wanderer
(*Translation*)

Often the solitary dweller awaits favor for himself, the mercy of the Lord, although he, anxious in spirit, has long been obliged to stir with his hands (i.e., row?) the ice-cold (lit. frost-cold) sea over the path of the waters, to travel the paths of exile. (5b) Fate is utterly inexorable (lit. resolute).

(6) So spoke the wanderer, mindful of hardships, of cruel slaughters, of the death of beloved kinsmen: Often alone each dawn I have had to bewail my sorrows; there is not now any one living (lit. none of the living) to whom I dare speak my mind openly. (11b) In truth I know that (it) is a very noble custom in a man that he should bind fast his mind, guard the treasury of his heart, let him think as he will. (15) (One) weary in spirit cannot resist fate nor (can) the troubled thought afford consolation (lit. perform help); therefore (those) eager for glorious reputation often bind fast in their hearts a gloomy (thought). (19) So I, often wretched, deprived of my native land, far from my noble kinsmen, have had to bind my mind with fetters, since (the time) years ago (when I) hid in the concealment of the earth (i.e., buried) my

    hrúsan heolstre be-wráh,   and ič héan þanan
    wód winter-čeariʒ   ofer waðuma ʒe-bind,
25   sóhte sele dréoriʒ   sinces bryttan
    hwǽr ič feorr oþþe néah   findan meahte
    þone-þe on medu-healle   míne wiste
    oþþe meč fréond-léasne   fréfran wolde,
    wéman mid wynnum.   Wát sé-þe cunnaþ
30   hú slíðen biþ   sorg to ʒe-féran
    þǽm-þe him lýt hafaþ   léofra ʒe-holena.
    Waraþ hine wræc-lást,   nealles wunden gold,
    ferhþ-loca fréoriʒ,   nealles foldan blǽd.
    ʒe-man hé sele-secgas   and sinc-þeʒe,
35   hú hine on ʒeoguðe   his gold-wine
    wenede to wiste.   Wynn eall ʒe-dréas!
     For-þon wát sé-þe sceal   his wine-dryhtnes
    léofes lár-cwidum   lange for-þolian,
    þonne sorg and slǽp| samod æt-gædre
40   earmne án-hagan   oft ʒe-bindaþ.
    Þynčeþ him on móde   þæt hé his mann-dryhten
    clyppe and cysse   and on cnéo lecge
    handa and héafod,   swá hé hwílum ǽr
    on ʒéar-dagum   ʒief-stóles bréac.
45   Þonne on-wæcneþ eft   wine-léas guma,
    ʒe-siehþ him be-foran   fealwe wǽgas,
    baðian brim-fuglas,   brǽdan feðera,
    hréosan hrím and snáw   hæʒle ʒe-menʒed.
    Þonne béoþ þý hefiʒran   heortan benna,
50   sáre æfter swǽsne.   Sorg biþ ʒe-níewod
    þonne mága ʒe-mynd   mód ʒeond-hweorfeþ;
    gréteþ gléo-stafum,   ʒeorne ʒeond-scéawaþ
    secga ʒe-seldan.   Swimmaþ eft on-weʒ.
    Fléotendra ferhþ   ná þǽr fela bringeþ
55   cúðra cwide-ʒiedda.   Čearu biþ ʒe-níewod
    þǽm-þe sendan sceal   swíðe ʒe-neahhe

gold-friend (i.e., generous lord), and I, abject, winter-grieving (i.e., in a mood as dreary as winter? oppressed by advancing years?) went from there over the surface (lit. binding) of the waves, wretched, I sought the dwelling of a dispenser of treasure (i.e., generous lord), (sought) where I might be able to find far or near some one who, in a mead-hall, might know of my (people) or might be willing to console me, friendless, comfort (me) with pleasures. (29b) He who experiences (it) knows how cruel is sorrow as a companion to him who has few friendly protectors for himself. (32) The path of exile attends him, not twisted gold, a mournful spirit, not earthly prosperity. He remembers the warriors in the hall (lit. hall-warriors) and the receiving of treasure, (remembers) how in his youth his gold-friend (i.e., generous lord) entertained him at feasting. Joy has all disappeared!

(37) Therefore he who must knows (how to) do without the instructive speeches of his beloved friendly lord for a long time, when sorrow and sleep together often bind the wretched solitary (one). (41) It seems to him in his mind that he is embracing and kissing his lord and laying his hands and head on his knee, as he sometimes formerly in the days of yore enjoyed the gift-throne (i.e., the throne where his lord sat dispensing gifts). (45) Then the friendless (lordless?) man awakens again, sees before him the dark waves, (sees) sea-birds bathe (and) spread their feathers, (sees) hoar-frost and snow fall mingled with hail.

(49) Then the wounds of the heart are the more severe, painful (with longing) for a loved one. Sorrow is renewed when the memory of kinsmen passes through his mind; (he) greets (them) joyfully, eagerly regards (his) comrades in arms (lit. companions of warriors). (53b) They float away again. The spirit of the floating ones (i.e., phantoms) does not bring there many familiar songs. Care is renewed for him who

ofer waðuma ȝe-bind   wériȝne sefan.

    For-þon ič ȝe-þenčan ne mæȝ   ȝeond þás weorold
for-hwon mód-sefa   mín ne ȝe-sweorce
60 þonne ič eorla líf   eall ȝeond-þenče,
hú híe fǽr-líče   flett of-ȝéafon,
móðȝe magu-þeȝnas.   Swá þes middan-ȝeard
eallra dógra ȝe-hwǽm   dréoseþ and fealleþ;
for-þon ne mæȝ weorðan wís   wer, ǽr hé áge
65 wintra dǽl on weorold-ríče.   Wita sceal ȝe-þyldiȝ,
né sceal ná tó hát-heort   né tó hræd-wyrde
né tó wác wiga   né tó wan-hyȝdiȝ
né tó forht né tó fæȝen   né tó feoh-ȝífre
né nǽfre ȝielpes tó ȝeorn   ǽr hé ȝeare cunne—
70 beorn sceal ȝe-bídan,   þonne hé béot spričeþ,
oþ-þæt collen-ferhþ   cunne ȝearwe
hwider hreðra ȝe-hyȝd   hweorfan wille.

    On-ȝietan sceal gléaw hæle   hú gæst-líč biþ
þonne eall þisse weorolde wela   wéste standeþ,
75 swá nú missen-líče   ȝeond þisne middan-ȝeard
winde be-wáwne   weallas standaþ
hríme be-hrorene,   hríðȝe þá eodoras.
Wóriaþ þá wín-salu,   wealdend licgaþ
dréame be-drorene,   duguþ eall ȝe-crang
80 wlanc be wealle.   Sume wíȝ for-nam,
ferede on forþ-weȝe;   sumne fugol oþ-bær
ofer héanne holm;   sumne se hára wulf
déaðe ȝe-dǽlde;   sumne dréoriȝ-hléor
on eorþ-scræfe   eorl ȝe-hýdde.
85 Íeðde swá þisne eard-ȝeard   ielda Scieppend,
oþ-þæt burg-wara   breahtma léase,
eald enta ȝe-weorc   ídlu stódon.
Sé þonne þisne weall-steall   wíse ȝe-þóhte
and þis deorce líf   déope ȝeond-þenčeþ,

154

must very often send forth his weary spirit over the surface (lit. binding) of the waves.

(58) Therefore I cannot imagine why throughout this world my mind will not grow gloomy when I consider all the life of men, how they suddenly left the hall (lit. floor of the hall), the courageous young retainers. (62b) So this world every day (lit. each of all days) is crumbling and falling; therefore a man cannot become wise before he has his portion of years in the world. (65b) A wise man must (be) patient, nor must he (be) at all too irascible nor too hasty of speech nor too weak a warrior nor too reckless nor too fearful nor too elated nor too avaricious nor ever (lit. never) too eager for glory before he really knows—a man must wait, when he makes a vow, until, bold-spirited, (he) really knows whither the thought of his heart will turn.

(73) A clever man ought to realize how terrible (it) will be when all the wealth of this world stands waste, as now variously (i.e., here and there) throughout this world walls stand wind-blown, covered with hoar-frost, the dwellings storm-beaten. (78) The wine-halls are crumbling, the rulers lie dead, deprived of revelry, all the band of warriors has fallen proud by the wall. (80b) War destroyed some, carried (them) away; a bird carried one off over the high sea; the gray wolf shared one with death; a sad-faced man hid (i.e., buried) one in a grave.

(85) Thus the Creator of men laid waste this dwelling-place, until the old works of giants (i.e., buildings) stood vacant, without the noise of the inhabitants. (88) He then thoughtfully (lit. wisely) reflected upon this place of ruins

90 fród on ferhþe,   feorr oft ʒe-man
    wæl-sliehta worn   and þás word a-cwiþ :
    Hwǽr cóm mearh? Hwǽr cóm magu?   Hwǽr
      cóm máðum-ʒiefa?
    Hwǽr cóm symbla ʒe-setu?   Hwǽr sindon
      sele-dréamas?
    Éa-lá beorht bune!   Éa-lá byrn-wiga!
95 Éa-lá þéodnes þrymm!   Hú séo þrág ʒe-wát,
    ʒe-náp under niht-helm,   swá héo ná wǽre!
    Standeþ nú on láste   léofre duʒuðe
    weall wundrum héah,   wyrm-líčum fág.
    Eorlas for-námon   æsca þrýðe,
100 wǽpen wæl-ʒífru,   wyrd séo mǽre,
    and þás stán-hliðu   stormas cnyssaþ,
    hríþ hréosende   hrúsan bindeþ,
    wintres wóma,   þonne wann cymeþ
    nípeþ niht-scua,   norðan on-sendeþ
105 hréo hæʒl-fære,   hæleðum on andan.
    Eall is earfoþ-líč   eorðan ríče,
    on-wendeþ wyrda ʒe-sceaft   weorold under
      heofonum.
    Hér biþ feoh lǽne,   hér biþ fréond lǽne,
    hér biþ mann lǽne,   hér biþ mæʒ lǽne,
110 eall þis eorðan ʒe-steall   ídel weorðeþ!
  Swá cwæþ snotor on móde,   ʒe-sæt him sundor æt rúne.
Til biþ sé-þe his tréowe ʒe-healdeþ,   né sceal nǽfre his torn tó
  recene
beorn of his bréostum a-cýðan,   nefne hé ǽr þá bóte cunne,
eorl mid ellne ʒe-fremman.   Wel biþ þǽm-þe him áre séčeþ,
115 frófre to Fæder on heofonum,   þǽr ús eall séo fæstnung
    standeþ.

(lit. wall-place) and profoundly meditates upon this sad life, wise in heart, (he) often remembers many slaughters in battle far (back in time) and speaks these words: (92) Where has the horse gone? Where has the warrior gone? Where has the giver of treasure gone? Where have (lit. has) the banquet seats gone? Where are the revelries in the hall? Alas, bright cup! Alas, armored warrior! Alas, princely splendor (lit. splendor of a prince)! How that time has passed away, grown dark under cover of night, as (if) it had never been! (97) Now the wall, wondrously high, decorated with serpent designs, outlasts the beloved band of warriors. (99) The force (lit. forces) of ash-wood spears destroyed the warriors, weapons greedy for slaughter, (and) fate, that famed (one), and storms beat upon these stone slopes (walls?), a driving (lit. falling) snowstorm binds the earth, the howling of winter, when (it) comes, (all) dark, the shadow of night grows dark, sends from the north a fierce hailstorm, to the vexation of men. (106) All the kingdom of the earth is full of hardships, the decree of the fates changes the world under the heavens. (108) Here wealth is transitory, here friend is transitory, here man is transitory, here kinsman is transitory, this whole foundation of the earth is becoming empty.

(111) So spoke the (man) wise in spirit, sat apart in secret meditation. Good is he who keeps his pledges, nor ought a man ever (lit. never) make known the grief from out of his breast too quickly, unless he, the man, should know beforehand how to bring about a remedy with fortitude. (114b) It will be well for him who seeks grace for himself, comfort from the Father in heaven, where for us is (lit. stands) all security.

The Seafarer

Mæʒ ič be mé selfum   sóþ-ʒiedd wrecan,
síðas secgan,   hú ič ʒe-swinc-dagum
earfoþ-hwíle   oft þrówode,
bitere bréost-čeare   ʒe-biden hæbbe,
5 ʒe-cunnod on čéole   čear-selda fela,
atol ýða ʒe-wealc,   þǽr meč oft be-ʒeat
nearu niht-wacu   æt nacan stefnan,
þonne hé be clifum cnossaþ.   Čealde ʒe-þrungen
wǽron míne fét,   forste ʒe-bunden,
10 čealdum clammum,   þǽr þá čeara seofodon
hát ymb heortan;   hungor innan slát
mere-wérʒes mód.   Þæt se mann ne wát
þe him on foldan   fæʒerost limpeþ,
hú ič earm-čeariʒ   ís-čealdne sǽ
15 winter wunode   wreččan lástum,
wine-mágum be-droren,
be-hangen hrím-ʒicelum;   hæʒl scúrum fléag.
Þǽr ič ne ʒe-híerde   bútan hlimman sǽ,
ís-čealdne wǽʒ.   Hwílum ielfete sang
20 dyde ič mé to gamene,   ganotes hléoðor
and hwilpan swéʒ   fore hleahtor wera,
mǽw singende   fore medu-drince.

The Seafarer
(*Translation*)

I am able to recite a true poem concerning myself, tell of my journeys, how I have often suffered times of hardship during days of toil, have endured bitter anxiety of heart, experienced on a ship many sorrowful abodes, the terrible tossing of the waves, when the strict night-watch often befell me at the prow of a ship, when it beats against the cliffs. (8b) My feet were pinched with cold, bound by the frost with cold fetters, when those cares sighed hot around my heart; from within, hunger tore the spirit of the sea-weary (one). (12b) The man to whom the fairest (lot) falls on land does not know this, how I, wretchedly care-worn, lived upon the ice-cold sea for a winter on the paths of exile, bereft of friendly kinsmen, hung about with frost-icicles; hail flew in storms. (18) There I did not hear (anything) except the sea resound, the ice-cold wave. At times I made the song of the swan into a pastime for myself, the voice of the gannet and the sound of the curlew for (lit. instead of) the laughter of men, the singing sea-gull in-

159

Stormas þǽr stán-clifu béoton,   þǽr him stearn on-cwæþ
    ísiȝ-feðera;   full oft þæt earn be-ȝeall,
25 úriȝ-feðera;   ne ǽniȝ hléow-mága
    féa-sceaftiȝ ferhþ   fréfran meahte.
    For-þon him ȝe-líefeþ lýt,   sé-þe áh lífes wynn
    ȝe-biden on burgum,   bealu-síða hwón,
    wlanc and wín-gál,   hú ič wériȝ oft
30 on brim-láde   bídan scolde.
    Náp niht-scua,   norðan sníwde,
    hrím hrúsan band,   hæȝl féoll on eorðan,
    corna čealdost.   For-þon cnyssaþ nú
    heortan ȝe-þóhtas   þæt ič héan stréamas,
35 sealt-ýða ȝe-lác,   self cunnie;
    manaþ módes lust   mǽla ȝe-hwelče
    ferhþ to féran,   þæt ič feorr heonan
    el-þéodiȝra   eard ȝe-séče.
    For-þon nis þæs mód-wlanc   mann ofer eorðan,
40 né his ȝiefena þæs gód,   né on ȝeoguðe to þæs hwæt,
    né on his dǽdum to þæs déor,   né him his dryhten to
        þæs hold,
    þæt hé á his sǽ-fóre   sorge næbbe,
    to hwon hine Dryhten   ȝe-dón wille.
    Ne biþ him to hearpan hyȝe   né to hring-þeȝe,
45 né to wífe wynn   né to weorolde hyht,
    né ymbe á-wiht elles   nefne ymb ýða ȝe-wealc;
    ac á hafaþ langunge   sé-þe on lagu fundaþ.
    Bearwas blóstmum nimaþ,   byriȝ fæȝriaþ,
    wangas wlitiȝiaþ,   weorold ónetteþ;
50 ealle þá ȝe-maniaþ   módes fúsne
    sefan to síðe,   þǽm-þe swá þenčeþ
    on flód-wegas   feorr ȝe-wítan.
    Swelče ȝéac manaþ   ȝeómran reorde,
    singeþ sumores weard,   sorge béodeþ

stead of mead-drinking. (23) Storms beat the rocky cliffs there, where the tern replied to them, icy-feathered; very often the eagle screamed, dewy-feathered; no (lit. not any) protecting kinsman was able to console (my) desolate spirit.

(27) Therefore he who possesses the joy of life (and has) experienced in cities few woeful journeys, proud and flushed with wine, will little believe how I, weary, have often been obliged to remain on the path of the sea. (31) The shadow of night grew dark, it snowed from the north, frost bound the soil, hail fell on earth, coldest of seeds. (33b) Therefore my thoughts are now urging (lit. beating on) my heart that I myself should try the high seas, the commotion of the salt waves; the heart's desire on every occasion exhorts my spirit to journey, (urges) that I visit the home of foreigners far from here. (39) Indeed there is not a man on earth so proud of spirit, nor so liberal of his gifts, nor so vigorous in his youth, nor so bold in his deeds, nor (with) a lord so gracious to him, that he will not always have anxiety about his seafaring, (have anxiety to find out) to what the Lord may wish to bring him. (44) For him there will not be any thought of the harp nor of ring-receiving, nor of delight in a woman nor of joy in the world, nor about anything else except about the tossing of the waves; but he who sets out on the water will always have a longing (for it). (48) Groves will bear (lit. take) blossoms, towns will become fair, fields will become beautiful, the world will hasten on; all these will incite to a voyage the eager spirit of the mind for him who is so minded to depart far on the sea-ways. (53) Likewise the cuckoo admonishes with sad voice, the sentinel of summer sings, inspires (lit. announces) bitter sorrow in the

55 biter on bréost-hord.   Þæt se beorn ne wát
    séft-éadiȝ secg,   hwæt þá sume dréogaþ
    þe þá wræc-lástas   wídost lecgaþ.
    For-þon nú mín hyȝe hweorfeþ   ofer hreðer-locan,
    mín mód-sefa   mid mere-flóde
60 ofer hwæles éðel   hweorfeþ wíde
    eorðan scéatas,   cymeþ eft to mé
    ȝífre and grǽdiȝ;   ȝielleþ án-floga,
    hweteþ on hwæl-weȝ   hreðer un-wearnum
    ofer holma ȝe-lagu.   For-þon mé hátran sind
65 Dryhtnes dréamas   þonne þis déade líf,
    lǽne on lande.   Ič ȝe-líefe ná
    þæt him eorþ-welan   éče standaþ.
    Simble þréora sum   þinga ȝe-hwelče,
    ǽr his tíd-dæȝe,   to twéon weorðeþ :
70 ádl oþþe ieldu   oþþe ecg-hete
    fǽȝum fram-weardum   feorh oþ-þringeþ.
    For-þon þæt biþ eorla ȝe-hwǽm   æfter-cweðendra,
    lof lifiendra   lást-worda betst,
    þæt hé ȝe-wyrče,   ǽr hé on-weȝ scyle,
75 fremum on foldan   wiþ féonda níþ,
    déorum dǽdum   déofle to-ȝeȝnes,
    þæt hine ielda bearn   æfter herien,
    and his lof siþþan   lifie mid enȝlum
    áwa to ealdre,   éčan lífes blǽd,
80 dréam mid duguðum.   Dagas sind ȝe-witene,
    ealle an-médlan   eorðan ríčes;
    nǽron nú cyningas   né cáseras
    né gold-ȝiefan   swelče ȝéo wǽron,
    þonne híe mǽst mid him   mǽrða ȝe-fremedon
85 and on dryht-líčestum   dóme lifdon.
    Ȝe-droren is þéos duguþ eall,   dréamas sind ȝe-witene ;
    wuniaþ þá wácran   and þás weorold healdaþ,

heart. (55b) The man—a man in easy circumstances—does not know what then some endure who travel most extensively the paths of exile.

(58) Therefore my thought ranges now beyond the confines of my heart, my mind ranges with the sea far and wide over the domain of the whale, the bosom of the earth, comes back to me greedy and eager; the lone flier screams, incites my heart irresistibly to the whale-way, over the expanse of the seas. (64b) Therefore the joys of the Lord are more intense to me than this dead, transitory life on earth. I by no means believe that worldly goods will last (lit. stand) forever. (68) Always one of three things in every circumstance will become doubtful before one's (lit. his) last day: illness or old age or war (lit. sword-hatred) will deprive a doomed, departing (man) of life. (72) Therefore for every man the praise of those who live and speak after (he is gone) is the best fame after death: that he bring it about, before he must (go) away, by means of good deeds on earth against the hostility of enemies, by means of bold deeds against the devil, that the sons of men shall praise him afterwards, and (that) praise of him shall afterwards live among the angels forever and ever, the glory of eternal life, joy among the hosts (of heaven). (80b) The days have departed, all the pomps of the kingdom of the earth; there have not been lately (lit. now) kings nor emperors nor gold-givers such as formerly were, when they performed the greatest of famous deeds among themselves and lived in the most splendid glory. (86) All this company has fallen, the joys have departed; the inferiors live on and

brúcaþ þurh bisgu.   Blǽd is ȝe-hnǽȝed,
eorðan inn-dryhtu   ealdaþ and séaraþ,
90 swá nú manna ȝe-hwelč   ȝeond middan-ȝeard.
Ieldu him on færeþ,   an-síen blácaþ,
gamol-feax gnornaþ,   wát his ȝéo-wine,
æðelinga bearn,   eorðan for-ȝiefene.
Ne mæȝ him þonne se flǽsc-hama,   þonne him þæt
  feorh losaþ,
95 né swéte for-swelgan   né sár ȝe-félan
né hand on-hréran   né mid hyȝe þenčan.
Þeah-þe græf wille   golde stréȝan
bróðor his ȝe-borenum,   byrȝan be déadum
máðum mis-líčum,   þæt hine mid wille,
100 ne mæȝ þǽre sáwle   þe biþ synna full
gold to ȝéoce   for Godes eȝesan,
þonne hé hit ǽr hýdeþ   þenden hé hér lifaþ.
Mičel biþ se Meotodes eȝesa,   for þone híe séo molde on-
čierreþ ;
    sé ȝe-staðolode   stíðe grundas,
105 eorðan scéatas   and upp-rodor.
Dol biþ sé-þe him his Dryhten ne on-drǽdeþ ;   cymeþ him se
déaþ un-þinged.
Éadiȝ biþ sé-þe éaþ-mód lifaþ ;   cymeþ him séo ár of heofonum.
Meotod him þæt mód ȝe-staðolaþ,   for-þon hé on his meahte
ȝe-líefeþ.
Stíeran man sceal strangum móde,   and þæt on staðolum healdan,
110 and ȝe-wiss werum,   wísum clǽne.
    Scyle manna ȝe-hwelč   mid ȝe-mete healdan
wiþ léofne and wiþ láðne   * * * bealu,
þéah-þe hé hine wille fýres   fullne * * *
oþþe on bǽle   for-bærnedne
115 his ȝe-worhtne wine.   Wyrd biþ swíðre,
Meotod mihtiȝra   þonne ǽniȝes mannes ȝe-hyȝd.
Wuton wé hycgan   hwǽr wé hám ágen

occupy the world, enjoy (it) through their labor. (88b) Glory is humbled, the nobility of the earth grows old and withers, as now every man (does) throughout the earth. (91) Old age comes upon him, his countenance grows pale, the gray-haired (lit. old-haired) (one) laments, he knows (that) his friends of former times, the sons of princes, (have been) committed to the earth (i.e., buried). (94) When life fails him, then his body (lit. flesh-coat) can neither swallow sweet (things) nor feel pain nor move a hand nor think with his mind. (97) Although a brother may wish to strew the grave with gold for his brother (lit. born one, i.e., one born of the same family), bury various treasures with the dead, in order that (it) will (go) with him, for the soul that is full of sins, gold can not (be) a help against the terror of God, although he hoards (lit. hides) it before while he lives here (i.e., in the world). (103) Great is the fear of God, on account of which the earth turns itself; he established firm foundations, the surface of the earth and the sky above. (106) Foolish is he who does not fear his Lord; death will come to him unexpected. Blessed is he who lives humbly (lit. humble); grace will come to him from heaven. (108) God will make steadfast the spirit for him, because he (i.e., the man) believes in his (i.e., God's) power. One must restrain a violent spirit, and keep it within bounds, and trustworthy to men, pure in its ways. (111) Every man should hold with (due) measure * * * evil toward friend (lit. dear) and foe (lit. hostile), although he may wish him full of fire * * * or (see) the friend (he has) made burned up in fire. (115b) Fate is stronger, God mightier than any man's thought. Let us consider where we have our home and then (let us) take

and þonne ȝe-þenčan   hú wé þider cumen;
and wé þonne éac tilien   þæt wé tó móten
120 on þá éčan   éadiȝ-nesse
þǽr is líf ȝe-lang   on lufan Dryhtnes,
hyht on heofonum.   Þæs síe þǽm Hálȝan þanc,
þæt hé úsič ȝe-weorðode,   wuldres Ealdor,
éče Dryhten,   on ealle tíd.

Amen.

thought how we may go there; and then may we also endeavor that we may (go) there into the eternal beatitude where life is dependent on the love of the Lord, joy in heaven. (122b) Thanks be to the Holy (one) for this, that he, the Lord of glory, the eternal Lord, exalted us for all time. Amen.

The Wife's Lament

Ič þis ჳiedd wrece   be mé full ჳeómorre,
mínre selfre síþ.   Ič þæt secgan mæჳ,
hwæt ič iermþa ჳe-bád,   siþþan ič upp wéox,
níewes oþþe ealdes,   ná má þonne nú.
5   Á ič wíte wann   mínra wræc-síða.

    Ærest mín hláford ჳe-wát   heonan of léodum
ofer ýða ჳe-lác ;   hæfde ič úht-čeare
hwǽr mín léod-fruma   landes wǽre.
Þá ič mé féran ჳe-wát   folgaþ sécan,
10   wine-léas wrečča,   for mínre wéa-þearfe.

    On-gunnon þæt þæs mannes   mágas hycgan
þurh dierne ჳe-þóht,   þæt híe to-dǽlden unc
þæt wit ჳe-wídost   on weorold-ríče
lifdon láþ-líčost—   and več langode.
15   Hét več hláford mín   hér eard niman ;
áhte ič léofra lýt   on þissum land-stede,
holdra fréonda.   For-þon is mín hyჳe ჳeómor,
þá ič mé full ჳe-mæčne   mannan funde,
heard-sǽliჳne,   hyჳe-ჳeómorne,
20   mód míðendne,   morðor hycgendne.
Blíðe ჳe-bǽru   full oft wit béotodon
þæt unc ne ჳe-dǽlde   nefne déaþ ána

The Wife's Lament
(*Translation*)

I am reciting this poem about myself, very sad (lit. about
my very sad self), my own experience. I can say this, what
miseries (lit. what of miseries) I lived through, after I grew
up, early or late, never more than now. Ever I have suffered
the torment of my exile (lit. journeys of exile).

(6) First my lord departed hence from (his) people over
the commotion of the waves; I had anxiety at dawn (as to)
where my prince on earth (lit. of the land) might be. (9)
Then I set out to seek service, a friendless exile, on account
of my woeful need.

(11) The man's kinsmen began to plot (lit. consider)
secretly (lit. through secret thought), that they might separate
us two, in such a way that we two, most widely (separated)
in the world lived most wretchedly—and I suffered longing.
(15) My lord commanded me to take up my dwelling here;
I had few dear, loyal friends in this region. (17b) Therefore
my heart is sad, since I had found the man very well suited to
me (to be) ill-starred, depressed, concealing his mind, plot-
ting a deadly sin. (21) With joyous demeanor, we two very
often had vowed that nothing (lit. not anything) else but

á-wiht elles ;   eft is þæt on-hworfen,
is nú * * *   swá hit ná wǽre,
25 fréond-scipe uncer.   Scealič feorr ӡe néah
mínes fela-léofan   fǽhþe dréogan.
   Hét meč man wunian   on wuda bearwe
under ác-tréo   on þǽm eorþ-scræfe.
Eald is þes eorþ-sele,   eall ič eom of-langod,
30 sindon dena dimme,   dúna upp-héa,
bitere burg-túnas   brǽrum be-weaxne,
wíč wynna léas.   Full oft meč hér wráðe be-ӡeat
fram-síþ fréan.   Fríend sind on eorðan,
léofe lifiende,   leӡer weardiaþ,
35 þonne ič on úhtan   ána gange
under ác-tréo   ӡeond þás eorþ-scrafu.
Þǽr ič sittan mót   sumor-langne dæӡ,
þǽr ič wépan mæӡ   míne wræc-síðas,
earfoða fela,   for-þon ič ǽfre ne mæӡ
40 þǽre mód-čeare   mínre ӡe-restan
né ealles þæs langaðes   þe meč on þissum lífe be-ӡeat.
   Á scyle ӡeong mann   wesan ӡeómor-mód,
heard heortan ӡe-þóht,   swelče habban sceal
blíðe ӡe-bǽru,   éac-þon bréost-čeare,
45 sin-sorgna ӡe-dréag—   síe æt him selfum ӡe-lang
eall his weorolde wynn,   síe full wíde fáh
feorres folc-landes,   þæt mín fréond siteþ
under stán-hlíðe,   storme be-hrímed,
wine wériӡ-mód,   wætere be-flówen
50 on dréor-sele.   Dréogeþ se mín wine
mičele mód-čeare ;   hé ӡe-man tó oft
wynn-líčran wíč.   Wá biþ þǽm-þe sceal
of langaðe   léofes a-bídan.

death alone would part us two; (but) this in turn is reversed, it is now * * * as if it had never been, our love. (25b) Far and near I must endure the hostility of my very dear (one). (27) I was commanded (lit. one commanded me) to dwell in a forest grove, under an oak tree in this cave in the earth. (29) This cave-dwelling is ancient, I am utterly oppressed with longing, the valleys are dark, the hills high, sharp (the) hedges (lit. town-enclosures), grown over with briars, a joyless dwelling. (32b) Very often the departure of my lord has afflicted (lit. seized) me cruelly here. There are beloved friends (i.e., lovers) living on earth, (who) occupy their bed, while (lit. when) I am walking alone at dawn under the oak tree through these caves in the earth. (37) There I may sit the long summer's day, there I can weep over my exile (lit. exile experiences), many hardships, for I cannot ever rest from this unhappiness (lit. heart-care) of mine nor from all the longing which has come upon (lit. seized) me in this life.

(42) Ever may a young man have to be sad of mind, grievous the thought of his heart, at the same time as (lit. likewise) he is obliged to keep a cheerful demeanor, and in addition (may he have) distress of heart, a multitude of perpetual sorrows—may all his joy in the world be dependent on himself (alone), may he be outlawed very far (away) in a distant country, so that my beloved will sit under a rocky slope, frosted by a storm, a weary-spirited lord, drenched with water in a gloomy hall (i.e., a ruined building?). (50b) My lord is suffering great distress of soul; he remembers too often a more joyful dwelling. Woe will be to the one who must wait for a loved one in (lit. out of) longing.

Maxims I (*lines 71–99*)

Forst sceal fréosan,   fýr wudu meltan,
eorðe grówan,   ís brycgian—
wæter helm wegan—,   wundrum lúcan
eorðan čiðas.   Án sceal on-bindan
5   forstes fetera,   fela-mihtiʒ God;
    winter sceal ʒe-weorpan,   weder eft cuman,
    sumor sweʒle hát,   sund un-stille.
    Déop déada weʒ   dierne biþ lenʒest;
    holen sceal on-ǽled,   ierfe ʒe-dǽled
10 déades mannes.   Dóm biþ sélest.
    Cyning sceal mid čéape   cwéne ʒe-bycgan,
    bunum and béagum;   bú sculon ǽrest
    ʒiefum gód wesan.   Gúþ sceal on eorle,
    wíʒ ʒe-weaxan,   and wíf ʒe-þéon
15 léof mid hire léodum,   léoht-mód wesan,
    rúne healdan,   rúm-heort béon
    méarum and máðmum,   medu-rǽdenne
    for ʒe-síþ-mæʒen   simble ǽʒ-hwǽr
    eodor æðelinga   ǽrest ʒe-grétan,
20 forman fulle   to fréan hand
    recene ʒe-rǽčan,   and him rǽd witan,
    bold-ágendum   bǽm æt-samne.

172

Maxims I
(*Translation*)

Frost must freeze, fire (must) disintegrate wood, earth
(must) flourish, ice (must) form a bridge—water (must)
wear a covering—, wonderfully lock up the young shoots in
(lit. of) the earth. (4b) One (alone) must unbind the fetters
of frost, God very mighty; winter must hasten away, fine
weather (must) come again, summer brightly hot, the sea
(must be) restless. (8) The solemn path of the dead will be
longest secret; holly must (be) burnt up, the inheritance of
a dead man (must be) divided. Glorious reputation is best.
(11) A king must buy a queen with goods, with cups and
rings; both must first be liberal with their gifts. (13b) Battle
and war must grow powerful in a warrior, and a woman
(must) thrive, beloved among her people, (must) be light-
hearted, (must) keep a secret, (must) be generous with horses
and treasures, (must) always and everywhere greet first her
lord (lit. protector of noblemen) with mead-serving before
the company, quickly offer the first cup to the hand of her
lord, and know what is best (lit. wise counsel) for them,
for both householders together.

Scip sceal ȝe-næȝled, scield ȝe-bunden,
léoht linden bord, léof will-cuma
25 Frísan wífe, þonne flota standeþ;
bíþ his čéol cumen and hire čeorl to hám,
ágen ǽt-ȝiefa, and héo hine inn laðaþ,
wæsceþ his wáriȝ hræȝl and him seleþ wǽde níewe,
líhþ him on lande þæs his lufu bǽdeþ.

(23) A ship must (be) nailed (i.e., joined together with nails), a shield (must be) bound, the linden-wood shield (must be) light, (her) dear one (must be) a welcome visitor to the wife of the Frisian, when his ship makes port (lit. stands); his ship has come, and her husband (is) home, (her) own provider, and she invites him in, washes his sea-stained clothing and gives him new clothes, grants him (now that he is) on land what his love requires.

Maxims II

Cyning sceal ríče healdan.   Čeastra béoþ feorran ӡe-síene,
or-þanc enta ӡe-weorc,   þá-þe on þisse eorðan sindon,
wrǽtt-líč weall-stána ӡe-weorc.   Wind biþ on lyfte swiftost,
þunor biþ þrágum hlúdost.   Þrymmas sindon Crístes mičele,
5   wyrd biþ swíðost.   Winter biþ čealdost,
    lengten hrímiӡost   (hé biþ lenӡest čeald),
    sumor sun-wlitiӡost   (sweӡel biþ hátost),
    hærfest hréþ-éadӡost,   hæleðum bringeþ
    ӡéares wæstmas,   þá-þe him God sendeþ.
10 Sóþ biþ sweotulost,   sinc biþ díerest,
    gold gumena ӡe-hwǽm,   and gamol snotorost,
    fyrn-ӡéarum fród,   sé-þe ǽr fela ӡe-bídeþ.
Weax biþ wundrum clibbor.   Wolcnu scríðaþ.
    Ӡeongne æðeling sculon   góde ӡe-síðas
15 bieldan to beadwe   and to béag-ӡiefe.
    Ellen sceal on eorle.   Ecg sceal wiþ helme
    hilde ӡe-bídan.   Hafoc sceal on glófe
    wilde ӡe-wunian.   Wulf sceal on bearwe,
    earm án-haga ;   eofor sceal on holte,
20 tóþ-mæӡenes trum.   Til sceal on éðle
    dómes wyrčan.   Daroþ sceal on handa,
    gár golde fág.   Ӡimm sceal on hringe

176

Maxims II
(*Translation*)

A king must rule (lit. hold dominion). Cities are visible from afar, skillful work of giants, which are on this earth, wondrous work of masonry (lit. building-stones). (3b) Wind is swiftest in the sky, thunder is loudest at times. The glories of Christ are great, fate is strongest. (5b) Winter is coldest, springtime (is) frostiest (it is longest cold), summer is sunniest and fairest (the sun is hottest), autumn (is) most glorious, brings to men the fruits of the year, which God sends them. (10) Truth is most evident, treasure is most precious, gold (is most precious) to every man, and an old man (is) wisest, experienced in bygone years, who formerly experiences a great deal. (13) Wax is wondrously sticky. Clouds glide by. Good companions ought to encourage a young prince in battle and in ring-giving. (16) Courage ought (to be) in a warrior. A sword must experience battle against a helmet. A hawk, (however) fierce, must get used to the glove (i.e., the falconer's wrist). A wolf must (dwell) in a grove, a wretched solitary dweller; a boar must (dwell) in a wood, secure in the strength of his tusks. (20b) A good (man) ought to attain glorious reputation in his native land. A javelin must (be) in the hand, a spear shining with gold. (22b) A gem must stand on a ring, high and broad. A cur-

standan stéap and ȝéap.   Stréam sceal on ýðum
menȝan mere-flóde.   Mæst sceal on čéole,
25 seȝl-ȝierd seomian.   Sweord sceal on bearme,
dryht-líč ísern.   Draca sceal on hlǽwe,
fród, frætwum wlanc.   Fisc sceal on wætere
cyn-ren cennan.   Cyning sceal on healle
béagas dǽlan.   Bera sceal on hǽðe,
30 eald and eȝes-full.   Éa of-dúne sceal
flód-grǽȝ féran.   Fierd sceal æt-samne,
tír-fæstra ȝe-trum.   Tréow sceal on eorle,
wís-dóm on were.   Wudu sceal on foldan
blǽdum blówan.   Beorg sceal on eorðan
35 gréne standan.   God sceal on heofonum,
dǽda Démend.   Duru sceal on healle,
rúm rečedes múþ.   Rand sceal on scielde,
fæst fingra ȝe-beorg.   Fugol uppe sceal
lácan on lyfte.   Leax sceal on wǽle
40 mid scote scríðan.   Scúr sceal on heofonum,
winde ȝe-blanden,   on þás weorold cuman.
Þéof sceal gangan þiestrum wederum.   Þyrs sceal on fenne ȝe-
    wunian
ána innan lande.   Ides sceal dierne cræfte,
fǽmne hire fréond ȝe-sécan,   ȝief héo nyle on folce ȝe-þéon,
45 þæt híe man béagum ȝe-bycge.   Brim sceal sealte weallan,
    lyft-helm and lagu-flód   ymb eallra landa ȝe-hwelč,
flówan fierȝen-stréamas.   Feoh sceal on eorðan
    týdran and tíeman.   Tungol sceal on heofonum
    beorhte scínan,   swá him be-béad Meotod.
50 Gód sceal wiþ yfele,   ȝeoguþ sceal wiþ ieldu,
    líf sceal wiþ déaðe,   léoht sceal wiþ þiestrum,
    fierd wiþ fierde,   féond wiþ óðrum,
    láþ wiþ láðe   ymb land sacan,
    synne stǽlan.   Á sceal snotor hycgan

rent must mingle in waves with the tide of the sea. A mast must (be) on a ship, a yardarm (must) hang (i.e., must hang from a mast). A sword must (lie) on (one's) lap, splendid iron sword. (26b) A dragon must (dwell) on a mound, old, glorying in his treasures. A fish must beget its offspring in the water. A king must give out rings in the hall. A bear must (dwell) on the heath, old and terrible. (30b) Water must flow (lit. go) downhill, flood-gray. An army must (stay) together, a troop of glorious (men). Fidelity must (be) in a warrior, wisdom in a man. (33b) A forest must flourish with foliage on earth. A hill must stand green on earth. God must (be) in heaven, the Judge of deeds. (36b) A door must (be) in a hall, the wide mouth of the house. A boss must (be) on a shield, a secure protection of the fingers. A bird must fly up in the sky. (39b) A salmon must dart (lit. move with a darting movement) through (lit. in) a pool. A storm in the skies must come into this world mingled with wind. (42) A thief must walk (abroad) in dark weather (lit. weathers). A demon must dwell in a fen, alone within (his) territory. A woman, a maiden, must seek her lover by secret art, if she does not (lit. does not wish to) prosper among the people, so that one may buy her with rings. (45b) The sea must surge with salt, cloud (lit. air-covering) and flood, mountain-streams (must) flow around every land (lit. each of all lands). Cattle must be prolific and multiply on earth. A star must shine brightly in the heavens, as God commanded it. (50) Good must against evil, youth must against age, life must against death, light must against darkness, army against army, (one) enemy against another, foe against foe (must) struggle over (lit. about) the land, avenge an injury. (54b) A wise man ought always to think about

55 ymb þisse weorolde ȝe-winn, wearg hangian,
   fæȝere on-ȝieldan þæt hé ǽr fácen dyde
   manna cynne. Meotod ána wát
   hwider séo sáwol sceal siþþan hweorfan,
   and ealle þá gástas þe for Gode hweorfaþ
60 æfter déaþ-dæȝe, dómes bídaþ
   on Fæder fæðme. Is séo forþ-ȝe-sceaft
   déogol and dierne; Dryhten ána wát,
   neriende Fæder. Nǽniȝ eft cymeþ
   hider under hrófas, þe þæt hér for sóþ
65 mannum secge, hwelč síe Meotodes ȝe-sceaft,
   siȝe-folca ȝe-setu, þǽr hé selfa wunaþ.

the trouble of this world, a criminal (must) hang, (must) fittingly atone to mankind for (the fact) that he committed (lit. did) a crime before. (57b) God alone knows whither the soul must go afterwards, and all the spirits that go into the presence of (lit. before) God after the day of death, await judgment in the Father's bosom. (61b) The future is dark and hidden; the Lord alone knows, the Father who saves (lit. saving Father). No one comes back hither under (our) roofs who may here in (lit. for) truth tell men this, what the nature of God may be, the habitations of the triumphant hosts, where he himself dwells.

Three Storm Riddles

1

    Hwelč is hæleða þæs horsc   and þæs hyӡe-cræftiӡ
þæt þæt mæӡe a-secgan,   hwá meč on síþ wrece,
þonne ič a-stíӡe strang,   stundum réðe,
þrymm-full þunie,   þrágum wræce
5 fére ӡeond foldan,   folc-salu bærne,
rečed réafie?   Ríečas stígaþ,
haswe ofer hrófum.   Hlynn biþ on eorðan,
wæl-cwealm wera,   þonne ič wudu hrére,
bearwas blǽd-hwæte,   béamas fielle,
10 holme ӡe-hréfed,   héahum meahtum
wrecen on wáðe,   wíde sended;
hæbbe mé on hrycge   þæt ǽr hádas wráh
fold-búendra,   flǽsc and gástas,
samod on sunde.   Sæӡe hwá meč þečče,
15 oþþe hú ič hátte,   þe þá hlæst bere.

Three Storm Riddles
(*Translation*)

1

Who (lit. which of men) is so wise and so clever that he can tell who drives me on my way, when I rise up strong, at times angry, resound violent, at times cruelly (lit. with persecution) pass over the land, burn houses, ravage buildings? (6b) Smoke rises (lit. smokes rise) up, dark over the roofs. There is noise on earth, violent death of men, when I shake the forest, the fruitful groves, I fell the trees, covered (lit. roofed) with water, driven into motion by the high powers, sent far and wide; I have on my back that which formerly covered the forms of the earth-dwellers (ref. to the Flood), flesh and spirits, together in the water. (14b) Say who covers me, or how I am called, who bear these burdens.

2

    Hwílum ič ȝe-wíte,   swá ne wénaþ menn,
under ýða ȝe-þræc   eorðan séčan,
gár-secges grund.   ȝeofon biþ ȝe-wréȝed,
fám ȝe-wealcen;
5 hwæl-mere hlimmeþ,   hlúde grimmeþ,
stréamas staðu béataþ,   stundum weorpaþ
on stealc hliða   stáne and sande,
wáre and wǽȝe,   þonne ič winnende,
holm-mæȝene be-þeaht,   hrúsan styrie,
10 síde sǽ-grundas.   Sund-helme ne mæȝ
losian ǽr meč lǽte   sé-þe láttéow biþ
on síða ȝe-hwǽm.   Sæȝe, þancol mann,
hwá meč breȝde   of brimes fæðmum,
þonne stréamas eft   stille weorðaþ,
15 ýða ȝe-þwǽre,   þe meč ǽr wrigon.

2

Sometimes I go, as men do not expect, to seek the earth under the tumult of the waves, the bottom of the sea. (3b) The ocean is stirred up, foam (is) tossed up; the sea (lit. whale-sea) resounds, roars loudly, currents beat upon the shores, violently hurl stone and sand, seaweed and wave, at the steep slopes, when I, struggling, covered by the might of the ocean, shake (lit. stir) the ground, the vast bottom (lit. bottoms) of the sea. (10b) I cannot escape the sea (lit. the covering of water) until (lit. before) he who is my guide on every journey lets me. (12b) Say, wise man, who draws me from the embraces of the sea, when the currents again grow still, the waves peaceful, which covered me before.

3

    Hwílum meč mín freâ   fæste ȝe-nearwaþ,
sendeþ þonne   under sǽl-wanges
bearm þone brádan,   and on bid wriceþ,
þrafaþ on þíestrum   þrymma sumne,
5 hǽste on enȝe,   þǽr mé heard siteþ
hrúse on hrycge.   Náh ič hwyrft-weȝes
of þǽm ágláče,   ac ič éðel-stól
hæleða hrére ;   horn-salu wagiaþ,
wera wíč-stede,   weallas bifiaþ,
10 stéape ofer stiȝ-witum.   Stille þynčeþ
lyft ofer lande   and lagu swíȝe,
oþ-þæt ič of enȝe   upp a-þringe,
efne swá meč wísaþ   sé meč wrǽðe on
æt frum-sceafte   furðum leȝde,
15 bende and clamme,   þæt ič on-búgan ne mót
of þæs ȝe-wealde   þe mé wegas tǽčneþ.
    Hwílum ič sceal ufan   ýða wréȝan,
stréamas styrian   and to stæðe þýwan
flint-grǽȝne flód.   Fámiȝ winneþ
20 wǽȝ wiþ wealle,   wann a-ríseþ
dún ofer díepe ;   hire deorc on lást,
éare ȝe-blanden,   óðer féreþ,

3

Sometimes my lord confines me securely, then sends (me)
under the broad bosom of the fertile plain, drives (me) to a
halt, forces one of the powers (i.e., me) into the darkness,
violently, in confinement, where the earth sits hard on my
back. (6b) I have not any way of escape from that oppression, but I shake the habitation of men; gabled halls tremble,
dwellings of men, walls shake, high over the householders.
(10b) The air seems quiet over the land and the water silent,
until I burst forth upward out of confinement, just as he
directs me who at first at the creation laid bands (lit. wreaths)
upon me, bonds and fetters, so that I may not escape (lit.
turn aside from) the power of the one that points me my
paths.

(17) At times from above I must stir up the waves, stir
the currents and drive the flint-gray sea to the shore. (19b)
Foamy, a wave fights against the wall (i.e., cliff), dark rises
the hill (i.e., wave) over the deep; in its wake, dark, mingled

þæt híe ȝe-mittaþ   mearc-lande néah
héa hlincas.   Þǽr biþ hlúd wudu,
25 brim-ȝiesta breahtm,   bídaþ stille
stealc stán-hliðu   stréam-ȝe-winnes,
hóp-ȝe-hnástes,   þonne héah ȝe-þring
on clifu crýdeþ.   Þǽr biþ čéole wén
slíðre sæčče,   ȝief hine sǽ bireþ
30 on þá grimman tíd,   gásta fullne,
þæt hé scyle ríče   be-rofen weorðan,
feore be-fohten   fámiȝ rídan
ýða hrycgum.   Þǽr biþ eȝesa sum
ieldum ȝe-íewed,   þára-þe ič híeran sceal
35 strang on stíþ-weȝ.   Hwá ȝe-stilleþ þæt?
    Hwílum ič þurh-rǽse   þæt mé on bæce rídeþ,
wann wǽȝ-fatu,   wíde to-þringe
lagu-stréama full,   hwílum lǽte eft
slúpan to-samne.   Sé biþ swéȝa mǽst,
40 breahtma ofer burgum,   and ȝe-brǽca hlúdost,
þonne scearp cymeþ   scúr wiþ óðrum,
ecg wiþ ecge;   eorpan ȝe-sceafte
fús ofer folcum   fýre swǽtaþ,
blácan líeȝe,   and ȝe-brecu féraþ
45 deorc ofer dryhtum   ȝe-dyne mičele,
faraþ feohtende,   feallan lǽtaþ
sweart sumsendu   séaw of bósme,
wǽtan of wambe.   Winnende færeþ
atol éorod-þréat;   eȝesa a-stíȝeþ,
50 mičel mód-þréa   manna cynne,
brógan on burgum,   þonne bláce scotiaþ
scríðende scinn   scearpum wǽpnum.
Dol him ne on-drǽdeþ   þá déaþ-speru;
swilteþ hwæðere,   ȝief him sóþ Meotod
55 on ȝe-rihtu   þurh reȝn ufan
of ȝe-stune lǽteþ   strǽle fléogan,

with the sea, comes another (wave), so that they meet the high hills near the seacoast. (24b) The wooden ship is loud there, the noise of the sailors (lit. sea-visitors), the steep stone slopes quietly await the strife of the waters, the clashing of the waves, when high the tumult presses on to the cliffs. (28b) For the ship there is the probability of a dangerous struggle there, if the sea carries it (away) in that terrible hour, full of souls (i.e., the men), so that it must be out of control (lit. bereft of power), robbed (lit. deprived by fighting) of its life, (must) ride, foamy, on the backs of the waves. (33b) There a certain terror, which I, violent on my rough path, must obey, is revealed to men. Who will calm that?

(36) At times I rush through that which rides on my back, the dark clouds (lit. water-vessels), scatter far and wide the cup of water-currents (i.e., the ocean), at times let them glide together again. (39b) It is the greatest of sounds, of noises over cities, and the loudest of crashes, when one cloud comes sharp against another, edge against edge (i.e., like sword against sword) ; the dark creatures, hastening over the people, sweat fire, bright flame, and the crashes (i.e., thunderclouds) pass dark over the people with a great din, they move on, fighting, let fall a dark, swishing moisture from their bosom, water from their womb. (48b) The terrible host moves on, fighting; terror mounts, a great panic (lit. mind-violence) in mankind, terrors in towns, when pallid, stalking specters shoot with sharp weapons. (53) (Only) a foolish (person) does not fear the deadly spears; he dies, however, if the true Lord lets fly arrows, speeding darts, from above out of

férende flán.   Féa þæt ȝe-díegaþ,
þára-þe ȝe-rǽčeþ   ryne-ȝiestes wǽpen.
  Ič þæs orleȝes   ór on-stelle,
60 þonne ȝe-wíte   wolcen-ȝe-hnáste
þurh ȝe-þræc þringan   þrymme mičele
ofer byrnan bósm.   Birsteþ hlúde
héah hlóþ-ȝe-crod;   þonne hníȝe eft
under lyfte helm   lande neâr,
65 and mé on hrycg hlade   þæt ič habban sceal,
meahtum ȝe-mæȝenod   mínes freân.
  Swá ič þrymm-full þéow   þrágum winne,
hwílum under eorðan,   hwílum ýða sceal
héan under-hnígan,   hwílum holm ufan,
70 stréamas styrie,   hwílum stíȝe upp,
wolcen-fære wréȝe,   wíde fére
swift and swíþ-feorm.   Sæȝe hwæt ič hátte,
oþþe hwá mеč rǽre,   þonne ič restan ne mót,
oþþe hwá mеč stæþþe,   þonne ič stille beom.

the whirlwind straight upon him through the rain. (57b) Few will survive it, whom the weapon of the swift foe (i.e., lightning) hits.

(59) I bring about the beginning of that strife, when I set out in the clash of the clouds, pressing (lit. to press) forward through the tumult with great violence, over the bosom of the torrent (lit. stream). (62b) Loudly (on) high crashes the throng of troops (i.e., stormclouds); then again I bend low under the covering of the air nearer the earth, and I load on my back that which I must hold, strengthened by the powers of my lord. (67) Thus I, a powerful servant, fight at times, sometimes under the earth, sometimes I must sink down, abject, under the waves, sometimes from above I stir up the water, the currents, sometimes I mount up, stir up the moving clouds (lit. cloud motion), I journey far and wide, swift and violent. (72b) Say what I am called, or who raises me up, when I may not rest, or who supports me, when I am still.

The Panther

Maniȝe sindon   ȝeond middan-ȝeard
un-rímu cynn,   þe wé æðelu ne magon
rihte a-reččan   né rím witan,
þæs wíde sind   ȝeond weorold innan
5 fugla and déora   fold-hrérendra
wornas wíd-scope,   swá wæter be-búgeþ
þisne beorhtan bósm,   brim grymetende,
sealt-ýða ȝe-swing.   Wé be sumum híerdon
wrǽtt-líče ȝe-cynd   wildra secgan
10 firum fréa-mǽrne   feorr-landum on
eard weardian,   éðles néotan
æfter dún-scrafum.   Is þæt déor pandher
be naman háten,   þæs-þe niþþa bearn,
wís-fæste weras,   on ȝe-writum cýðaþ
15 be þǽm án-stapan.   Sé is ǽȝ-hwǽm fréond,
duguða éstiȝ,   bútan dracan ánum,
þǽm hé on ealle tíd   and-wráþ lifaþ
þurh yfla ȝe-hwelč   þe hé ȝe-efnan mæȝ.
Þæt is wrǽtt-líč déor,   wundrum scíene
20 híewa ȝe-hwelčes;   swá hæleþ secgaþ,
gást-hálȝe guman,   þætte Ioséphes
tunece wǽre   tielȝa ȝe-hwelčes

The Panther
(Translation)

Many are the countless species throughout the world, of
which we cannot rightly explain the lineage nor know the
number, so widespread throughout the world are the ample
multitudes of birds and beasts walking on the earth, (as far)
as the water surrounds this beautiful earth (lit. bosom), the
roaring sea, the surge of the salt waves. (8b) We have heard
tell about one, (have heard that) a wondrous kind of wild
beast (lit. beasts) occupies a land very celebrated among
men, in distant regions, enjoys a home among mountain-caves.
(12b) That animal is called by the name of panther, according
to what the sons of men, wise men, make known in writings
concerning that solitary wanderer. (15b) He is a friend,
liberal of good deeds (lit. benefits), to every one except the
dragon alone, to whom he is (lit. lives) hostile for all time,
through every evil that he is able to perform.

(19) That is a rare beast, wondrously beautiful, of every
color; as men, holy men, say that Joseph's coat was varied
(lit. changing) in colors of every shade, each of those bright
(hues) shone more splendidly in every respect than the other

	bléom breȝdende,	þára beorhtra ȝe-hwelč
	ǽȝ-hwæs ǽn-líčra	óðrum líexte
25	dryhta bearnum;	swá þæs déores híew,
	blác briȝda ȝe-hwæs,	beorhtra and scíenra
	wundrum líexeþ,	þætte wrǽtt-líčra
	ǽȝ-hwelč óðrum,	ǽn-líčra ȝíen
	and fæȝerra	frætwum blíceþ,
30	simble seld-líčra.	Hé hafaþ sundor-ȝe-cynd,
	milde, ȝe-met-fæst.	Hé is mann-þwǽre,
	luf-sum and léof-tǽl;	nyle láðes wiht
	ǽniȝum ȝe-efnan	bútan þǽm átor-scaðan,
	his fyrn-ȝe-flitan,	þe ič ǽr fore sæȝde.
35	Simble fylle fæȝen,	þonne fódor þiȝeþ,
	æfter þǽm ȝe-reordum	reste séčeþ
	díeȝle stówe	under dún-scrafum;
	þǽr se þéod-wiga	þréo-nihta fæc
	swifeþ on sweofote,	slǽpe ȝe-bisgod.
40	Þonne ellen-róf	upp a-standeþ,
	þrymme ȝe-weliȝod,	on þone þriddan dæȝ,
	snéome of slǽpe.	Swéȝ-hléoðor cymeþ,
	wóða wynn-sumost	þurh þæs wildres múþ.
	Æfter þǽre stefne	stenč út cymeþ
45	of þǽm wang-stede,	wynn-sumra stéam,
	swétra and swíðra	swæcca ȝe-hwelčum,
	wyrta blóstmum	and wudu-blǽdum,
	eallum æðel-líčra	eorðan frætwum.
	Þonne of čeastrum	and cyne-stólum
50	and of burg-salum	beorn-þréat maniȝ
	faraþ fold-wegum	folca þrýðum,
	éorod-cystum,	ofstum ȝe-fýsde,
	daroþ-lácende;	déor efne swá same
	æfter þǽre stefne	on þone stenč faraþ.
55	Swá is Dryhten God,	dréama Rǽdend,
	eallum éaþ-méde	óðrum ȝe-sceaftum,

for the sons of men; so the animal's hue, bright with every play of color, gleams wondrously brighter and more beautiful, so that each shines more wonderful than the other, yet more splendid and fairer in its beauty (lit. ornaments), ever more wondrous. (30b) He has a peculiar nature, gentle, meek. He is kind, loving and agreeable; he will not do anything hostile to any one except the venomous foe, his ancient enemy, of which I spoke before. (35) Always rejoicing in his fill, when he partakes of food, he seeks rest after the feasting in a hidden place among the mountain-caves; there the great warrior rests in sleep for a space of three nights, given over to (lit. occupied in) slumber. (40) Then he rises up powerful, endowed (lit. enriched) with strength, on the third day, quickly from sleep. A melodious sound, the most delightful of voices, comes from (lit. through) the mouth of the beast. (44) After the voice a fragrance issues forth from that place, an exhalation pleasanter, sweeter and stronger than any odor, than the blossoms of plants and than the forest blossoms, finer than all the beautiful things of the earth. (49) Then out of the cities and royal dwellings and out of the town buildings many bands (lit. many a band) of men go on the roads in troops of people, in great companies, impelled hastily, spear-warriors; likewise animals after that voice (has been heard) go toward that fragrance.

(55) So is the Lord God, the Ruler of joys, gracious, (liberal with) every gift, to all other creatures except to the

    duguða ӡe-hwelčre,   bútan dracan ánum,
    átres ord-fruman.   Þæt is se ealda féond,
    þone hé ӡe-sǽlde   on súsla grund
60 and ӡe-feterode   fýrnum téagum,
    be-þeahte þréa-níedum,   and þý þriddan dæӡe
    of déagle a-rás,   þæs-þe hé déaþ fore ús
    þréo niht þolode,   Þéoden enӡla,
    sigora Sellend.   Þæt wæs swéte stenč,
65 wlitiӡ and wynn-sum   ӡeond weorold ealle.
    Siþþan to þǽm swicce   sóþ-fæste menn
    on healfa ӡe-hwone   héapum þrungon
    ӡeond eallne ymb-hwyrft   eorðan scéata.
    Swá se snotra ӡe-cwæþ   Sanctus Paulus :
70 "Maniӡ-fealde sind   ӡeond middan-ӡeard
    gód un-gníeðe   þe ús to ӡiefe dǽleþ
    and to feorh-nere   Fæder eall-mihtiӡ,
    and se ánga hyht   eallra ӡe-sceafta,
    uppe ӡe niðer."   Þæt is æðele stenč.

dragon alone, the instigator of evil (lit. poison). (58b) That is the ancient fiend, whom he bound in the abyss of torments and fettered with fiery chains, loaded (lit. covered) with grievous afflictions (ref. to the Harrowing of Hell), and on the third day arose from the grave, the Prince of angels, the Giver of victories, after he had suffered death for us for three nights. (64b) That was a sweet fragrance, lovely and pleasant throughout all the world. Then righteous men on every side throughout the whole expanse (lit. circuit) of the regions of the earth thronged in crowds to that odor. (69) Thus spoke the wise Saint Paul: "Manifold are the unstinted good things throughout the world which the Father almighty, who is (lit. and) the sole hope of all creatures, above and below, apportions to us as a gift and for the preservation of life." That is a fine perfume.

The Whale

Nú ič fitte ȝíen   ymb fisca cynn
wille wóþ-cræfte   wordum cýðan
þurh mód-ȝe-mynd   be þǽm mičelan hwæle.
Sé biþ un-willum   oft ȝe-méted,
5 frécne and ferhþ-grimm,   faroþ-lácendum,
niþþa ge-hwelčum;   þǽm is nama cenned,
fyrn-stréama ȝe-flotan,   Fastitocálon.
Is þæs híew ȝe-líč   hréofum stáne,
swelče wórie   be wædes ófre,
10 sand-beorgum ymb-seald,   sǽ-ríerica mǽst,
swá þæt wénaþ   wǽȝ-líðende
þæt híe on íeȝ-land sum   éagum wlíten,
and þonne ȝe-hýdaþ   héah-stefn scipu
to þǽm un-lande   ancor-rápum,
15 setlaþ sǽ-méaras   sundes æt ende,
and þonne on þæt íeȝ-land   upp ȝe-wítaþ
collen-ferhþe;   čéolas standaþ
be stæðe fæste,   stréame be-wunden.
Þonne ȝe-wíciaþ   wériȝ-ferhþe,
20 faroþ-lácende,   fréčnes ne wénaþ,
on þǽm íeȝ-lande   ǽled weččaþ,
héah-fýr ǽlaþ;   hæleþ béoþ on wynnum,

The Whale
(*Translation*)

Now by my intelligence I will further relate in words in a
poem, by the art of poetry, about a kind of fish (lit. fishes),
about the great whale. (4) He is often encountered, dangerous
and cruel-hearted, to the displeasure of seafarers, of every
man; to him, the swimmer of the ancient streams (i.e., the
ocean), the name Fastitocalon (Greek *aspidochelone,* lit.
shield-tortoise) is given (lit. named). (8) His form is like a
rough stone, as if the greatest (mass) of seaweeds were drift-
ing (lit. wandering) by the shore of the sea, surrounded by
sand dunes, so that seafarers believe that they are looking with
their eyes at some island, and then they make fast the high-
prowed ships with mooring lines (lit. anchor-ropes) to that
supposed land, place their ships (lit. sea-steeds) at the edge of
the water, and then they go boldly ashore on the "island";
the ships remain secure at the shore, surrounded by water.
(19) Then the weary seafarers make camp, they do not expect
danger, they build (lit. waken) a fire on the "island," kindle

réoniȝ-móde,   reste ȝe-lyste.

Þonne ȝe-féleþ   fácnes cræftiȝ

25 þæt him þá férend on   fæste wuniaþ,

wíč weardiaþ   wedres on luste,

þonne semninga   on sealtne wǽȝ

mid þá nóðe   niðer ȝe-wíteþ

gár-secges ȝiest,   grund ȝe-séčeþ,

30 and þonne on déaþ-sele   drenče be-fæsteþ

scipu mid scealcum.   Swá biþ scinna þéaw,

déofla wíse,   þæt híe drohtende

þurh dierne meaht   duguðe be-swícaþ,

and on teosu tyhtaþ   tilra dǽda,

35 wémaþ on willan,   þæt híe wraðe séčen,

frófre to féondum,   oþ-þæt híe fæste þǽr

æt þǽm wǽr-logan   wíč ȝe-čéosaþ.

Þonne þæt ȝe-cnáweþ   of cwic-súsle

fláh féond ȝe-mág,   þætte fíra ȝe-hwelč

40 hæleða cynnes   on his hringe biþ

fæste ȝe-féȝed,   hé him feorh-bana

þurh slíðen searu   siþþan weorðeþ,

wlancum and héanum,   þe his willan hér

firenum fremmaþ;   mid þǽm hé fǽringa,

45 heoloþ-helme be-þeaht,   helle séčeþ,

góda gǽsne,   grund-léasne wielm

under mist-glóme,   swá se mičela hwæl,

sé-þe be-senčeþ   sǽ-líðende

eorlas and ýþ-méaras.   Hé hafaþ óðre ȝe-cynd,

50 wæter-þyssa wlanc,   wrǽtt-líčran ȝíen.

Þonne hine on holme   hungor bisgaþ

and þone áglǽčan   ǽtes lysteþ,

þonne se mere-weard   múþ on-týneþ,

wíde weleras;   cymeþ wynn-sum stenč

55 of his innoðe,   þætte óðre þurh þone

sǽ-fisca cynn   be-swicen weorðaþ,

a high fire; the weary men are joyful (lit. in joys), desirous
of rest. (24) When, cunning in his deceit, he feels that the
sailors are remaining securely upon him, are making (lit.
occupying) camp, delighted at (lit. in joy of) the good
weather, then suddenly the stranger of the ocean (i.e., the
whale) dives (lit. goes) down with them boldly into the salt
wave, makes for the bottom, and then delivers over to drown-
ing the ships together with the men in the hall of death. (31b)
Such is the usage of demons, the way of devils, that they
continually (lit. continuing) deceive people through secret
power, incite them to the ruin (lit. harm) of good deeds, lead
them astray at will, so that they seek support, consolation,
from devils, until they firmly choose a dwelling-place among
the devils. (38) When, out of the torment of hell, the deceitful, wicked fiend perceives that any man of the human race
(lit. race of men) is caught (lit. fixed) fast in his fetter, he
thereupon slays him (lit. becomes a slayer to him) by cruel
cunning, (both) the rich and the poor, who sinfully do his will
here (i.e., on earth); concealed by a helmet of invisibility,
devoid of virtues, he suddenly goes with them to hell, the
bottomless surge (of fire) under the misty gloom, even as the
great whale, who sinks seafaring men and ships (lit. wave-
steeds). (49b) He, the proud swimmer (lit. water-rusher),
has another trait (lit. characteristic), even more marvelous.
When hunger afflicts him at sea and causes the monster to
desire food, then the lord of the sea opens his mouth, his wide
lips; a delightful fragrance issues from his insides, so that

swimmaþ sund-hwæte   þǽr se swéta stenč
út ȝe-wíteþ.   Híe þǽr-inn faraþ
un-wære weorode,   oþ-þæt se wída čeafl
60   ȝe-fylled biþ;   þonne fǽringa
ymbe| þá here-húðe   hlemmaþ to-gædre
grimme góman.   Swá biþ gumena ȝe-hwǽm,
sé-þe oftost his   un-wær-líče
on þás lǽnan tíd   líf be-scéawaþ,
65   lǽteþ hine be-swícan   þurh swétne stenč,
léasne willan,   þæt hé biþ leahtrum fáh
wiþ Wuldor-Cyning.   Him se a-wierȝda on-ȝeȝn
æfter hin-síðe   helle on-týneþ,
þǽm-þe léas-líče   líčes wynne
70   ofer ferhþ-ȝe-riht   fremedon on un-rǽd.
Þonne se fǽcna   on þǽm fæstenne
ȝe-bróht hafaþ,   bealwes cræftiȝ,
æt þǽm ed-wielme   þá-þe him on clifiaþ,
gyltum ȝe-hrodene,   and ǽr ȝeorne his
75   on hira líf-dagum   lárum híerdon,
þonne hé þá grimman   góman be-hlemmeþ
æfter feorh-cwæle   fæste to-gædre,
helle hlin-duru;   nágon hwyrft né swiče,
út-síþ ǽfre,   þá-þe þǽr-inn cumaþ,
80   þon-má-þe þá fiscas   faroþ-lácende
of þæs hwæles fenȝe   hweorfan móton.
For-þon is eallinga   [ús ofost sélest
þæt wé ȝe-cwémen   cyninga Wuldre],
dryhtna Dryhtne,   and á déoflum wiþ-sacen
85   wordum and weorcum,   þæt wé Wuldor-Cyning
ȝe-séon móten.   Wuton á sibbe to him
on þás hwílnan tíd   hǽlu sécan,
þæt wé mid swá léofne   on lofe móton
to wídan feore   wuldres néotan.

other kinds of fish are seduced by it, swim quickly to where the sweet odor comes out. (58b) They go in there in an incautious throng, until the wide jaw is filled; then suddenly the cruel jaws snap (lit. clash) together around that prey. (62b) Thus it shall be for every man who considers his life heedlessly in this transitory time, lets himself be seduced by a sweet odor, a false delight, until he is guilty of sins against the King of glory. (67b) After death (lit. departure) the accursed one opens hell for (lit. opposite) them who indulged in (lit. performed) the false joys of the flesh (lit. body) contrary to what is right for the spirit, in folly. (71) When the deceitful one, skillful at evil, has brought into that stronghold, into that whirlpool, those who, laden (lit. adorned) with crimes, adhere to him and formerly eagerly obeyed his instructions during the days of their life, then he snaps those cruel jaws firmly together, the prison door of hell, after death; those who enter there will not have (any) outlet nor escape, (nor) ever (any) passage out, any more than the fishes swimming the sea are permitted to turn back from the grasp of the whale. (82) Therefore it is indeed best that we hasten to please (lit. haste is altogether best for us that we please) the Glory of kings, the Lord of lords, and always strive against the devils by words and deeds, so that we may be permitted to see the King of glory. (86b) Let us ever seek peace and salvation from him in this transitory time, so that we will be permitted to enjoy glory forever and ever in praise with one so beloved.

A NOTE ON THE TEXTS

"The Voyages of Ohthere and Wulfstan" was inserted by King Alfred into the Old English translation of Orosius's *Compendious History of the World.*

"The Story of King Cynewulf of Wessex," a vivid account of a dynastic struggle in eighth-century England, is part of *The Anglo-Saxon Chronicle.* The date may possibly be slightly inaccurate.

"The Wars of King Alfred against the Vikings" is perhaps the most interesting part of *The Anglo-Saxon Chronicle.* It gives us a remarkable account of King Alfred's struggle to save his country.

When King Alfred translated (or ordered translated) Pope Gregory the Great's *Cura Pastoralis* into English, he added his own preface, about his efforts to repair the ravages of the viking invasions.

Cædmon's "Hymn" is included in the English translation which King Alfred ordered made of Bede's *Ecclesiastical History of the English People.*

The Battle of Brunanburg is one of the poems included in the various manuscript texts of *The Anglo-Saxon Chronicle.* The battle was an English victory in the year 937. The site of the battle has not been identified with certainty.

The Battle of Maldon is a fragment found in only one manuscript, fortunately copied before it was destroyed by fire in 1731. The poem is an account of a battle fought in the year 991.

The Dream of the Rood is preserved in The Vercelli Book. A portion of the poem has also been found carved in runes on the stone Ruthwell Cross, in Scotland.

The Wanderer, The Seafarer, The Wife's Lament, Maxims I, The Storm Riddles, The Panther, and *The Whale* are all from The Exeter Book, the greatest anthology of Old English poetry.

Maxims II is preserved in the same manuscript as one of the texts of *The Anglo-Saxon Chronicle.*

GLOSSARY

HOW TO USE THE GLOSSARY

Alphabetization

The digraph *æ* is not to be thought of as a combination of *a* and *e,* but as a separate letter; it follows *a.* The alphabetical order of the vowels is:

a æ e i o u y.

The only other departure from the normal order of the alphabet is that the letter *þ* follows *t.* The letters *þ* and *ð* are considered the same letter and are alphabetized the same.

The two forms of the letter *g* (*g* and *ʒ*) are considered the same letter and are alphabetized the same.

Prefixes

In looking up a word that begins with a prefix, look for the stem; that is, disregard the prefix and look under the first letter following the prefix. For example, *ʒe-weorc* will be found alphabetized under *w,* not *g.* In looking up a word that begins with more than one prefix, such as, for example, *un-for-bærned,* disregard both the prefix *un-* and the prefix *for-* and look it up under *bærned.*

Since prefixes are hyphenated in this book, it is sometimes impossible to distinguish a prefix from, for example, a preposition in a hyphenated adverb, such as *on-weʒ.* Accordingly, such expressions will be listed twice (all in boldface print). For example, *on-weʒ* will be found under *o* and also under *w.*

The list of prefixes is as follows:

a-	forþ-	þurh-
an-	ʒe-	un-
and-	ʒeond-	under-
æt-	of-	út-
be-	ofer-	wiþ-
ed-	on-	ymb-
for-	oþ-	
fore-	to-	

Grammatical Identification of Glossary Items

Nouns will be identified by an indication of grammatical gender: *masc.* or *fem.* or *neut.* or occasionally a combination of any or all of the three. Irregular noun plural forms will occasionally be given in parentheses.

Verbs will be glossed under infinitive forms. Weak verbs will be identified by a Roman numeral, *I, II,* or *III,* to indicate to which of the three classes of weak verbs each belongs. Irregular forms will be given in parentheses. Strong verbs will have the second, third, and fourth principal parts (i.e., preterite singular, preterite plural, and past participle) given in parentheses, followed by an Arabic numeral, *1–7,* to indicate to which ablaut class the verb belongs. Preterite-present verbs will have their principal parts given in parentheses in this order: (1) first- and third-person singular present indicative; (2) second-person singular present indicative; and (3) preterite singular.

All other parts of speech, such as adjectives, adverbs, prepositions, and conjunctions, will be identified by the appropriate abbreviation.

Parentheses

Parentheses will be used to indicate irregular forms (in addition to the principal parts of verbs, as explained above). For example, the numeral meaning "two" is glossed under its masculine form, *twézen,* followed by the feminine and neuter forms (*twá, tú*) in parentheses. Irregular comparatives and superlatives of adjectives and adverbs will also appear in parentheses.

Alternate Forms

Alternate forms will be separated by a slash mark /. For example, the masculine and neuter instrumental singular of the definite article can be either *pý* or *pon;* accordingly, it is glossed as *pý/pon;* there is a separate entry for *pon,* with directions to refer to *pý.*

Cross-referencing

All irregular forms encountered in the reader selections are glossed independently. For example, the irregular preterite verb form *éodon* will be found independently glossed, with an indication that it is the preterite plural of the verb *gán.*

Abbreviations

acc. accusative	*nom.* nominative
aj. adjective	*num.* numeral
av. adverb	*pers.* person
compar. comparative	*pl.* plural
conj. conjunction	*ppl.* participle, participial
correl. correlative	*prep.* preposition
dat. dative	*pres.* present
fem. feminine	*pret.* preterite
gen. genitive	*pron.* pronoun, pronominal
indic. indicative	*sg.* singular
instr. instrumental	*subj.* subjunctive
irreg. irregular	*superl.* superlative
masc. masculine	*vb.* verb
neg. negative	*w.* with
neut. neuter	

A

a- *prefix: see under first letter following prefix.*
á *av.* always, ever
ac *conj.* but, on the contrary
ác-tréo *neut.* oak tree
ád *masc.* pyre
ádl *fem.* illness, infirmity
ágan (áh, áhst, áhte) *pret.-pres.vb.* possess, have, rule
ágen *aj.* own
áglǽč *neut.* calamity, terror, distress, oppression
áglǽča *masc.* monster
áh *1st.3rd.pers.sg.pres.indic. of* ágan
áhte, áhton *pret. of* ágan
amber *masc.fem.neut.* a measure
ambyre *aj.* favorable
án *num.aj.pron.* one, single, a certain one
an- *prefix: see under first letter following prefix.*
ána *aj.* alone
ancor-ráp *masc.* anchor-rope, mooring-line, cable
and *conj.* and
and- *prefix: see under first letter following prefix.*
anda *masc.sg.* vexation, anger
án-floga *masc.* solitary flier
ánga *aj.* sole, only
án-haga *masc.* solitary dweller
án-líep/án-líepiȝ *aj.* single, individual
án-rǽd *aj.* resolute
án-stapa *masc.* lonely wanderer
án-streČes *av.* at one stretch, without stopping
ár *masc.* messenger
ár *fem.* honor, favor, grace, benefit
ár *fem.* oar
ár *fem.* property

ár-hwæt *aj.* eager for glory, glorious
áscian *II* ask, inquire, demand, seek
  ჳe-áscian hear, find out, learn
atol *aj.* terrible, evil
átor *neut.* poison
átor-scaða *masc.* poisonous enemy
áþ *masc.* oath, pledge
áwa *av.* always, ever
á-wiht *neut.sg.* anything

Æ

ǽ *fem.* law, rite, religion
ǽfen-tíd *fem.* evening
ǽfre *av.* ever, always
  ǽfre ymbe stunde ever and again
æftan *av.* after, behind, from behind
be-æftan *prep.av.* after, behind
æfter *av.prep.* after, along, among, afterwards, concern-
    ing, on account of
æfter-cweðende *ppl.aj.* speaking afterwards
ǽჳ-hwá *pron.* anyone, everyone
ǽჳ-hwǽr *av.* everywhere, anywhere
ǽჳ-hwæs *av.* completely, in every respect
ǽჳ-hwelč *pron.aj.* each, everyone
ǽჳðer *pron.av.* either, each, both
  ǽჳðer ჳe . . . ჳe both . . . and
  ǽჳðer oþþe . . . oþþe either . . . or
ǽht *fem.* property, possessions
ǽlan *I* burn; kindle
  on-ǽlan burn, consume
ǽlč *aj.pron.* each, every, all, any
ǽled *masc.sg.* fire
ჳe-ǽmettiჳian *II* empty, void
ǽniჳ *pron.aj.* any, anyone

211

ǽn-líč *aj.* unique, noble, splendid
ǽr *av.conj.prep.* before, formerly, earlier
ærče-biscop *masc.* archbishop
ǽrende *neut.* message
ǽrend-ʒe-writ *neut.* written message, letter
ǽrend-raca *masc.* messenger, representative
ǽrest *av.* first, at first
ǽr-ʒe-winn *neut.* former strife
ærnan *I* ride, gallop
ǽr-þǽm-þe *conj.* before
ǽr-þon *conj.* before
ǽs *neut.sg.* carrion
æsc *masc.* ash-wood, spear, viking ship
æsc-here *masc.* naval force, viking fleet, spear-army
æsc-holt *neut.* ash-wood spear
æstel *masc.* book-mark
æt *prep.* at, in, near, from
æt- *prefix: see under first letter following prefix*
ǽt *masc.fem.neut.* food ; eating
ǽterne *see* ǽtren
ǽt-ʒiefa *masc.* provider, food-giver
ǽtren/ǽterne *aj.* poisonous, deadly
æðele *aj.* noble, excellent, fine
ʒe-æðele *aj.* natural, fitting
æðeling *masc.* prince, nobleman
æðel-líč *aj.* noble, excellent
æðelu *fem.* lineage
ǽwisc-mód *aj.* abashed, ashamed

B

bád *pret.sg. of* bídan
bán *neut.* bone, ivory, whalebone
bana *masc.* slayer, death
band *pret.sg. of* bindan
baðian *II* bathe

bæc *neut.* back

  ofer **bæc** *av.* back

bæc-bord *neut.* port (side of a ship), larboard

bæd *pret.sg. of* biddan

bǽdan *I* compel, urge, require

bǽdon *pret.pl. of* biddan

bǽl *neut.sg.* fire, flame, funeral pyre

bǽm *dat. of num.* béȝen

bær *pret.sg. of* beran

ȝe-**bǽre** *neut.* behavior, demeanor; scream

bǽren *pret.subj.pl. of* beran

bærnan *I* burn

  for-**bærnan** burn up, cremate

  un-for-**bærned** *ppl.aj.* uncremated

bǽron *pret.pl. of* beran

bærst *pret.sg. of* berstan

be/bí *prep.* by, at, along, beside, about, concerning, **in,** according to

be- *prefix: see under first letter following prefix*

béacen *neut.* sign, symbol, token, beacon, apparition

béad *pret.sg. of* béodan

beadu *fem.sg.* battle

beadu-rǽs *masc.* rush of battle, onslaught

beadu-weorc *neut.* warlike deed

béag *masc.* ring; *pl.* jewelry, treasure

béag *pret.sg. of* búgan

béag-ȝiefa *masc.* ring-giver, lord

béag-ȝiefu *fem.* ring-giving

beald-líče *av.* boldly

bealu *neut.* evil, harm

bealu-síþ *masc.* woeful journey, distressing experience

bealu-ware *masc.pl.* evil-doers

bealwes *gen.sg. of* bealu

béam *masc.* tree, cross

bearm *masc.* bosom, lap

bearn *neut.* child, son

bearu (bearwas) *masc.* grove

bearwas *pl. of* bearu

bearwe *dat.sg. of* bearu

béatan (béot, béoton, béaten) *7* strike, beat

béč *gen.dat.sg., nom.acc.pl. of* bóc

béӡen (bá, bú) *num.* both

benč *fem.* bench

bend *masc.fem.* bond, fetter

benn *fem.* wound

béodan (béad, budon, boden) *2* offer, command, announce

    a-**béodan** offer, command, announce

    be-**béodan** offer, command

    ӡe-**béodan** offer, command

beom *1st.pers.sg.pres.indic. of* béon

béon/wesan *anomalous vb.* be

beorg *masc.* hill

ӡe-**beorg** *neut.* defense, protection

beorgan (bearg, burgon, borgen) *3* protect, save

beorht *aj.* bright

beorn *masc.* man, warrior

beorn-þréat *masc.* band of men

béot *neut.* vow, threat

    on **béot** threateningly

béotian *II* vow, pledge

béoton *pret.pl. of* béatan

béoþ *pres.indic.pl. of* béon

bera *masc.* bear (animal)

beran (bær, bǽron, boren) *4* bear, carry, bring

    oþ-**beran** carry off

berstan (bærst, burston, borsten) *3* burst; crash

    to-**berstan** burst apart, shatter

ȝe-bétan *I* make amends for, atone for, amend, improve
betera *aj.* better
betst *aj.* best
bí *see* be
bid *neut.sg.* delay, halt
  on bid to a halt
bídan (bád, bidon, biden) *1* wait, await
  a-bídan await
  ȝe-bídan wait, await, experience, endure, live through
biddan (bæd, bǽdon, beden) *5* ask, order, pray
  ȝe-biddan pray to
biden *past ppl. of* bídan
bieldan *I* embolden, encourage
bierȝan (bieriȝde) *I* taste
  on-bierȝan taste
bifian *II* tremble
bill *neut.* sword
bill-ȝe-slieht *masc.* sword-slaughter, battle
ȝe-bind *neut.* binding
bindan (band, bundon, bunden) *3* bind
  ȝe-bindan bind
  on-bindan unbind, untie, loosen
binnan *prep.av.* inside, within
biren *aj.* of a bear, bear-skin
bireþ/birþ *3rd.pers.sg.pres.indic. of* beran
birsteþ *3rd.pers.sg.pres.indic. of* berstan
biscop *masc.* bishop
biscop-stól *masc.* bishopric, diocese
bisgian *II* occupy (oneself) ; afflict
  a-bisgian occupy (oneself)
bisgu *fem.* occupation, preoccupation, labor, business
bisiȝ *aj.* busy
bismerian *II* mock
biter *aj.* sharp, angry, cruel, severe, bitter

biþ *3rd.pers.sg.pres.indic.* of béon
blác *aj.* bright, shining; pale, pallid
blácian *II* turn pale
blandan (blénd, bléndon, blanden) *7* mingle, mix
blanden-feax *aj.* gray-haired
blǽd *masc.* prosperity, glory
blǽd *fem.* foliage, fruit
blǽd-hwæt *aj.* copious, fruitful
bléo *neut.* color
blícan (blác, blicon, blicen) *1* shine, glitter, sparkle
bliss *fem.* bliss
blíðe *aj.* happy, glad, cheerful
blód *neut.* blood
blódiȝ *aj.* bloody
blóstma *masc.* blossom
blówan (bléow, bléowon, blówen) *7* bloom, flourish
bóc (béč) *fem.neut.* book
boda *masc.* messenger
boden *past ppl.* of béodan
boga *masc.* bow, longbow
boht *past ppl.* of bycgan
un-be-boht *ppl.aj.* unsold
bold-ágend *masc.* homestead-owner, househoulder
bord *neut.* board, shield
bord-weall *masc.* shield-wall
boren *past ppl.* of beran
bósm *masc.* bosom, breast, lap
bót *fem.* remedy
brád *aj.* broad, wide
bræc *pret.sg.* of brecan
ȝe-bræc/ȝe-brec *neut.* crash, noise
brǽcon *pret.pl.* of brecan
brǽdan *I* spread out
bræȝd *pret.sg.* of breȝdan
brǽr *masc.* briar

bréac *pret.sg. of* brúcan

breahtm *masc.* noise

ȝe-**brec** *see* ȝe-bræc

brecan (bræc, brǽcon, brocen) *4* break
  a-**brecan** break, destroy
  to-**brecan** break to pieces, break up

breȝdan (bræȝd, brugdon, brogden) *3* move quickly,
  pull, draw; change, be changed

bregu *masc.sg.* lord, ruler

brenȝan (bróhte) *I* bring, lead

bréost *neut.* breast, chest, heart (*commonly in pl.*)

bréost-čearu *fem.* anxiety of heart

bréost-cofa *masc.* heart

bréost-hord *neut.* heart, thought, mind

a-**bréoðan** (bréaþ, bruðon, broðen) *2* fail, come to grief

bréowan (bréaw, bruwon, browen) *2* brew

briȝd *neut.* play (of color)

brim *neut.* sea

brim-fugol *masc.* sea bird

brim-ȝiest *masc.* sailor

brim-lád *fem.* path of the sea, sea journey

brim-liðend *masc.* seafarer

brim-mann *masc.* seaman, seafarer

bringan *defective vb.* (*past ppl.* brungen) *3* bring
  ȝe-**bringan** bring

brocen *past ppl. of* brecan

brocian *II* afflict, hurt
  ȝe-**brocian** afflict, hurt

bróga *masc.* terror

bróht *past ppl. of* brenȝan

bróhte, bróhton *pret. of* brenȝan

bróðor *masc.* brother
  ȝe-**bróðor** brother

browen *past ppl. of* bréowan

brúcan (bréac, brucon, brocen) *2* use, enjoy *w.gen.*
brún-ecg *aj.* bright-edged
brycg *fem.* bridge, causeway
brycgian *II* make a bridge
brycg-weard *masc.* bridge-defender
byrne *masc.sg.* burning, fire
brytta *masc.* dispenser, distributor
bryttian *II* distribute, break up
bú *neut. of num.* béȝen
búan (búde, bún/búd) *7-III* dwell, settle, cultivate
budon *pret.pl. of* béodan
bufan *prep.av.* above
búgan (béag, bugon, bogen) *2* bend, turn, bow, retreat
   be-**búgan** surround, encompass
   for-**búgan** avoid, flee from
   on-**búgan** turn aside
bugon *pret.pl. of* búgan
bún *past ppl. of* búan
bunden *past ppl. of* bindan
bune *fem.* cup
búr *masc.* apartment, cottage, chamber
burg (byriȝ) *fem.* stronghold, fortress, fortified town, city
burgon *pret.pl. of* beorgan
burg-sæl (-salu) *neut.* town building
burg-tún *masc.* town enclosure
burg-waran *masc.pl.* townspeople, inhabitants
búr-þeȝn *masc.* chamberlain
bútan *prep.* except, out of, without
bútan *conj.* unless, but, except that
bútan *av.* outside
búte *conj.* but
bú-tú *neut.* both
bycgan (bohte) *I* buy
  be-**bycgan** sell

ȝe-**bycgan** buy, acquire
býn *aj.* inhabited, cultivated
ȝe-**byrd** *fem.neut.* birth, lineage, rank
byrde *aj.* of high rank
byre *masc.sg.* opportunity
byrȝan *I* bury, conceal
byriȝ *gen.dat.sg., nom.acc.pl. of* burg
byrne *fem.* byrnie, coat of chain-mail
byrne *fem.sg.* stream, brook
byrn-wiga *masc.* soldier in armor, byrnied warrior

C

cáf *aj.* bold
cáf-líče *av.* boldly
camp *masc.* battle
ȝe-**camp** battle
camp-stede *masc.* battlefield
candel *fem.* candle
cásere *masc.* emperor
čeafl *masc.* jaw
čeald *neut.sg.* cold
čeald *aj.* cold
čeallian *II* call, shout
čéap *masc.* cattle; goods, property
čear-seld *neut.* sorrowful abode
čearu *fem.* care, sorrow, distress, anxiety
čéas *pret.sg. of* čéosan
čeaster *fem.* city
cellod *aj.* hollow (?)
cempa *masc.* fighter, warrior
céne *aj.av.* bold, boldly, fiercely
cennan *I* name; declare
cennan *I* beget
čéol *masc.* ship

219

** čeorfan** (čearf, curfon, corfen) *3* cut
čeorl *masc.* man, fellow, husband
3e-čéosan (čéas, curon, coren) *2* choose
čiele *masc.* chill, cool
čierlisc *aj.* rustic
    čierlisc menn peasants
čierm *masc.* noise
čierr *masc.* time, occasion, turn, change
čierran *I* turn, change, go, convert (to a religion)
    on-čierran turn
čiriče *fem.* church
číþ *masc.* seed, young shoot
clamm *masc.* fetter, vise
clǽne *aj.* clean, pure
clǽne *av.* entirely
cléofan (cléaf, clufon, clofen) *2* split
clibbor *aj.* sticky, clinging
clif *neut.* cliff
clifian *II* adhere
clipian *II* call, call out
clúdi3 *aj.* rocky
clufon *pret.pl. of* cléofan
clyppan *I* embrace
    ymb-clyppan embrace
cnáwan (cnéow, cnéowon, cnáwen) *7* know, recognize
    3e-cnáwan know, recognize, understand, perceive
    on-cnáwan know, understand, perceive
cnearr *masc.* ship
cnéo *neut.* knee; generation
cnéo-mǽ3 *masc.* ancestor, kinsman
cniht *masc.* boy, young man
cnossian *II* knock, pound
cnyssan *I* strike, beat against
cólian *II* grow cool

collen-ferhþ *aj.* bold, brave
cóm, cómon *pret. of* cuman
corn *neut.* grain
crang *pret.sg. of* cringan
cræft *masc.fem.* power, strength; ability, art, skill
cræftiӡ *aj.* powerful; cunning, skillful
créad *pret.sg. of* crúdan
cringan (crang, crungon, crungen) *3* fall in battle
  ӡe-**cringan** fall in battle
crúdan (créad, crudon, croden) *2* crowd, press, hasten
crungon *pret.pl. of* cringan
crýdeþ *3rd.pers.sg.pres.indic. of* crúdan
cuman (cóm, cómon, cumen) *4* come, go
  be-**cuman** come, come to, happen, befall
  ofer-**cuman** overcome
cumbol-ӡe-hnást *neut.sg.* clash of banners, battle
cumpæder *masc.* a godfather in his relationship to the
    natural father of his godson (*Latin* compater)
cunnan (cann, cannst, cúðe) *pret.-pres.vb.* know, know
    how to
cunnian *II* attempt, test, put to the test, experience
curfon *pret.pl. of* čeorfan
cúþ *aj.* known, familiar
un-**cúþ** *aj.* unknown
un-for-**cúþ** *aj.* dauntless; honorable
cúðen *pret.subj.pl. of* cunnan
cúðon *pret.indic.pl. of* cunnan
cwǽden *pret.subj.pl. of* cweðan
cwǽdon *pret.indic.pl. of* cweðan
cwæþ *1st.3rd.pers.sg.pret.indic. of* cweðan
cweahte *pret.sg. of* cweččan
a-**cweččan** (cweahte) *I* shake, brandish
cwelan (cwæl, cwǽlon, cwolen) *4* die

a-**cwelan** die

ȝe-**cwéman** *I* please; serve

cwén *fem.* woman; wife; queen

cweðan (cwæþ, cwǽdon, cweden) *5* say, speak

  a-**cweðan** speak

  ȝe-**cweðan** say, speak

  on-**cweðan** reply

cwic *aj.* alive, living

cwic-súsl *neut.* torment of hell

cwide-ȝiedd *neut.* song, speech

cwield *masc.fem.neut.* pestilence

cwiþ *3rd.pers.sg.pres.indic. of* cweðan

cwíðan *I* bewail, lament

cwolen *past ppl. of* cwelan

cymeþ/cymþ *3rd.pers.sg.pres.indic. of* cuman

ȝe-**cynd** *neut.* nature, kind, race, species; quality, property, characteristic

cyne-ríče *neut.* kingdom

cyne-stól *masc.* royal dwelling

cyning *masc.* king

cynn *neut.* kind, race, family, species

cyn-ren *neut.sg.* generation, kind

cyrtel *masc.* kirtle, coat, gown

cyssan *I* kiss

cyst *fem.* choice; the best of; excellence

cýðan *I* make known, relate

  a-**cýðan** make known, show, proclaim

  ȝe-**cýðan** make known

cýþþ *fem.* home, native land

D

daga *gen.pl. of* dæȝ

dagan *dat.pl. of* dæȝ

dagas *nom.acc.pl. of* dæȝ

dagum *dat.pl. of* dæӡ
daroþ *masc.* spear, javelin
daroþ-lácend *masc.* spear-warrior
dǽd *fem.* deed, action
dæӡ (dagas) *masc.* day
dæӡ-weorc *neut.* day's work
dǽl *masc.* part, portion, deal, number
dǽlan *I* divide, apportion, distribute, share with, take
    part in
  be-**dǽlan** deprive of
  ӡe-**dǽlan** divide, share
  to-**dǽlan** divide, apportion, separate
déad *aj.* dead
déag *1st.3rd.pers.sg.pres.indic. of* dugan
déagol *neut.* grave
dealf *pret.sg. of* delfan
déaþ *masc.* death
déaþ-dæӡ *masc.* death-day
déaþ-sele *masc.* hall of death, hell
déaþ-spere *neut.* deadly spear
be-**delfan** (dealf, dulfon, dolfen) *3* bury
déman *I* judge
démend *masc.* judge
dennian *II* flow (?), be wet (?)
denu *fem.* valley
déofol *masc.neut.* devil
déogol *aj.* concealed, dark
déop *aj.* deep ; solemn
déop *neut.* the deep, depth, deep water
déor *aj.* bold
déor *neut.* animal
deorc *aj.* dark, gloomy, sad
derian *I* harm, hurt
ӡe-**diegan** *I* survive, escape

díeȝle *aj.av.* secret, secretly
díepe *fem.sg.* the deep, sea
díere *aj.av.* precious, dear, valuable
dierne *aj.* secret, concealed
dimm *aj.* dark, dim
dógor *masc.neut.* day
dol *aj.* foolish
dolg *neut.* wound
dóm *masc.* judgment, opinion, glory, glorious reputation
dóm-ȝeorn *aj.* eager for glorious reputation
dón (dyde, ȝe-dón) *anomalous vb.* do, make, put
   ȝe-dón arrive at, get to, do, bring about, effect
dorste, dorston *pret. of* durran
draca *masc.* dragon
on-drǽdan (dréd, drédon, drǽden) 7 fear, dread
drǽfan *I* drive away, exile
   a-drǽfan drive away, exile
ȝe-dréag *neut.* crowd
dreahte, dreahton *pret. of* dreččan
dréam *masc.* revelry, gaiety, happiness
dréas *pret.sg. of* dréosan
dreččan (dreahte) *I* oppress, annoy, harass
dréfan *I* disturb, afflict
dreng *masc.* warrior
dréogan (dréag, drugon, drogen) 2 experience, suffer,
   endure
dréoriȝ *aj.* dreary, wretched ; bloody
dréoriȝ-hléor *aj.* sad-faced
dréor-sele *masc.* dreary hall, gloomy hall
dréosan (dréas, druron, droren) 2 fall, crumble, disintegrate
   be-dréosan deprive of
   ȝe-dréosan fall, decline, fail, perish
drífan (dráf, drifon, drifen) *1* drive

be-drífan cover
þurh-drífan pierce
drincan (dranc, druncon, druncen) *3* drink
drohtian *II* behave; continue
droren *past ppl. of* dréosan
drýȝe *aj.* dry
on drýȝum on dry ground
dryht *fem.* multitude, people, army; *pl.* men
dryhten *masc.* lord
dryht-líč *aj.* lordly, noble
ȝe-drynč *masc.* drinking
dugan (déag, déaht, dohte) *pret.-pres.vb.* be good, avail
duguþ *fem.* army, host, comitatus; people; power; bene-
    fit, gift
dún *fem.* hill
of-dúne *av.* down, downward, downhill
dún-scræf (-scrafu) *neut.* mountain-cave
durran (dearr, dearrst, dorste) *pret.-pres.vb.* dare
duru *fem.* door
dyde, dydon *pret. of* dón
ȝe-dyn *masc.neut.sg.* din, noise

E

éa *fem.* river, water
éac *av.* also, moreover
éac *prep.w.dat.* in addition to
éaca *masc.* addition, increase, reinforcement
    to éacan *w.gen.* in addition to
éac-þon *av.* in addition
éadiȝ *aj.* happy, blessed, fortunate
éadiȝ-ness *fem.* blessedness, beatitude
eafora *masc.* son, heir
éage *neut.* eye
eahta *num.* eight

éa-lá *interjection* alas
eald (ieldra, ieldest) *aj.* old, ancient
eald-ȝe-wyrht *neut.* ancient deeds
ealdian *II* grow old
ealdor *masc.* lord
ealdor *neut.* life; eternity
   to ealdre forever
ealdor-lang *aj.* life-long; eternal
ealdor-mann *masc.* chief, nobleman, ealdorman
ealgian *II* defend
   ȝe-ealgian defend
eall *aj.* all, entire
eall *av.* altogether, entirely
eall *pron.* everything
ealles *av.* entirely, altogether
eallinga *av.* entirely, altogether
eall-mihtiȝ *aj.* almighty
ealneȝ *av.* always
ealu (ealuþ) *neut.* ale
éar *masc.* sea, water
eard *masc.* land, home, dwelling
eard-ȝeard *masc.* dwelling-place
eardian *II* dwell, inhabit, remain
eard-stapa *masc.* wanderer
earfoþ *neut.* hardship
earfoþ-hwíl *fem.* time of hardship
earfoþ-líč *aj.* difficult, full of hardship
earg *aj.* cowardly
   un-earg *aj.* dauntless, brave
éar-ȝe-bland *neut.sg.* the turbulence of the sea, the blend-
     ing of the waves
earm *masc.* arm
earm *aj.* poor, wretched
earm-čeariȝ *aj.* wretched, sorrowful

earn *masc.* eagle
ȝe-**earnian** *II* earn, deserve
ȝe-**earnung** *fem.* favor
eart *2nd.pers.sg.pres.indic. of* béon
éast *av.aj.* east
   be **éastan** east of
éastan *av.* from the east
éa-stæþ *masc.neut.* rivcr-bank
éast-ende *masc.* the eastern part
éaste-weard *av.aj.* eastward, eastern
éast-healf *fem.* the east side
éast-lang *av.aj.* extending eastward
éaðe *av.* easily
éaþ-mód/éaþ-méde *aj.* gentle, gracious, humble
eaxl *fem.* shoulder
eaxl-ȝe-spann *neut.sg.* intersection of the beams of a
   cross
ebba *masc.* ebb-tide
ebbian *II* ebb, flow out
   a-**ebbian** ebb, flow out, recede
   be-**ebbian** strand, leave aground by the ebb-tide
éče *aj.av.* eternal, forever
ecg *fem.* edge, sword
ecg-hete *masc.sg.* sword-hostility, war
ed- *prefix: see under first letter following prefix*
and-**efen** *fem.* amount, proportion, measure
on-**efen** *prep.* beside
to-**efenes** *prep.* alongside, beside, parallel to
efen-lang *aj.* stretching all along, parallel to
efen-níehþ *fem.* neighborhood, vicinity
efes *fem.* edge, side
ȝe-**efnan** *I* accomplish, perform, do
efne *av.* just, even
efstan *I* hasten

eft *av.* again, in turn, later, back

eʒesa *masc.* terror, fear, awe

eʒes-full *aj.* terrible

eʒes-líč *aj.* terrible, dreadful

ellen *masc.neut.sg.* courage, valor, zeal
  on ellen courageously

ellen-róf *aj.* powerful, courageous

elles *av.* else, otherwise

eln *fem.* ell

el-þéodiʒ *aj.* foreign

ende *masc.* end, district, portion, boundary, border

enʒel *masc.* angel

enʒu *fem.* confinement, narrowness

ent *masc.* giant

éode *pret.sg. of* gán

éoden *pret.subj.pl. of* gán

éodon *pret.pl. of* gán

eodor *masc.* dwelling, enclosure; protector, prince

eofor *masc.* boar

eoh *masc.neut.* horse, steed

eom *1st.pers.sg.pres.indic. of* béon

eorl *masc.* warrior, man, hero, earl, jarl, nobleman

eornoste *av.* earnestly

éorod-cyst *fem.* elite troop, company

éorod-þréat *masc.* troop, host

eorp *aj.* dark

eorðe *fem.* earth

eorþ-scræf (-scrafu) *neut.* cave, grave

eorþ-sele *masc.* cave-dwelling

eorþ-weʒ *masc.* earth

eorþ-wela *masc.* wealth, worldly goods

éow *dat.acc. of pron.* ʒé

éower *pron.aj.* your; *gen. of pron.* ʒé

erian *I* plow

éstiȝ *aj.* gracious, liberal
ettan *I* graze
éðel *masc.* native land, country, domain, home
éðel-stól *masc.* habitation

F

fácen *neut.* deceit, crime
fág *aj.* colored, stained; decorated; shining
fáh *aj.* outlawed; guilty
fám *neut.sg.* foam
fámiȝ *aj.* foamy
fandian *II* search out, find out, attempt
fangen *past ppl. of* fón
faran (fór, fóron, faren) ó go, journey
    a-faran go, go out, depart, travel
    for-faran go before, get in front of, obstruct
    ȝe-faran go, journey, die
    of-faran intercept, overtake, cut off
    to-faran disperse, separate, split up, divide
faroþ-lácend *masc.* sailor, seafarer
faroþ-lácende *ppl.aj.* swimming the sea
faru *fem.* passage, march, journey
fæc *neut.* space of time
fǽcne *aj.* deceitful
fæder *masc.* father
fǽȝe *aj.* fated to die, doomed
fæȝen *aj.* glad, willing, joyful, rejoicing
fǽȝer *aj.* beautiful, fair
fǽȝere *av.* fairly, beautifully, properly, well
fæȝrian *II* become beautiful
fǽhþ *fem.* hostility, feud, revenge
fǽmne *fem.* maiden
færeþ *3rd.pers.sg.pres.indic. of* faran
fǽringa *av.* suddenly

229

fǽr-líče *av.* suddenly
fǽr-scaða *masc.* sudden enemy
fæst *aj.* firm, fast, secure
fæstan *I* fasten, establish
   be-**fæstan** put in safekeeping, establish, implant, deliver
   oþ-**fæstan** set to (a task), commit, entrust
fæsten *neut.* stronghold, safe retreat
fæst-líče *av.* steadily
fæstnian *II* fasten, secure
   ʒe-**fæstnian** fasten, make fast
fæstnung *fem.* security
fǽtels *masc.sg.* vessel, receptacle, bag
fæðm *masc.* embrace
féa *aj.* few
feaht *pret.sg. of* feohtan
feallan (féoll, féollon, feallen) 7 fall, fall dead, extend
   a-**feallan** fall, fall off, fall down
   oþ-**feallan** fall away, fail, lapse
fealu *aj.* dark
fealu-hilte *aj.* golden-hilted
féa-sceaftiʒ *aj.* destitute, miserable
féawa *nom.acc.pl. of* féa
féawum *dat.pl. of* féa
ʒe-**feččan** (feah) *I* fetch, seize
féʒan *I* join; fix
fela *indeclinable noun w.gen* much, many
fela *av.* greatly
fela-léof *aj.* very dear
fela-mihtiʒ *aj.* very mighty, most mighty
ʒe-**félan** *I* feel, touch
feld *masc.* field, open country
fell *neut.* skin, hide
fenʒ *masc.* grasp

féng, féngon *pret. of* fón

fenn *masc.* fen, marsh

féo *dat.sg. of* feoh

feoh *neut.* wealth, property, cattle

feoh-ȝífre *aj.* avaricious, greedy for money

feoh-léas *aj.* without money, destitute

feoht *neut.* battle, fight

   ȝe-**feoht** battle, fight

feohtan (feaht, fuhton, fohten) *3* fight

   be-**feohtan** take by fighting

   ȝe-**feohtan** fight, gain by fighting

feohte *fem.* battle, fight

féolan (fealh, fulgon/fǽlon, folgen) *3* penetrate, enter, press on

   be-**féolan** commit, apply oneself, devote oneself

féol-heard *aj.* file-hardened (?), hard as a file (?)

féoll, féollon *pret. of* feallan

féond (fíend) *masc.* enemy; fiend, the devil

feore *dat.sg. of* feorh

feorh (feoras) *masc.neut.* life

   to wídan feore forever and ever

feorh-bana *masc.* slayer

feorh-bold *neut.* body

feorh-cwalu *fem.sg.* slaughter, death

feorh-hús *neut.* body

feorh-neru *fem.sg.* preservation of life

feorm *fem.* food, sustenance, benefit

feorr (fierr, fierrest) *av.aj.* far

feorran *av.* from afar

feorr-land *neut.* distant land

féos *gen.sg. of* feoh

féower *num.* four

féowertiȝ *num.* forty

ȝe-**féra** *masc.* companion, comrade

231

féran *I* journey, go
  forþ-**féran** depart, die
  ofer-**féran** traverse
férend *masc.* sailor
ferhþ *masc.neut.* mind, spirit
ferhþ-ʒe-riht *neut.* what is right for the spirit
ferhþ-grimm *aj.* savage, cruel-hearted
ferhþ-loca *masc.* breast, thoughts, feelings
ferian *I* carry, transport; go, depart
fersc *aj.* fresh, fresh-water
fét *dat.sg., nom.acc.pl. of* fót
feter *fem.* fetter, bond
ʒe-**feterian** *II* fetter
fetian *II* fetch
  ʒe-**fetian** *fetch,* carry off
féða *masc.* foot-soldier, troop
feðer *fem.* feather
fiell *masc.* fall, death
fiellan *I* fell, kill, lay low
  ʒe-**fiellan** fell, kill, lay low
fielþ *3rd.pers.sg.pres.indic. of* feallan
fíend *dat.sg., nom.acc.pl. of* féond
fierd *fem.* army, militia, English army
fierdian *II* serve with the army
fierd-léas *aj.* without an army, undefended by an army
fierd-rinc *masc.* warrior, English soldier
fierʒen-stréam *masc.* mountain-stream
fierrest *superl. of* feorr
fíf *num.* five
fíftíene *num.* fifteen
fíftiʒ *num.* fifty
findan (fand, fundon, funden) *3* find
    on-**findan** find out
finger *masc.* finger

fíras *masc.pl.* men, mankind
firenum *av.* wickedly
first *masc.* time, period
fisc *masc.* fish
fiscere *masc.* fisherman
fiscoþ *masc.* fishing
fitt *fem.* poem, song
flá *fem.* arrow
fláh *aj.* deceitful
flán *fem.* arrow
flæsc *neut.sg.* flesh
flæsc-hama *masc.* body
fléag *pret.sg.* of fléogan
fléam *masc.* flight (fleeing)
fléogan (fléag, flugon, flogen) *2* fly; flee
fléon (fléah, flugon, flogen) *2* flee, escape
fléotan (fléat, fluton, floten) *2* float
flett *neut.* floor, hall
flíeman *I* put to flight
   a-**flíeman** put to flight
   ʒe-**flíeman** put to flight
flint-græʒ *aj.* flint-gray, gray like flint
flocc *masc.* company, troop
flocc-rád *fem.* troop, mounted detachment
flód *masc.* flood, tide, sea
flód-græʒ *aj.* flood-gray
flód-weʒ *masc.* sea-way
flot *neut.sg.* sea
flota *masc.* sailor; ship
   ʒe-**flota** swimmer, floater; whale
flówan (fléow, fléowon, flówen) *7* flow
   be-**flówan** flow over, drench
flugon *pret.pl.* of fléogan, fléon
flyht *masc.* flight, flying

fódor *neut.sg.* food, fodder
un-ʒe-**fóge** *av.* excessively, exceedingly
un-be-**fohten** *ppl.aj.* unopposed
folc *neut.* people; army
folc-ʒe-feoht *neut.* major battle, pitched battle, **general**
    engagement
folc-land *neut.* country
folc-sæl (-salu) *neut.* house
folc-stede *masc.* battlefield
fold-búend *masc.* earth-dweller, human being
folde *fem.* earth, land
fold-hrérende *ppl.aj.* walking on the earth
fold-weʒ *masc.* road, path, way
folgaþ *masc.* service; retinue
folgian *II* follow
folm *fem.* hand
fón (féng, féngon, fangen) *7* seize, take, grasp, **catch**
    fón to ríče succeed to the throne
    fón to wǽpnum take up arms
    ʒe-**fón** seize, take, grasp
    on-**fón** receive; *w.gen.* stand sponsor in baptism
for *prep,* on account of, for, before
for- *prefix: see under first letter following prefix*
fór, fóron *pret. of* faran
foran *av.prep.* before, ahead, forward, in front, from **in**
    front
    æt-**foran** *av.prep.* before
    be-**foran** *av.prep.* before
    on-**foran** *av.prep.* before, forward, in front of
ford *masc.* ford
fore *prep.* for, before
fore- *prefix: see under first letter following prefix*
fóre *pret.subj.sg. of* faran
fore-weard *aj.* early

forht *aj.* frightened, afraid, fearful
  un-**forht** fearless, unafraid
forhtian *II* become frightened
for-hwon *adv.conj.* why
forma *aj.* first
forst *masc.* frost
forþ *av.* forth, forward, away, henceforth, continuing
forþ- *prefix: see under first letter following prefix*
for-þǽm *conj.* because
for-þǽm-þe *conj.* because
forþ-ʒeorn *aj.* eager to advance
forþ-ʒe-sceaft *fem.* creation, destiny, the future
ʒe-forðian *II* carry out, perform
for-þon *av.* therefore, for that reason
for-þon *conj.* because
forþ-weʒ *masc.* journey, departure
  on **forþ-weʒe** away
for-þý *av.* therefore, for that reason
for-þý-þe *conj.* because
fót (fét) *masc.* foot
fót-mǽl *neut.* foot (measure)
fóþ *pres.indic.pl. of* fón
fracuþ *aj.* wicked, criminal
fram *av.prep.* from, away, away from, concerning
fram-síþ *masc.* departure
fram-weard *aj.* departing, doomed to die
franca *masc.* spear (of Frankish design)
frǽt, frǽton *pret. of* fretan
frǽtwa *fem.pl.* treasures, trappings, ornaments
fréa *masc.* lord
fréa-mǽre *aj.* very celebrated
fréčen *neut.* danger
frécne *aj.* bold, dangerous
fréfran *I* console

fremd *aj.* strange, foreign, alien
fremman *I* do, make
ȝe-**fremman** perform, bring about
fremu *fem.* goodness, good deed
fréo *aj.* free, noble, generous
fréod *fem.* peace
fréo-mǽȝ *masc.* noble kinsman
fréond (fríend) *masc.* friend, lover
fréond-léas *aj.* friendless
fréond-líče *av.* in friendly fashion
fréond-scipe *masc.* friendship, love
fréoriȝ *aj.* freezing cold; mournful
fréosan (fréas, fruron, froren) *2* freeze
ofer-**fréosan** freeze over
fretan (frǽt, frǽton, freten) *5 irreg.* eat, eat up, devour
frettan *I* feed on, eat up, graze
fríend *dat.sg., nom.acc.pl. of* fréond
friȝnan (fræȝn, frugnon, frugnen) *3* inquire; learn
ȝe-**friȝnan** find out, hear of
friþ *neut.* peace
un-**friþ** hostility
fród *aj.* wise, old, experienced
frófor *fem.* consolation
froren *past ppl. of* fréosan
frugnon *pret.pl. of* friȝnan
frum-sceaft *fem.* creation; origin
frymdiȝ *aj.* desirous, inquiring
fugol (fuglas) *masc.* bird
fugolere *masc.* fowler, bird-catcher
fuhton *pret.pl. of* feohtan
fulgon *pret.pl. of* féolan
fúlian *II* decompose, putrefy, become foul
full *neut.sg.* cup
full *aj.* full

be fullan fully, entirely
full *av.* fully, entirely, very
fultum *masc.* help, aid
funde *pret.subj.sg. of* findan
funden *past ppl., pret.subj.pl. of* findan
fundon *pret.pl. of* findan
fundian *II* try, attempt; go
furlang *neut.* furlong
furðor *av.* farther, further
furðum *av.* at first, just, even
fús *aj.* striving forward, eager, hastening
ʒe-fylče *neut.* army, band, division
fyllan *I* fill
fyllu *fem.sg.* plenty, fill
fylstan *I* help
fýr *neut.* fire
fýren *aj.* fiery, burning
fyrmest *aj.av.* first, foremost
ʒe-fyrn *av.* formerly, long ago, once
fyrn-ʒéar *neut.* former year, bygone year
fyrn-ʒe-flita *masc.* ancient enemy, long-standing enemy
fyrn-stréamas *masc.pl.* ocean, the ancient streams
fyrst *aj.* first, foremost
fýsan *I* impel, hasten
    a-fýsan drive, drive away, hasten, impel, urge

G

gadrian *II* gather, assemble
    ʒe-gadrian gather, assemble
gafol *neut.* tribute
galan (gól, gólon, galen) 6 sing
gamen *neut.sg.* mirth, sport
gamol *aj.* old
gamol-feax *aj.* gray-haired

237

gán (éode, ʒe-gán) *anomalous vb.* go, come, walk
  a-**gán** go
  be-**gán** surround (on foot), traverse, visit, get to, **care**
    for, practice, serve
  forþ-**gán** go forth, proceed
gang *masc.* going, passage, flow
gangan (ʒéong, ʒéongon, gangen) 7 go, walk
  ʒe-**gangan** go, happen, obtain
gann *pret.sg. of* ʒinnan
ganot *masc.* gannet (a sea bird)
gár *masc.* spear, javelin
gár-berend *masc.* spear-bearer, warrior
gár-mitting *fem.sg.* spear-conflict, battle
gár-rǽs *masc.* onslaught, battle, spear-**rush**
gár-secg *masc.sg.* sea, ocean
gást *masc.* ghost, soul, spirit
gást-háliʒ *aj.* holy in spirit, holy
æt-gædre *av.* together
to-gædre *av.* together
gǽsne *aj.* barren; deprived of, wanting
gæst-líč *aj.* terrible
gǽþ *3rd.pers.sg.pres.indic. of* gán
ʒe *conj.* and, also
  ʒe . . . **ʒe** both . . . and
ʒé *2nd.pers.pl.pron.* you
ʒe- *prefix: see under first letter following prefix*
ʒéac *masc.* cuckoo
ʒeaf *pret.sg. of* ʒiefan
ʒéafon *pret.pl. of* ʒiefan
ʒealga *masc.* gallows
ʒealg-tréo *neut.* gallows-tree, gallows, cross
ʒeall *pret.sg. of* ʒiellan
ʒéap *aj.* broad
ʒéar *neut.* year

ȝéar-dagas *masc.pl.* former days, time past
ȝeare *see* ȝearwe
ȝearu *aj.* ready, complete
ȝearwe/ȝeare *av.* readily, entirely, well, indeed, really
ȝearwe *nom.pl. of aj.* ȝearu
ȝeat *neut.* gate
ȝeat *pret.sg. of* ȝietan
ȝéaton *pret.pl. of* ȝietan
on-ȝeȝn *av.prep.* opposite, against, towards, in reply to,
   w.vb. of motion to meet, back
to-ȝeȝnes *av.prep.* against, in opposition to
ȝéo *av.* formerly, long ago
ȝéoc *fem.* help, consolation
ȝeofon *neut.sg.* sea, ocean
ȝeoguþ *fem.* youth
ȝeómor *aj.* sad, mournful
ȝeómor-mód *aj.* sorrowful, sad in mind
ȝeond *prep.* through, throughout, among, over, beyond,
   along
ȝeond- *prefix: see under first letter following prefix*
be-ȝeondan *prep.* beyond
ȝeong (ȝienȝra, ȝienȝest) *aj.* young
ȝeorn *aj.* eager
forþ-ȝeorn *aj.* eager to advance
ȝeorne *av.* eagerly, well, completely
ȝeorn-full *aj.* eager
ȝeorn-líče *av.* earnestly, zealously
be-ȝéotan (ȝéat, guton, goten) 2 pour, pour over, cover
   with
ȝéo-wine *masc.* departed friend, friend of former times
ȝiedd *neut.* poem
ȝief *conj.* if
ȝiefan (ȝeaf, ȝéafon, ȝiefen) 5 give
  a-ȝiefan give, give back, give up

for-ʒiefan give, grant, forgive, commit
of-ʒiefan leave, give up
ʒief-stól *masc.* throne, gift-throne
ʒiefu *fem.* gift
ʒieldan (ʒeald, guldon, golden) *3* pay
    for-ʒieldan pay for, buy off
    on-ʒieldan pay, be punished, atone for
ʒiellan (ʒeall, gullon, gollen) *3* scream, yell
    be-ʒiellan scream
ʒielp *masc.neut.sg.* glory, boast
ʒielpan (ʒealp, gulpon, golpen) *3* boast
ʒielp-word *neut.* boasting word
ʒielt *3rd.pers.sg.pres.indic. of* ʒieldan
ʒíeman *I* care about
ʒíen *av.* yet, still, further
ʒierwan *I* prepare; decorate; dress
    on-ʒierwan undress
ʒiest *masc.* visitor, guest, stranger
ʒíet/ʒíeta *av.* yet, still
and-ʒiet *neut.sg.* understanding, intelligence, sense,
    meaning
ʒíeta *see* ʒíet
ʒietan (ʒeat, ʒéaton, ʒieten) *5* get
    be-ʒietan get, take, seize, catch
    on-ʒietan understand, perceive, make out, realize
a-ʒíetan *I* kill, destroy
and-ʒiet-ful-líče *av.* sensibly, intelligibly
ʒífre *aj.* greedy
ʒimm *masc.* gem
an-ʒinn *neut.sg.* beginning, undertaking
on-ʒinnan (gann, gunnon, gunnen) *3* begin, undertake
ʒísl *masc.* hostage
    fore-ʒísl hostage, preliminary hostage
glád *pret.sg. of* glídan

gléaw *aj.* clever, wise
gléo-stæf (-stafas) *masc.* joy
glídan (glád, glidon, gliden) *1* glide, move
glóf *fem.* glove
un-gníeðe *aj.* generous, not stingy, unstinted
gnornian *II* grieve, lament
god *masc.* god, God
gód *aj.* good; liberal
gód *neut.* good, goods, goodness, benefit, advantage, virtue
god-cund *aj.* divine, holy
god-sunu *masc.* godson
gold *neut.* gold
gold-ȝiefa *masc.* gold-giver, lord
gold-wine *masc.* lord, generous lord
góma *masc.* jaws
goten *past ppl. of* ȝéotan
gram *aj.* cruel, fierce
grǽdiȝ *aj.* greedy, eager
græf (grafu) *neut.* grave
grǽȝ *aj.* gray
gremian *I* enrage
gréne *aj.* green
gréot *neut.* sand, dust, earth
gréotan (gréat, gruton, groten) *2* weep, lament
grétan *I* greet, salute; approach, attack
    ȝe-**grétan** greet
grimm *aj.* fierce, wild, savage, dire
grimman (gramm, grummon, grummen) *3* rage, roar
grindan (grand, grundon, grunden) *3* grind
    for-**grindan** destroy
griþ *neut.sg.* truce, peace
grówan (gréow, gréowon, grówen) *7* grow, increase, flourish

grund *masc.* ground, abyss, bottom, foundation
grunden *past ppl. of* grindan
grund-léas *aj.* bottomless
grymettan *I* roar
gryre-léoþ *neut.* song of terror
guma *masc.* man
gunnon *pret.pl. of* ȝinnan
gunnen *past ppl. of* ȝinnan
gúþ *fem.* battle, war
gúþ-hafoc *masc.* war-hawk
gúþ-plega *masc.* battle
gúþ-rinc *masc.* warrior
gylt *masc.* guilt, crime, sin

H

habban (hæfde) *III* have, hold, keep
hád *masc.* condition, rank, order, office; form, nature
hafast *see* hæfst
hafaþ *see* hæfþ
hafen *past ppl. of* hebban
hafenian *II* hold up, lift
hafoc *masc.* hawk, falcon
hál *aj.* healthy, unharmed
háliȝ *aj.* holy
háliȝ *masc.* saint
hám *masc.* dwelling, home, village, estate
hamor *masc.* hammer
hám-weard *av.aj.* homeward, on the way home
hand *fem.* hand
hand-plega *masc.* hand-to-hand fighting
hangen *past ppl. of* hón
hangian *II* hang, be hanged
hár *aj.* hoary, gray, old
hasu *aj.* dark, dusky

hasu-pád gray-coated
haswe *pl. of aj.* hasu
hát *aj.* hot
hátan (hét, héton, háten) 7 call, command, name, bid;
    be called, be named
  3e-hátan promise
hát-heort *aj.* hot-tempered, irascible
hátte *irreg.1st.pers.sg. of* hátan (be called, be named)
3e-háwian *II* view, observe, survey, inspect
hæbbe *1st.pers.sg.pres.indic., pres.subj.sg. of* habban
hæbben *pres.subj.pl. of* habban
hæfde, hæfdon *pret. of* habban
hæfst/hafast *2nd.pers.sg.pres.indic. of* habban
hæfþ/hafaþ *3rd.pers.sg.pres.indic. of* habban
hæӡl *masc.* hail, sleet
hæӡl-faru *fem.* hailstorm
hǽlan *I* heal, save
hæle *masc.* warrior, man
hǽlend *masc.sg.* the Savior
hæleþ *masc.* warrior, man, hero
hǽlu *fem.sg.* salvation
hærfest *masc.* autumn, harvest season
hæste *av.* violently
hǽþ *masc.neut.* heath
hǽðen *aj.* heathen
hé (héo, hit) *3rd.pers.pron.* he (she, it)
héafdum *variant dat.sg., dat.pl. of* héafod
héafod (héafdas) *masc.neut.* head
héah (híerra, híehst) *aj.* high
héah-fæder *masc.* the great Father, God
héah-fýr *neut.* a high fire, towering flame
héah-stefn *aj.* high-prowed (of a ship)
héah þungon *aj.* of high rank, distinguished

healdan (héold, héoldon, healden) 7 hold, keep, rule,
    control, defend, occupy, guard
  be-**healdan** behold, look on
  ȝe-**healdan** hold, grasp, maintain, keep
healf *fem*. half, side, behalf
healf *aj*. half
heall *fem*. hall, residence
heals *masc*. neck
héan *aj*. vile, base, degraded, abject, poor
héan *masc.acc.pl. of* héah
héan-líč *aj*. abject
un-**héan-líče** *av*. not ignobly, creditably
héanne *masc.acc.sg. of* héah
héap *masc*. crowd, troop
heard *aj*. hard, strong, brave, cruel
  for-**heard** very hard
heard-líče *av*. bravely
heard-sǽliȝ *aj*. unfortunate, ill-starred
hearm *masc*. harm, grief
hearpe *fem*. harp
hearra *masc*. lord
heaðu-lind *fem*. linden-wood battle-shield
héawan (héow, héowon, héawen) 7 hew, cut
  a-**héawan** cut down, cut off
  for-**héawan** cut to pieces, cut down, kill
hebban (hóf, hófon, hæfen) 6 raise, lift
  a-**hebban** raise, lift
hefiȝ *aj*. heavy, severe
hell *fem.sg*. hell
hell-scaða *masc*. hell-foe, devil
helm *masc*. protection; helmet; covering
help *fem.sg*. help
ȝe-**hende** *aj.av*. at hand, near
héo *fem.nom.sg. of pron*. hé

heofon *masc.fem.* heaven, sky
heofon-líč *aj.* heavenly
heofon-ríče *neut.* kingdom of heaven
héold *pret.sg. of* healdan
héolden *pret.subj.pl. of* healdan
héoldon *pret.pl. of* healdan
heoloþ-helm *masc.sg.* helmet of invisibility
heolstor *masc.* hiding place, darkness
heonan *av.* from here, hence
be-**heonan** *prep.* on this side of
heorte *fem.* heart
heorþ-ʒe-néat *masc.* hearth-companion, retainer
heorþ-weorod *neut.* band of household retainers
héow, héowon *pret. of* héawan
hér *av.* here
here (herʒas) *masc.* army, the Scandinavian army
here-flíema *masc.* fugitive from battle
here-ʒeatwe *fem.pl.* battle-gear, military equipment
here-húþ *fem.* booty; prey
here-láf *fem.* remnant of an army
herʒaþ *masc.* raid, harrying expedition
herʒe *dat.sg. of* here
herʒes *gen.sg. of* here
hergian *II* ravage, lay waste, harry, raid, plunder
   for-**hergian** plunder, devastate, destroy
   ʒe-**hergian** plunder, ravage
herian *I* praise
hét, héton *pret. of* hátan
hettend *masc.* enemy
hider *av.* here, hither
híe *fem.acc.sg., nom.acc.pl. of pron.* hé
hieldan *I* incline, bend, bow
híenan *I* humiliate, bring low

híeran *I* hear, obey
   híeran inn on belong to
   híeran inn to belong to
   híeran to belong to
   ȝe-híeran hear, obey
hierde-bóc *fem.* shepherd book, pastoral book
híerra *compar. of* héah
híer-sumian *II* obey
híew *neut.* color ; form
hild *fem.* battle, war
hilde-rinc *masc.* warrior
him *masc.neut.dat.sg., dat.pl. of pron.* hé
hindan *av.* behind, from behind
be-hindan *av.prep.* behind
hine *masc.acc.sg. of pron.* hé
hin-síþ *masc.* departure, death
hira *gen.pl. of pron.* hé
híred-mann *masc.* household retainer
his *masc.neut.gen.sg. of pron.* hé
hit *neut.nom.acc.sg. of pron.* hé
hladan (hlód, hlódon, hladen) *6* load, pile up
hláford *masc.* lord
hláford-léas *aj.* lordless
hlæst *neut.* burden
hlǽw *masc.* mound, barrow
hleahtor *masc.sg.* laughter, noise
ȝe-hléapan (hléop, hléopon, hléapen) *7* jump on, mount
hlemman *I* clash
   be-hlemman dash together
hléop *pret.sg. of* hléapan
hléoðor *neut.* voice, sound
hléoðrian *II* speak
hléow *masc.sg.* protection, protector
hléow-mǽȝ *masc.* protecting kinsman

hliehhan (hlóg, hlógon) *I–6* laugh, rejoice
hlífian *II* tower, stand high
hlimman (hlamm, hlummon, hlummen) *3* resound, roar
hlinč *masc.* hill
hlin-duru *fem.sg.* prison door
hliþ *neut.* slope
hlóg *pret.sg. of* hliehhan
hlóþ *fem.* troop, band, crowd
hlóþ-ʒe-crod *neut.* mass of troops, throng of troops
hlúd *aj.* loud
hlynn *masc.sg.* noise
ʒe-**hlystan** *I* listen, listen to
hnág *pret.sg. of* hnígan
hnǽgan *I* humble
hnígan (hnág, hnigon, hniʒen) *1* bow down, bend low
    under-**hnígan** sink under
hóf, hófon *pret. of* hebban
hogode, hogodon *pret. of* hycgan
ʒe-**hola** *masc.* protector, defender
hold *aj.* loyal, gracious
holen *masc.sg.* holly
holm *masc.* sca, water
holm-mæʒen *neut.* might of the ocean, force of the waves
holt *neut.* wood, grove
holt-wudu *masc.* forest, the trees of the forest
hón (héng, héngon, hangen) *7* hang
    a-**hón** hang
    be-**hón** drape
hóp-ʒe-hnást *neut.sg.* clashing of waves, dashing of
        waves
hord *neut.* hoard, treasure
hord-cofa *masc.* treasure-chamber; breast, heart,
        thoughts
horn-sœl (-salu) *neut.* gabled building

247

hors *neut.* horse
horsc *aj.* wise
hors-hwæl *masc.* walrus
hors-þeʒn *masc.* marshal, master of the horse (the title of a royal officer)
hrán *masc.* reindeer
hræd *aj.* quick, ready, active
hræd-wyrde *aj.* hasty of speech
hræfn *masc.* raven
hræʒl *neut.* garment, clothing
hræðe *av.* quickly
hrǽw *neut.* body, corpse
hréam *masc.* cry, alarm
hreddan *I* save, rescue, recover
  a-**hreddan** save, rescue, recover
ʒe-**hréfan** *I* roof, roof over
hréman *I* exult
hrémiʒ *aj.* exultant
hréodan (hréad, hrudon, hroden) *2* adorn
hréof *aj.* rough, scabby
hréoh *aj.* rough, angry, fierce; troubled
hréosan (hréas, hruron, hroren) *2* fall, fall down
  be-**hréosan** fall on, cover
hréow-čeariʒ *aj.* sorrowful, troubled, sad
hréran *I* move, stir, disturb, shake, agitate
  on-**hréran** move
hréþ-éadiʒ *aj.* glorious
hreðer *masc.* heart, breast
hreðer-loca *masc.* breast, heart, confines of the heart
hrím *masc.sg.* hoarfrost
be-**hríman** *I* cover with hoarfrost
hrím-čeald *aj.* frosty, as cold as frost
hrím-ʒicel *masc.* frost-icicles
hrímiʒ *aj.* frosty

hring *masc.* ring ; fetter ; *pl.* ornaments, jewelry
hring-loca *masc.* coat of chain-mail
hring-þegu *fem.* ring-receiving
hríþ *fem.* snowstorm
hríðer *neut.* cattle
hríðiȝ *aj.* storm-beaten
hroden *past ppl. of* hréodan
hróf *masc.* roof
hroren *past ppl. of* hréosan
hrúse *fem.* earth
hrycg *masc.* back
hryre *masc.sg.* fall, death
hú *av.* how
hund *num.* hundred
hund-twelftiȝ *num.* hundred and twenty
huneȝ *masc.* honey
hungor *masc.sg.* hunger
hunta *masc.* hunter, huntsman
huntoþ *masc.* hunting
húru *av.* at least, certainly
hús *neut.* house, building
hwá *pron.* who (*interrogative*), someone
ȝe-hwá *pron.* each one
hwalas *nom.acc.pl. of* hwæl
hwæl (hwalas) *masc.* whale
hwæl-hunta *masc.* whale-hunter, whaler
hwæl-huntoþ *masc.* whale-hunting, whaling
hwæl-mere *masc.* sea
hwæl-weȝ *masc.* sea, whale-way
hwǽm *dat. of pron.* hwá
hwǽr *av.* where, somewhere
ȝe-hwæs *gen. of pron.* ȝe-hwá
hwæt *pron.* what
hwœt *aj.* quick, vigorous, valiant

hwæt *interjection* lo, indeed, behold
hwæðer *pron.* whichever, which (of two)
hwæðer *conj.* whether
ȝe-**hwæðer** *pron.aj.* either, each, both
hwæðere *av.* however, nevertheless
for-**hwega** *av.* at least, about
hwelč *pron.* which, what, whichever, any
ȝe-**hwelč** *aj.* each, all, any
hwéne *av.* a little, somewhat
hweorfan (hwearf, hwurfon, hworfen) *3* turn, return,
  go, move about, turn back
 ȝeond-**hweorfan** pass through
 on-**hweorfan** reverse
hwettan *I* incite, rouse
hwider *av.* whither, where
hwíl *fem.* time, period, while
hwílen *aj.* transitory, passing
hwilpe *fem.* curlew (a sea bird)
hwílum *av.* at times, sometimes, once
hwít *aj.* white
hwón *av.aj.* a little, a few ; somewhat
hwon *instr.sg. of pron.* hwá
for-**hwon** *av.conj.* why
hwone *acc.sg. of pron.* hwá
hwonne *av.conj.* when, until
hworfen *past ppl. of* hweorfan
hwyrft *masc.* outlet
 ymb-**hwyrft** circuit ; region
hwyrft-weȝ *masc.* escape, way of escape
hycgan (hogode) *III* think, consider, intend
 for-**hycgan** despise, reject
hýd *fem.* hide, skin
hýdan *I* hide
 ȝe-**hýdan** hide

ȝe-hýdan *I* make fast with a cable (of hide)
ȝe-hyȝd *fem.neut.* mind, thought
hyȝe *masc.* mind, heart, spirit; thought; courage
hyȝe-cræftiȝ *aj.* wise, clever
hyȝe-ȝeómor *aj.* sad in mind
hyht *masc.* hope; joy; expectation
hyrned-nebba *aj.* horny-beaked
hyse (hyssas) *masc.* young man
hyssa *gen.pl. of* hyse
hyssas *nom.acc.pl. of* hyse
hysses *gen.sg. of* hyse

I

ič *1st.pers.sg. pron.* I
ídel *aj.* empty
ides *fem.* woman, lady
íeȝ-land *neut.* island
íegoþ *masc.* island
ielde *masc.pl.* men, human beings
ieldra *masc.* parent, forebear, ancestor
ieldu *fem.* age, old age
ielfetu *fem.* swan
ierfe *neut.* inheritance
ierȝþu *fem.sg.* slackness, cowardice
iermþu *fem.* misery
iernan (earn, urnon, urnen) *3* run, gallop
   ȝe-iernan get by racing
ierre *aj.* angry
íeðan *I* devastate, lay waste
un-íeðe-líče *av.* with difficulty, disadvantageously
íewan *I* show, reveal
ilca *aj.* same
inn *av.* in, inside
innan *av.prep.* from inside, inside, in

innan-bordes *av.* at home
inn-dryhten *aj.* very noble, distinguished
inn-dryhtu *fem.* honor, glory, nobility
inne *av.* inside, in, inwardly
innoþ *masc.fem.sg.* insides
inwidda *masc.* adversary, evil one
inwitt-hlemm *masc.* treacherous wound, malicious
       wound
íren *neut.* iron, iron sword
is *3rd.pers.sg.pres.indic. of* béon
ís *neut.sg.* ice
ís-čeald *aj.* ice-cold
ísern *neut.* iron, iron sword
ísiʒ-feðera *aj.* icy-feathered

L

ʒe-lác *fem.neut.* commotion, tumult
lácan (leolc) *defective vb.* 7 move, fly
láf *fem.* remainder, survivor, leavings, what is left
       to láfe béon be left
láge *pret.subj.sg. of* licgan
lágon *pret.pl. of* licgan
lagu *masc.sg.* water, sea
       ʒe-lagu extent, surface (of the sea)
lagu-flód *masc.* flood, waters, sea
lagu-lád *fem.* water-path
lagu-stréam *masc.* water, current, ocean
land *neut.* land, country, territory
       un-land supposed land, false land
land-stede *masc.* region
lang (lenʒra, lenʒest) *aj.* long, lasting, tall
and-lang *aj.* continuous, entire
ʒe-lang *aj.* dependent on
langaþ *masc.* longing

lange (len3, len3est) *av.* long, a long time, far, late
langian *II* long for, be grieved
  of-**langian** long for, be oppressed with longing
lang-scip *neut.* warship
langung *fem.* longing
langung-hwíl *fem.* time of longing
lár *fem.* instruction, teaching, learning, lore
lár-cwide *masc.* instructive speech, precept, maxim
láréow *masc.* teacher
lást *masc.* track, trail
  lástas lecgan go
  on lást lecgan pursue
  on láste standan *w.dat.* remain behind, outlast
lást-word *neut.* reputation left behind, fame after death
láttéow *masc.* leader, guide
láþ *aj.* hostile, hateful
láþ *neut.* foe
láþ-líče *av.* wretchedly, unpleasantly
laðian *II* invite
lǽdan *I* lead, bring
  a-**lǽdan** lead, bring
  ȝe-**lǽdan** lead, bring
lǽfan *I* leave
læȝ *pret.sg. of* licgan
lǽn *fem.neut.sg.* loan
  to lǽne on loan
lǽne *aj.* temporary, transitory
lǽran *I* teach, instruct
ȝe-lǽred *ppl.aj.* learned
lǽriȝ *masc.* border, edge
lǽs *av.* less; *compar. of* lýt
lǽssa *aj.* smaller; *compar. of* lýtel
lǽst *aj.* smallest; *superl. of* lýtel
lǽst *av.* least; *superl. of* lýt

ȝe-lǽstan *I* serve, stand by; perform, carry out
lǽtan (lét, léton, lǽten) *7* let, leave
   for-lǽtan abandon, give up, leave, forsake, let go
leahtor (leahtras) *masc.* vice, sin
wiðer-léan *neut.* requital
léas *aj.* lacking; false
léas-líč *aj.* false, empty
leax *masc.sg.* salmon
lecgan (leȝde) *I* lay
   a-lecgan lay down, lay out
leȝd *past.ppl. of* lecgan
leȝde, leȝdon *pret. of* lecgan
leȝer *neut.* bed, resting place, lying, funeral wake
ȝe-lendan *I* land, arrive, go
lenȝ *compar. of av.* lange
lenȝest *superl. of* lang, lange
lenȝra *compar. of aj.* lang
lengten *masc.sg.* springtime
léod *fem.* people, nation; *pl.* people
léod-fruma *masc.* prince
léof *aj.* dear, beloved, friendly, agreeable, pleasant
léof *masc.sg.* beloved one, dear one
léof-tǽl *aj.* loving, agreeable
léoht *neut.sg.* light
léoht *aj.* light
léoht-mód *aj.* light-hearted, easy-going
léon (láh) *defective vb. 1* lend, give, grant
leornian *II* learn
   ȝe-leornian learn, study
leornung *fem.* learning
lét, léton *pret., of* lǽtan
ȝe-lettan *I* hinder, prevent
libban (lifde) *III* live
líč *neut.* body, corpse

ȝe-líč *aj.* like, similar
licgan (læȝ, lágon, leȝen) *5* lie, lie dead, extend
    to-licgan separate, lie between
lid *neut.* ship
lid-mann *masc.* sailor, seafarer, seaman
líefan *I* allow, permit
    a-líefan allow, grant, hand over, yield up
    ȝe-líefan believe
líeȝ *masc.* fire, flame
líehtan *I* dismount; illumine
líesan *I* release, redeem
    on-líesan release, redeem
líexan *I* shine, gleam
líf *neut.* life
líf-dæȝ *masc.* life-day, lifetime
lifdon *pret.pl. of* libban
lifian *II* live
liȝeþ *3rd.pers.sg.pres.indic. of* licgan
líhþ *3rd.pers.sg.pres.indic. of* léon
limpan (lamp, lumpon, lumpen) *3* happen, come to pass
    be-limpan concern, belong
lim-wériȝ *aj.* limb-weary
lind *fem.* linden-wood shield
linden *aj.* of linden wood
locen *past ppl. of* lúcan
lócian *II* look, see
lof *masc.neut.sg.* praise, glory
losian *II* be lost, fail, perish, escape
lúcan (léac, lucon, locen) *2* close, lock, weave, inter-
    twine
    be-lúcan close, shut
lucon *pret.pl. of* lúcan
lufian *II* love
luf-líče *av.* kindly, affectionately

luf-sum *aj.* loving
lufu *fem.* love
lust *masc.* desire; joy
lútan (léat, luton, loten) *2* bend down, bow down
   on-lútan bend down, bow down, incline
lyft *masc.fem.neut.* air, sky
   on lyft aloft
lyft-helm *masc.* air, mist, cloud
ȝe-lyst *ppl.aj.* desirous
lystan *I* cause desire
lýt (lǽs, lǽst) *av.* little
lýtel (lǽssa, lǽst) *aj.* small
lytiȝian *II* become guileful (?)
lýtlian *II* grow less, diminish

M

má *av.* more
má *indeclinable noun, w.gen.* more
ȝe-mág *aj.* bad, wicked
mága *gen.pl. of* mǽȝ
magan (mæȝ, meaht, meahte) *pret.-pres.vb.* be able, can
mágas *nom.acc.pl. of* mǽȝ
magu *masc.* man, kinsman
mágum *dat.pl. of* mǽȝ
magu-þeȝn *masc.* young retainer
man *pron.* one
man *1st.3rd.pers.sg.pres.indic. of* munan
ȝe-mána *masc.* intercourse, dealings
mancus *masc.* mancus, a coin
on-ȝe-mang *prep.* among
manian *II* exhort, urge
   ȝe-manian exhort, urge
maniȝ *aj.* many, many a
   for-maniȝ very many, very many a

maniȝ-feald *aj.* manifold
mann (menn) *masc.* man, human being
mann-cynn *neut.sg.* mankind
mann-dryhten *masc.* lord
mann-þwǽre *aj.* gentle, kind
mára *compar. of* micel
maðelian *II* speak, discourse
máðum (máðmas) *masc.* treasure
máðum-ȝiefa *masc.* treasure-giver
ȝe-mǽč *aj.* suitable, companionable
mæȝ *1st.3rd.pers.sg.pres.indic. of* magan
mǽȝ (mágas) *masc.* kinsman, son
mæȝe *pres.subj.sg. of* magan
mæȝen *neut.* strength
mæȝen *pres.subj.pl. of* magan
mæȝenian *II* gain strength
mǽȝþ *fem.* clan, tribe, nation
mǽl *neut.* time, occasion
mǽlan *I* speak, discourse
  ȝe-mǽlan speak, discourse
mǽre *aj.* splendid, illustrious, famous
mǽrðu *fem.* glory, fame, famous deed
mæsse *fem.* mass, religious festival
mæsse-préost *masc.* mass-priest, priest
mæst *masc.* mast (of a ship)
mǽst *av.* most, mostly
mǽst *superl. of* micel
ȝe-mǽtan *I* dream
mǽte *aj.* moderate, small
mǽþ *fem.sg.* measure, fitness, what is right
mæðel-stede *masc.* place of assembly
mǽw *masc.* sea gull
mé *dat.acc. of* ič
meaht *fem.* power, might

257

meaht *2nd.pers.sg.pres.indic. of* magan
meahte, meahton *pret. of* magan
mearc-land *neut.* seacoast
méare *dat.sg. of* mearh
mearh (méaras) *masc.* horse, steed
mearþ *masc.* marten
méarum *dat.pl. of* mearh
meč *acc. of* ič
méče *masc.* sword
an-**médla** *masc.* pomp, pride
medu *masc.* mead
medu-drinc *masc.* mead-drinking
medu-heall *fem.* mead-hall
medu-rǽden *fem.sg.* responsibility for serving mead
meltan (mealt, multon, molten) *3* melt, disintegrate
menȝan *I* mingle, mix
　ȝe-**menȝan** mingle, mix
meniȝu *fem.sg.* multitude
menn *dat.sg., nom.acc.pl. of* mann
meoluc *fem.* milk
meotod *masc.* Creator, God
mere *masc.* lake, pond, sea
mere-flód masc. sea, tide
mere-weard *masc.* guardian of the sea
mere-wériȝ *aj.* sea-weary
ȝe-met *neut.* measure, limit
métan *I* meet, encounter
　ȝe-**métan** meet, encounter
mete *masc.* food
mete-líest *fem.* lack of food, starvation
ȝe-met-fæst *aj.* modest, meek
méðe *aj.* tired, weary
mičel (mára, mǽst) *aj.* big, large, great, much
mičelum *av.* much, greatly

mid *prep.av.* with, among, together
midd *aj.* middle, the middle of
middan-ʒeard *masc.sg.* world, earth
midde-weard *aj.av.* middle, central, centrally, in the middle
míere *fem.* mare
a-**mierran** *I* wound, injure
mihtiʒ *aj.* mighty
míl *fem.* mile
milde *aj.* gentle, merciful
milds *fem.* kindness, mercy
mín *pron.aj.* my, mine; *gen. of* ič
mis-líč *aj.* various
missen-líče *av.* variously
mist-glóm *masc.sg.* misty gloom
ʒe-**mittan** *I* meet
míðan (máþ, midon, miden) *I* conceal
mód *neut.* mind, spirit, disposition, courage, pride
  ofer-**mód** overconfidence
mód-čeariʒ *aj.* sorrowful of heart, anxious in spirit
mód-čearu *fem.* sorrow, grief
mód-ʒe-mynd *neut.* mind, thought, intelligence
mód-ʒe-þanc *masc.* purpose of mind
módiʒ *aj.* courageous
módiʒ-líče *av.* boldly
módor *fem.* mother
mód-sefa *masc.* mind, heart, spirit, thought
mód-þréa *masc.fem.neut.* anguish, violence of mind
mód-wlanc *aj.* proud of spirit
mold-ærn *neut.* earth-chamber, tomb
molde *fem.* earth
mónaþ *masc.* month
mónða *gen.pl. of* mónaþ
mónðas *nom.acc.pl. of* mónaþ

mónðes *gen.sg. of* mónaþ
mónðum *dat.pl. of* mónaþ
mór *masc.* upland, mountain
morgen *masc.* morning, the next day
morgen-tíd *fem.* morning
morðor *neut.* murder, slaying; deadly sin
móst *2nd.pers.sg.pres.indic. of* mótan
mósten *pret.subj.pl. of* mótan
móste, móston *pret. of* mótan
ʒe-mót *neut.* meeting, encounter, assembly, council
mótan (mót, móst, móste) *pret.-pres.vb.* be permitted,
    may
munan (man, manst, munde) *pret.-pres.vb.* remember,
    consider, bear in mind
  ʒe-munan remember, recall
  on-munan consider worthy
mund-byrd *fem.sg.* protection
murnan (mearn, murnon, mornen) *3* care about
múþ *masc.* mouth
múða *masc.* river mouth
mylen-scearp *aj.* sharp from the grindstone
ʒe-mynd *fem.neut.* memory, mind, thought
ʒe-myndiʒ *aj.* mindful
mynster *neut.* cathedral; monastery

N

ná *av.* not at all, never, by no means
nabban (næfde) *III* not have, lack
naca *masc.* ship
nágon *neg.pres.indic.pl. of* ágan
náh *neg.1st.3rd.pers.sg.pres.indic. of* ágan
náht/nán-wiht *neut.sg.* nothing; *av.* not, not at all,
    by no means
ná-hwæðer *see* nǽʒðer

nam *pret.sg. of* niman
nama *masc.* name
náme *pret.subj.sg. of* niman
námon *pret.pl. of* niman
nán *pron.aj.* none, no one, no
nán-wiht *see* náht
náp *pret.sg. of* nípan
næbbe *1st.pers.sg.pres.indic., pres.subj.sg. of* nabban
næfde, næfdon *pret. of* nabban
næfre *av.* never
næȝl *masc.* nail
ȝe-næȝled *ppl.aj.* nailed, studded
næȝled-cnearr *masc.* nailed ship, ship fastened with nails
nǽȝðer/ná-hwæðer né . . . **né** *correl.conj.* neither . . .
    nor
nǽniȝ *pron.aj.* none, no, no one
nǽre *neg.2nd.pers.sg.pret.indic., neg.pret.subj.sg. of* béon
nǽren *neg.pret.subj.pl. of* béon
nǽron *neg.pret.indic.pl. of* béon
næs *neg.1st.3rd.pers.sg.pret.indic. of* béon
ne *av.* not
né *conj.* nor
    né . . . **né** neither . . . nor
néah (néar, níehst) *av.prep.* near, near to, nearly
ȝe-neahhe *av.* enough, very much, often
nealles *av.* not at all, by no means
néar *compar. of* néah
nearu *aj.* narrow, strict
ȝe-nearwian *II* confine, oppress
ȝe-néat *masc.* comrade, companion, retainer
néa-wist *fem.* vicinity, neighborhood
nefne *conj.prep.* except, unless
nemnan (nemde, nemned) *I* name, call by name
néotan (néat, nuton, noten) *2* use, enjoy *w.gen.*

nerian *I* save, rescue
   3e-**nerian** save, rescue
níed *fem.* necessity
níed-be-þearf *aj.* necessary
níehst *superl. of* néah
níewe *aj.av.* new, newly
níewian *II* renew
nigun *num.* nine
niht *fem.* night
niht-helm *masc.* cover of night
niht-scua *masc.* shadow of night
niht-wacu *fem.* night watch
niman (nam, námon, numen) *4* take, seize, get
   be-**niman** *w.gen.* deprive of
   for-**niman** destroy, take away
   3e-**niman** take, seize, get, carry off
   to-**niman** separate, take apart
nípan (náp, nipon, nipen) *I* grow dark
   3e-**nípan** grow dark
nis *neg.3rd.pers.sg.pres.indic. of* béon
niste, niston *pret. of* nytan
níþ *masc.* enmity, strife, battle, affliction, grief
niðer *av.* below, down
niþþas *masc.pl.* men
3e-**nóg** *aj.* enough, many
nolde, noldon *pret. of* nyllan
norþ *aj.av.* north
   be **norðan** north of
norðan *av.* from the north
norðe-weard/norþ-weard *aj.av.* northern, northward
norþ-mǽst *av.* farthest north
norþ-rihte *av.* due north
norþ-weard *see* norðe-weard
notu *fem.* employment, use, office

nóðe *av.* boldly

nú *av.conj.* now, now that

numen *past ppl. of* niman

nyllan (nylle, nylt, nolde) *anomalous vb.* not wish, be unwilling

nytan (nát, nást, niste) *pret.-pres.vb.* not know

nyttian *II* use, use up, enjoy

nytt-weorðe *aj.* useful, efficient

O

of *prep.* from, out of, concerning

of *av.* off, away

of- *prefix: see under first letter following prefix*

of-dúne *av.* down, downward, downhill

ofer *prep.av.* over, above, across, in spite of, contrary to, after

ofer- *prefix: see under first letter following prefix*

ófer (ófras) *masc.* river bank, seashore

ofost *fem.* haste

ofost-líče *av.* hastily

ofstum *av.* hastily

oft *av.* often

on *prep.* in, into, on, to, among, at, toward, against

on- *prefix: see under first letter following prefix*

ónettan *I* hasten, hasten on

on-ʒe-mang *prep.* among

on-weʒ *av.* away

open *aj.* open, evident, clear

ór *neut.* beginning, origin

ord *neut.* point, spear-point, spear; front rank, vanguard

ord-fruma *masc.* instigator

orleʒe *neut.* war, hostility

un-orne *aj.* honest

or-þanc *aj.* ingenious, skillful

oþ *prep.conj.* until, to, up to
oþ- *prefix: see under first letter following prefix*
óðer *aj.* other; second
óðer *pron.* one
    óðer . . . óðer the one . . . the other
oþ-þæt *conj.* until
oþ-þe *conj.* until
oþþe *conj.* or
    oþþe . . . oþþe either . . . or

P

pandher *masc.* panther
plega *masc.* game, sport, festivity
plegian *II* fight
port *masc.neut.* market town, trading center, port
prass *masc.sg.* proud array (?)

R

rád *fem.* raid, sortie, expedition, journey, riding, way
rád *pret.sg. of* rídan
rand *masc.* border, rim; shield-boss; shield
rás *pret.sg. of* rísan
raðe *av.* quickly
rǽčan (rǽhte) I reach
    ȝe-rǽčan reach, hit; offer
rǽd *masc.* advice, counsel, what is best to do
    un-rǽd folly
rǽdan (reord/rǽdde) *7-I* advise, instruct; rule
    a-rǽdan read
    ȝe-rǽdan decide, determine
ȝe-rǽde *neut.* armor, trappings
rǽdend *masc.* ruler, adviser
rǽhte *pret.sg. of* rǽčan
rǽran *I* raise
    a-rǽran raise, lift up, set up

ráesan *I* attack, rush at
  þurh-**ráesan** rush through
réaf *neut.* garment, armor
réafian *II* plunder, ravage
reččan (reahte) *I* expound
  a-**reččan** translate, expound, relate
reččan (róhte) *I* care, trouble about
rečed *masc.* house, hall
réče-léas *aj.* careless, reckless
recene *av.* quickly
ʒe-réfa *masc.* reeve, sheriff, prefect, government official
reʒn *masc.* rain
ʒe-reʒnod *ppl.aj.* adorned, ornamented
be-réofan (réaf, rufon, rofen) *2* rob, bereave
réoniʒ-mód *aj.* mournful, weary
reord *fem.neut.* voice, speech, language
ʒe-reord *fem.* meal, feast
reord-berend *masc.* speech-bearer, human being
réow, réowon *pret. of* rówan
rest *fem.* rest, resting place, repose
restan *I* rest, repose
  ʒe-**restan** rest, repose, cease
réðe *aj.av.* angry, cruel, fierce
ríče *neut.* rule, dominion, power, kingdom, empire
ríče *aj.* rich, powerful
rícsian *II* rule, reign
rídan (rád, ridon, riden) *1* ride
  be-**rídan** surround on horseback
  for-**rídan** intercept on horseback
  on-**rídan** ride
ridon *pret.pl. of* rídan
ríeč *masc.* smoke
rihtan *I* direct
riht *aj.* right, just, straight

un-**riht** wrong, unlawful, wicked, unjust
rihte *av.* rightly, correctly
ȝe-**rihte** *neut.* straight direction
riht-fæderen-cynn *neut.* direct paternal ancestry
riht-norðan-wind *masc.* wind from due north
rím *neut.* number, count
un-**rím** multitude, countless number
ríman *I* count
rinc *masc.* man, warrior
rip *neut.* harvest, harvesting
ripan (ráp, ripon, ripen) *I irreg.* harvest, reap
ȝe-**ripan** harvest, reap
a-**rísan** (rás, rison, risen) *I* rise, arise
ród *fem.* cross
rofen *past ppl. of* réofan
róhton *pret.pl. of* reččan
rówan (réow, réowon, rówen) *7* row
be-**rówan** row past, row around
oþ-**rówan** escape by rowing
rúm *aj.* large, spacious, wide
rúm-heort *aj.* large-hearted, generous
rún *fem.* secret, private counsel
ȝe-**rýman** *I* extend, enlarge, make room for, make way for, clear away
rýmet *neut.* room, space
ryne-ȝiest *masc.* swift foe, lightning (?)

S

sacan (sóc, sócon, sacen) *6* struggle, fight
wiþ-**sacan** oppose, strive against
ság *pret.sg. of* sígan
salwiȝ-pád *aj.* dark-coated
sam . . . sam *correl.conj.* whether . . . or
same *av.* likewise

æt-**samne** *av.* together
to-**samne** *av.* together
samnian *II* assemble, gather
  ȝe-**samnian** assemble, gather
samod *av.* together
sám-worht *ppl.aj.* unfinished, half built
sand *neut.* sand
sand-beorg *masc.* sand dune
sang *masc.* song
sang *pret.sg. of* singan
sár *neut.* pain, wound
sár *aj.* painful, grievous
sárgian *II* wound
  ȝe-**sárgian** wound
sáwe *pret.subj.sg. of* séon
sáwol *fem.* soul
sáwon *pret.pl. of* séon
sǽ *masc./fem.* sea
sæčč *fem.* strife, contest
sæd *aj.* sated with, weary of
sǽ-fisc *masc.* sea-fish
sǽ-fór *fem.sg.* seafaring
sæȝde, sæȝdon *pret. of* secgan
sæȝe *imperative sg. of* secgan
sæȝeþ *3rd.pers.sg.pres.indic. of* secgan
sǽ-grund *masc.* bottom of the sea, abyss
sǽl *masc./fem.* time, occasion
sǽlan *I* tie up, bind
  ȝe-**sǽlan** tie up, bind
sǽ-lida *masc.* sailor, seafarer, viking
ȝe-**sǽliȝ-líč** *aj.* happy, fortunate
sǽ-líðende *aj.* seafaring
sǽl-wang *masc.* fertile plain
sǽ-mann *masc.* seaman, seafarer

sǽ-mearh (-méaras) *masc.* ship, sea-steed
sǽ-ríerič *neut.* sea-reed, seaweed (?)
sǽ-rima *masc.* coast
sǽ-rinc *masc.* seafarer, viking
sæt *pret.sg. of* sittan
sǽton *pret.pl. of* sittan
a-scacan (scóc, scócon, scæcen) *6* shake, brandish
scadu *fem.* shadow
scæpen *past ppl. of* scieppan
scéaf *pret.sg. of* scúfan
sceaft *masc.* shaft
ʒe-sceaft *fem.* creation; creature; decree; nature, con-
    dition
forþ-ʒe-sceaft *fem.* creation; destiny, the future
sceal *1st.3rd.pers.sg.pres.indic. of* sculan
scealc *masc.* man
scéap *neut.* sheep
sceard *aj.* deprived of
scearp *aj.* sharp
scéat *masc.* region; surface
scéat *pret.sg. of* scéotan
sceatt *masc.* money, coin
scéaþ *fem.* sheath, scabbard
scéawian *II* look, look at
    be-scéawian consider
    ʒeond-scéawian look upon, regard
scéawung *fem.* inspection, exploration
scéotan (scéat, scuton, scoten) *2* shoot
    of-scéotan shoot down, hit, kill
scield *masc.* shield
scield-burg *fem.sg.* shield-fortress
scíene *aj.* fair, beautiful, bright
scieppan (scóp, scópon, scæpen) *6* create, shape, des-
    tine, design
scieppend *masc.sg.* Creator

scieþþan (scód, scódon, scæden) 6 injure, harm
scíma *masc.* radiance
scínan (scán, scinon, scinen) *1* shine
scinn *neut.* specter, phantom, demon
scip *neut.* ship, boat
scip-flota *masc.* sailor, seafarer
scip-here *masc.* fleet, viking fleet
ȝe-scipian *II* provide with ships
scip-ráp *masc.* ship-rope, ship-cable, line
scír *fem.* shire, division, district, province
scír *aj.* clear, bright
scóc *pret.sg. of* scacan
scolde, scoldon *pret. of* sculan
scóp *pret.sg. of* scieppan
scot *neut.* shot, shooting movement
scoten *past ppl. of* scéotan
scotian *II* shoot
scríðan (scráþ, scridon, scriden) *1* go, move, stalk, stride, glide
scúfan (scéaf, scufon, scofen) *2* push, shove, thrust
a-scúfan push, push off, launch
sculan (sceal, scealt, scolde) *pret.-pres.vb.* be obliged to, have to, must, be destined to, be supposed to, shall
scúr *masc.* storm
scyle *pres.subj.sg. of* sculan
sě (séo, þæt) *article, pron.* the, this, that, this one, that one, he, she, it, *rel.* who, which, that, that which
seah *pret.sg. of* séon
seald *past ppl. of* sellan
sealde, sealdon *pret. of* sellan
sealt *aj.* salt, salty
sealt-ýþ *fem.* salt wave
séarian *II* become dry, wither
searu *neut.* cunning

269

séaþ *masc.* pit
séaw *masc.sg.* moisture, juice
sécan (sóhte) *I* seek, visit
  ჳe-**sécan** seek, visit
secg *masc.* warrior, man
secgan (sæჳde) *III* say, speak
  a-**secgan** say, tell
  ჳe-**secgan** say, speak
sefa *masc.* mind, heart, spirit, understanding
séft-éadiჳ *aj.* prosperous, blessed with comfort, in easy
    circumstances
seჳl *masc.* sail
seჳl-ჳierd *fem.* yardarm
seჳlian *II* sail
  ჳe-**seჳlian** sail, get by sailing
ჳe-**selda** *masc.* companion, comrade, retainer
seld-líč *aj.* unusual, wonderful
sele *masc.* hall, house, dwelling
sele-dréam *masc.* hall-revelry
sele-secg *masc.* hall-warrior, retainer
sélest *aj.* best
self *pron.* himself, herself, itself, etc.
sellan (sealde) *I* give, hand over
  ჳe-**sellan** give, give up
  ymb-**sellan** surround
sellend *masc.* giver
sélra *aj.* better
ჳe-**séman** *I* settle, reconcile
semninga *av.* immediately, suddenly
be-**senčan** *I* cause to sink
sendan *I* send
  a-**sendan** send
  on-**sendan** send, send forth
séo *fem.nom.sg. of* sě

270

seofian *II* sigh, lament
seofon *num.* seven
séoles *gen.sg. of* seolh
seolfor *neut.sg.* silver
seolh (séolas) *masc.* seal (animal)
seomian *II* hang; wait
séon (seah, sáwon, sewen) *5* see
  ȝe-séon see, perceive
set *neut.* camp
ȝe-set *neut.* seat, habitation
seten *past ppl. of* sittan
setl *neut.* seat, residence, place
setlan *I* settle; place
settan *I* set, place
  a-settan place, transfer, set, put
  ȝe-settan set, place, seat
sé-þe *relative pron.* who, which, that
sibb *fem.* peace; relationship
síd *aj.* extensive, wide
síde *fem.* side
sidu *masc.sg.* custom, morality
síe *pres.subj.sg. of* béon
siehþ *3rd.pers.sg.pres.indic. of* séon
síen *pres.subj.pl. of* béon
an-síen *fem.* face
ȝe-síene *aj.* visible, seen
ȝe-sierwed *ppl.aj.* armed
siex *num.* six
  hé siexa sum he as one of six, he and five others
siextiȝ *num.* sixty
sígan (ság, sigon, siȝen) *I* sink
siȝe *masc.* victory
siȝe-béam *masc.* tree of victory
siȝe-folc *neut.* victorious people, triumphant host

271

siʒlan *I* sail

  ʒe-siʒlan sail, get by sailing

sigor *masc.* victory

sigor-fæst *aj.* victorious

ʒe-sihþ *fem.* sight, vision

simble *av.* always, ever

sinc *neut.* treasure

sinc-ʒiefa *masc.* treasure-giver, lord, chief

sinc-þegu *fem.* receiving of treasure

sind *pres.indic.pl. of* béon

sindon *pres.indic.pl. of* béon

sin-gál *aj.* continual, perpetual

singan (sang, sungon, sungen) *3* sing

sin-sorg *fem.* perpetual sorrow

sint *pres.indic.pl. of* béon

sittan (sæt, sǽton, seten) *5* sit, remain, be stationed

  a-sittan be stranded, run aground

  be-sittan besiege, surround

  ʒe-sittan sit, sit out, finish

  ymb-sittan besiege

síþ *masc.* journey, trip, errand; occasion, time; experi-
    ence

ʒe-síþ *masc.* companion, retainer

út-síþ *masc.* passage out

síþ-fæt *masc.sg.* expedition, journey

síðian *II* journey

ʒe-síþ-mæʒen *neut.* band of warriors, company

siþþan *conj.* since, after, when

siþþan *av.* afterwards, then, subsequently, after that,
    thereupon

slát *pret.sg. of* slítan

slæʒen *past ppl. of* sléan

slǽp *masc.* sleep, slumber

sléan (slóg, slógon, slæȝen) *6* strike
  be-**sléan** strike, deprive
  ȝe-**sléan** get by striking, win
  of-**sléan** slay
slítan (slát, sliton, sliten) *1* cut, rend
slíðe/slíðen *aj.* cruel, hard, dangerous
slóg *pret.sg. of* sléan
slóge *pret.subj.sg. of* sléan
slógon *pret.pl. of* sléan
slúpan (sléap, slupon, slopen) *2* slip, glide
smæl *aj.* narrow
snáw *masc.* snow
snell *aj.* active, bold
snéome *av.* quickly
sníwan *I* snow
snotor *aj.* wise
sófte (séft, softost) *av.* softly, gently, easily
sóhte, sóhton *pret. of* séčan
sóna *av.* immediately
sorg *fem.* sorrow, anxiety
sorg-léoþ *neut.* dirge
sóþ *neut.* truth
sóþ *aj.* true
sóþ-fæst *aj.* true, righteous
sóþ-ȝiedd *neut.* a true poem
spéd *fem.* success, wealth, prosperity
spédan *I* succeed, prosper, be wealthy
spédiȝ *aj.* prosperous, successful
  un-**spédiȝ** poor
spell *neut.* story, discourse, message
a-**spendan** *I* spend, expend, consume
  for-**spendan** spend, expend, consume, squander
spéow *pret.sg. of* spówan
spere *neut.* spear

273

spillan *I* kill, destroy
spor *neut.sg.* track, course
spówan (spéow, spéowon, spówen) *7* prosper
sprang *pret.sg. of* springan
spræc *pret.sg. of* sprecan
sprǽcon *pret.pl. of* sprecan
sprecan (spræc, sprǽcon, sprecen) *5* speak
fore-**sprecen** *ppl.aj.* aforesaid
sprenȝan *I* break, shiver
spričeþ *3rd.pers.sg.pres.indic. of* sprecan
springan (sprang, sprungon, sprungen) *3* spring
spyrian *II* pursue, follow
stág *pret.sg. of* stígan
stán *masc.* stone
stán-clif *neut.* stone cliff
standan (stód, stódon, standen) *6* stand, remain, **stop**
  a-**standan** stand up
  be-**standan** stand around
  for-**standan** understand
  ȝe-**standan** stand
  under-**standan** understand
  wiþ-**standan** withstand, resist
stang *pret.sg. of* stingan
stán-hliþ *neut.* stone slope
staðol *masc.* foundation, position
ȝe-**staðolian** *II* establish
staðu *acc.pl. of* stæþ
stǽlan *I* avenge
stæl-here *masc.* predatory army, marauding **army**
stæl-hrán *masc.* decoy-reindeer
stæl-weorðe *aj.* serviceable
stæþ (staðas) *masc.neut.* shore, bank
stæþþan *I* support
stealc *aj.* steep

stealde *pret.sg. of* stellan
an-steall *masc.neut.* store, supply
ȝe-steall *masc.neut.* foundation
stéam *masc.* moisture, blood; exhalation
stéap *aj.* high, towering
stearn *masc.* tern (a sea bird)
stede *masc.* place, position
stede-fæst *aj.* steadfast
stefn *masc.* stem, trunk
stefn *fem.* voice; term of military service
stefna *masc.* prow of a ship
stefnettan *I* stand fast
on-stellan (stealde) *I* place, put, bring about, establish
stenč *masc.* odor, fragrance
stent *3rd.pers.sg.pres.indic. of* standan
stéor-bord *neut.* starboard
steppan (stóp, stópon, stæpen) *6* advance, go forward, march
be-stíeman *I* wet, suffuse, moisten
stíeran *I* direct, guide, restrain
stígan (stág, stigon, stiȝen) *1* go, move, set out; ascend, mount
   a-stígan rise, ascend, mount
   ȝe-stígan go up, ascend, mount
stiȝ-wita *masc.* householder
stihtan *I* direct, order, arrange
ȝe-stillan *I* calm, still
stille *aj.* still, quiet
   un-stille restless
still-ness *fem.* peace, quiet, tranquility
   un-still-ness disturbance, trouble
stingan (stang, stungon, stungen) *3* stab
   of-stingan stab, stab to death
stíþ *aj.* stiff, strong, stern, fierce, firm

stíþ-hycgende *aj.* resolute
stíþ-líče *av.* sternly, stoutly
stíþ-mód *aj.* resolute, unflinching
stíþ-weȝ *masc.* rough way
stód *pret.sg. of* standan
stóden *pret.subj.pl. of* standan
stódon *pret.pl. of* standan
stóp *pret.sg. of* steppan
storm *masc.* storm
stów *fem.* place, position
strang *aj.* strong, violent
strǽl *masc.fem.* arrow
stréam *masc.* stream, current
stréam-ȝe-winn *neut.* strife of waters
stréȝan *I* strew, spread
ȝe-stréon *neut.* treasure, property
ȝe-stun *neut.* crash, noise, whirlwind
stund *fem.* time, moment
    ǽfre ymbe stunde ever and again
styčče-mǽlum *av.* piecemeal, here and there
styrian *I* disturb, stir, move
    a-**styrian** move, remove
sum *aj.pron.* one, some, someone, a certain, a certain one
    hé siexa sum he as one of six, he and five others
sumor *masc.* summer
sumor-lang *aj.* summer-long, of the length of a summer's day
sumor-lida *masc.* summer fleet
sumsende *aj.* swishing (of rain)
sund *neut.sg.* sea, water
ȝe-sund *aj.* healthy, unharmed
sund-helm *masc.* covering of water, sea
sund-hwæt *aj.* quick at swimming
sundor *av.* apart, aloof

sundor-ȝe-cynd *fem.* special quality, peculiar nature
sunne *fem.* sun
sunu *masc.* son
sun-wlitiȝ *aj.* sunny and fair, fair with sunshine
súsl *neut.* torment
súþ *aj.av.* south
  be súðan south of
súðan *av.* from the south
súðerne *aj.* southern
súðe-weard *aj.av.* southern, southward
súþ-rihte *av.* due south
súþ-rima *masc.* the south coast
súþ-stæþ *masc.neut.* the south coast
swá *av.conj.* so, as, likewise, thus, such, as if
swá-hwæðer *pron.* whichever
swá-hwelč-swá *pron.* whoever
swán *masc.* peasant
and-swaru *fem.sg.* answer
swát *masc.sg.* blood ; sweat
swæcc *masc.* fragrance, odor
swǽs *aj.* dear, beloved ; one's own
swǽtan *I* sweat ; bleed
swæþ (swaðu) *neut.* track, path
sweart *aj.* black, dark
a-swebban (swefede) *I* put to sleep, slay
swefan (swæf, swǽfon, swefen) *5* sleep, rest
swefed *past ppl. of* swebban
swefn *neut.* sleep, dream
swéȝ *masc.* sound, melody
sweȝel *neut.sg.* sun ; sky
swéȝ-hléoðor *neut.* sound, melody
sweȝle *av.* brightly
swclč *pron.* such

swelče *av.conj.* likewise, similarly, as if
   swelče swá just as
for-swelgan (swealg, swulgon, swolgen) *3* swallow
sweltan (swealt, swulton, swolten) *3* die
swenȝ *masc.* blow, stroke
sweofot *neut.sg.* sleep
ȝe-sweorcan (swearc, swurcon, sworcen) *3* grow dark,
   become grievous
sweord *neut.* sword
sweostor *fem.* sister
sweotul *aj.* clear, evident
swéte *aj.* sweet
be-swícan (swác, swicon, swicen) *1* deceive, betray,
   seduce
swicc *masc.sg.* odor
swiče *masc.sg.* escape
swicen *past ppl. of* swícan
swifeþ *3rd.pers.sg.pres.indic. of* swefan
swift *aj.* swift
swíȝe *aj.* silent
be-swillan *1* wash, drench
swilteþ *3rd.pers.sg.pres.indic. of* sweltan
swimman (swamm, swummon, swummen) *3* swim, float
swín *neut.* pig, hog, boar
ȝe-swinc-dæȝ *masc.* day of toil
ȝe-swing *neut.* surge
swíþ *aj.* strong
swíðe *av.* very, exceedingly, strongly, much, fiercely
   for-swíðe very much, utterly
swíþ-feorm *aj.* violent
swíðost *av.* chiefly
swíðre *fem.sg.* right hand
symbel *neut.* banquet, feast
synn *fem.* sin, crime ; injury

T

tam *aj.* tame
tǽčan (tǽhte) *I* teach, instruct, direct
tǽčnan *I* designate, mark out
tǽhte *pret.sg. of* tǽčan
tǽsan *I* wound
téag *fem.* cord, chain
téon (téah, tugon, togen) *2* draw, pull
téon (téode) *II* make, prepare
teosu *fem.* harm, injury
téþ *dat.sg., nom.acc.pl. of* tóþ
tíd *fem.* time; hour
tíd-dæȝ *masc.* last day, final hour, lifetime, life-span
tielȝ *masc.sg.* dye, color
tíeman *I* multiply, beget
tíen *num.* ten
til *aj.* good
tilian *II* strive for, endeavor
timbran/timbrian *I-II* build
tír *masc.* glory
tír-fæst *aj.* glorious
to *prep.* to, at, toward, from; *w.dat* as a
tó *av.* too, also, there, thereto
to- *prefix: see under first letter following prefix*
ȝe-toht *neut.sg.* battle
torn *neut.* anger, grief
tóþ (téþ) *masc.* tooth, tusk
tóþ-mæȝen *neut.* strength of tusks
tó-weard *prep.* toward
trem *neut.sg.* space, step
tréo *neut.* tree, cross
tréow *fem.* trust, fidelity; agreement, pledge, treaty
trum *aj.* firm, secure, strong

ȝe-**trum** *neut.* troop
ȝe-**truma** *masc.* troop
trymian *I* arrange; strengthen, encourage, exhort
tú *neut. of num.* twéȝen
tú *av.* twice
tugon *pret.pl. of* téon
tún *masc.* enclosure, homestead, village
tunece *fem.sg.* tunic, coat
tungol *masc.neut.* star, luminary
tuwa *av.* twice
twá *fem. of num.* twéȝen
twǽm *dat. of num.* twéȝen
to-**twǽman** *I* divide
twéȝa *gen. of num.* twéȝen
twéȝen (twá, tú) *num.* two
twelf *num.* twelve
twéntiȝ *num.* twenty
twéo *masc.* doubt
   to **twéon weorðan** become doubtful
be-**twéonan** *prep.* between, among
be-**tweox** *prep.* between, among
týdran *I* produce offspring, be prolific
tyhtan *I* teach, incite, lead astray
on-**týnan** *I* open

Þ

þá *av.conj.* then, when, since
þá *fem.acc.sg., nom.acc.pl. of* sě
þá-ȝíet *av.* still, yet
þá-hwíle-þe *conj.* while
þanan *av.* from there, thence
þanc *masc.* thought; thanks; grace, favor
ȝe-**þanc** *masc.neut.* purpose
ȝe-**þancian** *II* thank

þancol *aj.* thoughtful, wise

þára *gen.pl. of* sĕ

þás *fem.acc.sg., nom.acc.pl. of* þes

þǽm *masc.neut.dat.sg., dat.pl. of* sĕ

for-þǽm *conj.* because

for-þǽm-þe *conj.* because

þǽr *av.conj.* there, where, if

þǽre *fem.gen.dat.sg. of* sĕ

þǽr-inn *av.* therein, in there

þǽr-inne *av.* therein, in there

þǽr-on *av.* therein, in there

þǽr-tó *av.* thereto, to it, to that place, besides, for that
    purpose

þæs *masc.neut.gen.sg. of* sĕ

þæt/þætte *conj.* that, so that, in order that, in such a
    way that, until, because

þæt *neut.nom.acc.sg. of* sĕ

oþ-þæt *conj.* until

þætte *see* þæt

þe *relative particle* who, which, that

þe *conj.* when, where, than

þé *dat.acc. of pron.* þú

oþ-þe *conj.* until

þéah *av.conj.* however, though, although, yet, never-
    theless

þeaht *past ppl. of* þeccan

þeahte *pret.sg. of* þeccan

þéah-þe *conj.* although

þearf *fem.* need

þearf *1st.3rd.pers.sg.pres.indic. of* þurfan

þearle *av.* severely, strongly

þéaw *masc.* custom, usage; *pl.* virtues, morals

þeč *acc. of pron.* þú

þecčan (þeahte) *I* cover
  be-þecčan cover, cover over, conceal
þeȝn *masc.* retainer, royal officer, thane
þeȝn-líče *av.* as a thane ought to do
þeȝnung *fem.* service; mass-book
þenčan (þohte) *I* think, consider, intend
  ȝe-þenčan think, consider, think of, imagine
  ȝeond-þenčan consider, contemplate
þenden *av.conj.* meanwhile, while
þenian *I* stretch, stretch out
þéod *fem.* people, nation; host
ȝe-þéode *neut.* language; nation, clan, tribe
þéoden *masc.* prince, lord, chieftain
þéod-wiga *masc.* great warrior
þéof *masc.* thief
ȝe-þéon (þáh, þungon, þungen) *1-3* thrive, prosper
þéos *fem.sg. of* þes
þéow/þéowa *masc.* servant, slave, serf
þéowot-dóm *masc.* service
þes (þéos, þis) *pron.aj.* this
þicgan (þeah, þǽgon, þeȝen) *5* receive, partake of
  ȝe-þicgan receive
þider *av.* there, thither
þider-weard *av.aj.* there, on the way there
þider-weardes *av.* on the way there
þíestre *fem.neut.* darkness; *pl.* (þíestru) shades of night
þíestre *aj.* dark
þiȝeþ *3rd.pers.sg.pres.indic. of* þicgan
þín *pron.aj.* your, thy, thine; *gen. of pron.* þú
þing *neut.* circumstance, condition
un-þinged *ppl.aj.* unexpected
þis *neut.sg. of* þes
þisne *masc.acc.sg. of* þes
þissum *dat.pl. of* þes

ʒe-þóht *masc.* thought
þolian *II* endure, hold out, suffer
    for-þolian do without, lack, forego
    ʒe-þolian endure, tolerate
þon *see* þý
for-þon *av.* therefore, for that reason
for-þon *conj.* because
þone *masc.acc.sg. of* sĕ
þon-má-þe *conj.* any more than
þonne *av.conj.* then, when, since, than
þorfte, þorfton *pret. of* þurfan
þrafian *II* compel, press, urge, push
þrág *fem.* time, occasion
ʒe-þrang *neut.* throng, crowd, tumult
ʒe-þræc *neut.* throng, press, tumult
þréa-níed *fem.* affliction
þréo *fem.neut. of num.* þríe
þréo-niht *fem.* period of three days
þréora *gen. of num.* þríe
þridda *aj.* third
þríe (þréo) *num.* three
þrim *dat. of num.* þríe
ʒe-þring *neut.sg.* commotion, tumult, press, throng
þringan (þrang, þrungon, þrungen) *3* crowd, throng,
    press forward
    a-þringan rush forth, break out
    ʒe-þringan press, pinch
    oþ-þringan deprive of
    to-þringan drive asunder
þrítiʒ *num.* thirty
þrungen *past.ppl. of* þringan
þrungon *pret.pl. of* þringan
þrówian *II* suffer

þrymm *masc.* troop, crowd; might, power, violence; splendor, majesty, glory

þrymm-fæst *aj.* glorious

þrymm-full *aj.* powerful, violent; majestic

þrýþ *fem.* force, might, strength; troop

þú *2nd.pers.sg.pron.* you, thou

þúhte, þúhton *pret. of* þyncan

ȝe-þungen *aj.* excellent, noble, distinguished, prosperous

þunian *II* resound, roar

þunor *masc.sg.* thunder

þurfan (þearf, þearft, þorfte) *pret.-pres.vb.* need

þurh *prep.* through, by, by means of

þurh- *prefix: see under first letter following prefix*

þus *av.* thus

þúsend *num.* thousand

ȝe-þwǽre *aj.* gentle, peaceful

þý/þon *masc.neut.instr.sg. of* sě

þý/þon *av.* any

for-þý *av.* therefore, for that reason

þyncan (þúhte) *I* seem

ȝe-þyldiȝ *aj.* patient

þyrs *masc.sg.* giant, demon

þýs *masc.neut.instr.sg. of* þes

for-þý-þe *conj.* because

þýwan *I* press, urge, force

U

ufan *av.* above, from above

ufe-weard *aj.* upper

úhta *masc.* dawn, early morning

úht-čearu *fem.* sorrow at dawn

un- *prefix: see under first letter following prefix*

unc *dat.acc. of pron.* wit

uncer *pron.aj., gen. of pron.* wit

under *prep.av.* under, beneath
under- *prefix: see under first letter following prefix*
unnan (ann, annst, úðe) *pret.-pres.vb. w.gen.* grant
   ȝe-**unnan** grant
upp/uppe *av.* up, upward, above, upstream, inland,
   ashore
upp-gang *masc.* passage onto land
upp-héah *aj.* high
upp-rodor *masc.* the sky above, firmament
úre *pron.aj.* our, ours ; *gen. of pron.* wé
úriȝ-feðera *aj.* dewy-feathered
urnon *pret.pl. of* iernan
ús *dat.acc. of pron.* wé
úsič *acc. of pron.* wé
út *av.* out, outside, abroad
út- *prefix: see under first letter following prefix*
útan *av.* out, from outside
ymb-útan *av.* out around
útan-bordes *av.* abroad
úte *av.* outside, abroad
úter-mere *masc.* outer sea, outer bay
úte-weard *aj.* outer, outside
úðe, úðon *pret. of* unnan
úþ-wita *masc.* scholar

W

wá *masc.sg.* woe
wác *aj.* weak ; slender
wácian *II* grow weak
un-**wác-líče** *av.* strongly, without wavering
wadan (wód, wódon, waden) *6* go, proceed, advance,
   traverse
   ȝe-**wadan** go, advance
   þurh-**wadan** pierce, penetrate

wagian *II* shake, move
wamb *fem.* belly, womb
wamm *masc.neut.* stain; crime, sin
wand *pret.sg. of* windan
wandian *II* hesitate
wang *masc.* field, plain
wang-stede *masc.* place
wan-hyȝdiȝ *aj.* rash, reckless
wann *aj.* dark
wann *pret.sg. of* winnan
wár *neut.sg.* seaweed
warian *II* guard, hold, possess, attend
wáriȝ *aj.* sea-stained
wascan (wéosc, wéoscon, wascen) *7* wash
wát *1st.3rd.pers.sg.pres.indic. of* witan
ȝe-wát *pret.sg. of* ȝe-wítan
wáþ *fem.sg.* motion, journey, wandering
waðum *masc.* wave, billow
be-wáwan (wéow, wéowon, wáwen) *7* blow
on-wæcnan (wóc, wócon, wæcned) *I-6* awaken
wæd (wadu) *neut.* water, sea
wǽd *fem.* garment
wǽfer-síen *fem.sg.* spectacle
wǽȝ (wǽgas) *masc.* wave
ȝe-wǽȝan *I* afflict
wǽȝ-fæt (-fatu) *neut.* water-vessel, cloud
wǽȝ-líðend *masc.* seafarer
wǽgon *pret.pl. of* wegan
wæl *neut.* slaughter, corpse, the slain (collectively)
wǽl *masc.* pool
wæl-cwealm *masc.* violent death
wæl-feld *masc.* battlefield
wæl-ȝífre *aj.* greedy for slaughter

wæl-rest *fem.* bed of slaughter, resting place among the slain

wæl-slieht *masc.* slaughter

wæl-spere *neut.* deadly spear

wæl-stów *fem.* battlefield, place of slaughter

wæl-wulf *masc.* warrior, murderous wolf

wǽpen *neut.* weapon

wǽpen-ʒe-wrixle *neut.sg.* battle, exchange of weapons

un-wær *aj.* incautious

wǽre *2nd.pers.sg.pret.indic., pret.subj.sg. of* béon

wǽren *pret.subj.pl. of* béon

un-wær-líč *aj.* unwary, heedless

wǽr-loga *masc.* liar, devil

wǽron *pret.indic.pl. of* béon

wæs *1st.3rd.pers.sg.pret.indic. of* béon

wæsceþ *3rd.pers.sg.pres.indic. of* wascan

wæstm *masc.fem.neut.* fruit

wǽta *masc.* moisture, fluid, juice

wæter *neut.* water

wæter-fæsten *neut.* water stronghold, place protected by water

wæter-þyssa *masc.* water-rusher, swimmer, whale

wé *1st.pers.pl.pron.* we

ʒe-wealc *neut.* rolling, tossing

wealcan (wéolc, wéolcon, wealcen) 7 roll, surge, toss

weald *masc.* forest, wood

an-weald *masc.fem.neut.* authority, power, rule

ʒe-weald *neut.* control, authority, dominion, possession, power

an-wealda *masc.* lord, ruler

wealdan (wéold, wéoldon, wealden) 7 rule, control, wield

ʒe-wealden *aj.* inconsiderable, small

wealdend *masc.* ruler

wealh-stód *masc.* interpreter
weall *masc.* wall
weallan (wéoll, wéollon, weallen) 7 well up, surge
weall-stán *masc.* stone used for building
weall-steall *masc.neut.* wall-place, foundation
un-**wealt** *aj.* steady, stable
weard *masc.* guardian, watchman, guard
fore-**weard** *aj.* early
fram-**weard** *aj.* departing, doomed to die
tó-**weard** *prep.* toward
weardian *II* guard, occupy
wearg *masc.* criminal, outlaw
un-**wearnum** *av.* irresistibly, without restraint
wearp *pret.sg. of* weorpan
wearþ *pret.sg. of* weorðan
wéa-þearf *fem.* woeful need
weax *neut.sg.* wax
weaxan (wéox, wéoxon, weaxen) 7 grow
  be-**weaxan** grow over
  ȝe-**weaxan** grow, grow powerful
un-**weaxen** *ppl.aj.* not fully grown
weččan (weahte) *I* waken
weder *neut.* weather, fine weather, bad weather
weȝ *masc.* way, route, path
  his **weȝes** *adverbial* on his way
forþ-weȝ *masc.* journey, departure
  on **forþ-weȝe** away
on-**weȝ** *av.* away
wegan (wæȝ, wǽgon, weȝen) 5 carry, wear
  for-**wegan** destroy, kill
wel *av.* well, rightly, fully, very much
wela *masc.* wealth
weleras *masc.fem.pl.* lips
wel-hwǽr *av.* everywhere

288

weliȝian *II* abound; enrich
wéman *I* comfort, console; allure, lead astray
wén *fem.* expectation, probability
wénan *I* expect, believe, think, *w.gen.*
wendan *I* go, turn, change, translate
  a-**wendan** translate
  on-**wendan** change
wenian *I* entertain, honor
wéop *pret.sg. of* wépan
weorc *neut.* work, deed; pain
  ȝe-**weorc** fortification, military work, work
weorod *neut.* troop, band, company, host, throng
weorold *fem.* world
weorold-cund *aj.* secular
weorold-ȝe-sǽliȝ *aj.* prosperous in worldly goods
weorold-ríče *neut.* the kingdom of the world
weorold-þing *neut.* affair of the world
weorpan (wearp, wurpon, worpen) *3* throw, cast
  ȝe-**weorpan** hasten away
weorðan (wearþ, wurdon, worden) *3* become, happen, be
  for-**weorðan** perish, come to grief
ȝe-weorðian *II* honor, exalt; adorn
weorþ-líč *aj.* worthy, honorable, splendid
wéox *pret.sg. of* weaxan
wépan (wéop, wéopon, wépen) *7* weep, lament
wer *masc.* man
werian *I* defend, protect
wériȝ *aj.* weary, tired
wériȝ-ferhþ *aj.* weary
wériȝ-mód *aj.* weary in spirit, downcast
wesan *see* béon
west *av.aj.* west, westward
  be **westan** west of

westan *av.* from the west
westan-wind *masc.* wind from the west
wéste *aj.* waste, desolate, barren, uninhabited
wésten *masc.neut.* desert, wasteland, unoccupied territory
west-lang *av.aj.* extending westward
west-weard *av.aj.* westward, western
wíč *neut.* dwelling place, camp
wicg *neut.* horse, steed
wíč-ʒe-féra *masc.* bailiff
wícian *II* encamp, dwell, inhabit
  ʒe-**wícian** encamp
wíčing *masc.* viking, pirate
wíč-stede *masc.* dwelling
wíd *aj.* wide, extensive
  to wídan feore forever and ever
wíde *av.* far and wide, extensively
  ʒe-**wíde** widely
wíd-sǽ *masc.fem.* the open sea
wíd-scop *aj.* ample
wielm *masc.* boiling, welling, surging
  ed-**wielm** whirlpool
a-**wierʒda** *ppl.aj.* accursed
wiernan *I* refuse, prevent, withhold
  for-**wiernan** prevent, hinder
wíf *neut.* woman, wife
wíf-cýþþu *fem.* intercourse with a woman
wíʒ *neut.* war, combat
wiga *masc.* warrior
wiʒena *gen.pl. of* wiga
wíʒend *masc.* warrior
wíʒ-haga *masc.sg.* shield-wall, battle-hedge
wíʒ-heard *aj.* brave in battle
wíʒ-plega *masc.* combat, battle-play

wíȝ-smiþ *masc.* warrior
wiht *fem.neut.* being ; thing, anything
wilde *aj.* wild, untamed
wildor *neut.* wild beast
wile *3rd.pers.sg.pres.indic. of* willan
willa *masc.* wish, will, desire ; delight, pleasure
  un-**willa** displeasure
willan (wolde) *anomalous vb.* wish, be willing, be
    about to
will-cuma *masc.* welcome visitor
wilnung *fem.* desire, wish
wind *masc.* wind
windan (wand, wundon, wunden) *3* turn, move, wind,
    twist, brandish, wheel, fly
  be-**windan** wind around, envelop, encompass, surround
  oþ-**windan** escape
wine *masc.* friend, lord
wine-dryhten *masc.* friendly lord, lord and friend
wine-léas *aj.* friendless, lordless
wine-mǽȝ *masc.* dear kinsman
wín-gál *aj.* flushed with wine
ȝe-winn *neut.* strife, struggle, war, trouble
winnan (wann, wunnon, wunnen) *3* strive, contend,
    struggle, fight ; bear, endure
  ȝe-**winnan** to gain by fighting, wrest
wín-sæl (-salu) *neut.* wine-hall
winter *neut.* winter, year
winter-čeariȝ *aj.* winter-grieving
winter-setl *neut.* winter quarters
wís *aj.* wise, learned
wís-dóm *masc.* wisdom
wíse *fem.* manner, way
wís-fæst *aj.* wise
wísian *II* direct, guide

ʒe-**wiss** *aj.* certain, trustworthy

wist *masc.fem.* food, feast

wiste, wiston *pret. of* witan

wit *1st.pers. dual pron.* we two

wita *masc.* councilor, wise-man, learned man

witan (wát, wást, wiste) *pret.-pres.vb.* know

æt-**wítan** (wát, witon, witen) *1* reproach, blame for, twit
ʒe-**wítan** depart, go

wíte *neut.* torment, trouble

witen *past ppl. of* wítan

witon *pret.pl. of* wítan

wiþ *prep.* against, opposite, toward, in relation to, in
return for, along

wiþ- *prefix: see under first letter following prefix*

wiðer-léan *neut.* requital

wlanc *aj.* proud, rich, glorying in

wlát *pret.sg. of* wlítan

wlítan (wlát, wliton, wliten) *1* look, gaze

wlitiʒ *aj.* beautiful

wlitiʒian *II* become beautiful

wód, wódon *pret.sg. of* wadan

wolcen (wolcnas) *masc.neut.* cloud, sky

wolcen-faru *fem.* motion of clouds

wolcen-ʒe-hnást *neut.sg.* clash of clouds

wolde, woldon *pret. of* willan

wóma *masc.* noise, howling

word *neut.* word

worden *past ppl. of* weorðan

worht *past ppl. of* wyrčan

worhte, worhton *pret. of* wyrčan

wórian *II* roam, wander; crumble

worn *masc.* large number, great many, multitude

wóþ *fem.* voice

wóþ-cræft *masc.* art of poetry

wráh *pret.sg. of* wréon
wráþ *aj.* angry, fierce, cruel
and-**wráþ** hostile, enraged
wraðu *fem.sg.* prop, support
wræc *neut.sg.* misery, persecution, exile
wræc *pret.sg. of* wrecan
wrǽce *pret.subj.sg. of* wrecan
wræc-lást *masc.* path of exile
wræc-síþ *masc.* journey of exile, exile experience
wrǽtt-líč *aj.* wondrous, rare
wrǽþ *fem.* wreath, band ; bond (?)
wrecan (wræc, wrǽcon, wrecen) 5 drive, drive out,
  avenge ; recite
ʒe-**wrecan** avenge
wrečča *masc.* exile, refugee
wréʒan *I* stir up, excite
wréoh *imperative sg. of* wréon
wréon (wráh, wrigon, wriʒen) *1* hide, cover
be-**wréon** hide, cover
wriceþ *3rd.pers.sg.pres.indic. of* wrecan
wriʒen *past ppl. of* wréon
wrigon *pret.pl. of* wréon
ʒe-**writ** *neut.* writing, document
wrítan (wrát, writon, writen) *1* write
a-**wrítan** write
writen *past ppl. of* wrítan
wucu *fem.* week
wudu *masc.* wood, forest ; tree, cross ; ship
wudu-blǽd *fem.* forest blossom
wudu-fæsten *neut.* forest stronghold, place protected by
  woods
wuldor *neut.* glory
wuldor-cyning *masc.* king of glory
wuldor-fæder *masc.* father of glory

293

wulf *masc.* wolf
wund *fem.* wound
wund *aj.* wounded
wunden *past ppl. of* windan
wundian *II* wound
  for-**wundian** wound severely
  ȝe-**wundian** wound
wundon *pret.pl. of* windan
wundor *neut.* wonder, miracle
wundrian *II* wonder, marvel
wundrum *av.* wonderfully, wondrously
wunian *II* remain, dwell, be accustomed to
  ȝe-**wunian** inhabit, dwell
wurde *pret.subj.sg. of* weorðan
wurdon *pret.pl. of* weorðan
wuton *adhortative vb., w. infinitive* let us
wynn *fem.* joy, delight, pleasure
wynn-líč *aj.* joyful, pleasant
wynn-sum *aj.* delightful, pleasant
wynnum *av.* beautifully, joyfully
wyrčan (worhte, worht) *I* work, build, make, do, attain
  for-**wyrčan** obstruct, barricade; destroy, do wrong
  ȝe-**wyrčan** make, bring about
wyrd *fem.* fate
and-**wyrdan** *I* answer
wyrm-líča *masc.* serpent image
wyrt *fem.* plant, herb

Y

yfel *neut.* evil, harm
ymb/ymbe *prep.* around, about, at
ymb- *prefix: see under first letter following prefix*
ymbe *see* ymb

ymb-útan *av.* out around
yteren *aj.* otter-skin
ýþ *fem.* wave
ýþ-mearh (-méaras) *masc.* ship, wave-steed

PROPER NOUNS

Most Anglo-Saxon names of persons were composed of two meaningful elements, which did not necessarily make any sense in combination.

Ádam Adam
Andred Andred Forest, the Weald, in Kent and Sussex
Angel-cynn the English people, England
Angle *pl.* the Angles, the Anglians, Anglia, the district of Angel
An-láf the Anglo-Saxon form of the Scandinavian name *Olaf*
Apulder Appledore, Kent
Asser a ninth-century monk, the biographer of King Alfred
Axan-mynster Axminster, Devonshire
Æbbe a Frisian name
Ælf-here an Anglo-Saxon name (elf-army)
Ælf-nóþ an Anglo-Saxon name (elf-boldness)
Ælf-ráed an Anglo-Saxon name (elf-counsel)
Ælf-ríč an Anglo-Saxon name (elf-strong)
Ælf-wine an Anglo-Saxon name (elf-friend)
Æsces-dún Ashdown, Berkshire
Æsc-ferhþ an Anglo-Saxon name (spear-mind)

Æðel-ferhþ an Anglo-Saxon name (noble-mind)
Æðel-gár an Anglo-Saxon name (noble-spear)
Æðel-helm an Anglo-Saxon name (noble-protector)
Æðel-nóþ an Anglo-Saxon name (noble-boldness)
Æðel-ræd an Anglo-Saxon name (noble-counsel)
Æðel-ríč an Anglo-Saxon name (noble-strong)
Æðel-stán an Anglo-Saxon name (noble-stone)
Æðel-wulf an Anglo-Saxon name (noble-wolf)
Bac-secg an Anglo-Saxon form of an otherwise unknown Scandinavian name
Basingas *pl.* Basing, Hampshire
Béam-fléot Benfleet, Essex
Beorht-helm an Anglo-Saxon name (bright-protector)
Beorht-nóþ an Anglo-Saxon name (bright-boldness)
Beorht-weald an Anglo-Saxon name (bright-powerful)
Beorht-wulf an Anglo-Saxon name (bright-wolf)
Beormas *pl.* the Permians, the Biarmians, a Finno-Ugric people
Beorn-wulf an Anglo-Saxon name (warrior-wolf)
Blécinga-ég Blekinge, a district in southern Sweden
Breotone *pl.* the Britons, the Celts, Britain
Bret-Wéalas *pl.* the Welsh, the Celts
Brúnan-burg unidentified site of a battle fought in the year 937
Brycg Bridgnorth, Shropshire
Bunne Boulogne-sur-mer, in northern France
Burgenda-land Bornholm, an island in the Baltic, off the southern tip of Sweden
Butting-tún Buttington, Gloucestershire
Cent Kent
Čéola an Anglo-Saxon name (possibly "seafarer," from *čéol,* "ship")
Čéol-mund an Anglo-Saxon name (ship-protection)

Čérdič an Anglo-Saxon name of doubtful, possibly Celtic, origin, the legendary founder of the West Saxon dynasty

Čisse-čeaster Chichester, Sussex

Coln the river Colne, in Hertfordshire, Middlesex, and Buckinghamshire

Constantínus the Latin form of *Constantine*

Crécas *pl.* the Greeks

Críst Christ

Crísten Christian

Cumbra the Anglo-Saxon form of the Welsh word *cymro*, "Welshman," identical with the first element in the place name *Cumberland*

Cwénas *pl.* the Suomi-Finns

Cyne-heard an Anglo-Saxon name (royal-brave)

Cyne-wulf an Anglo-Saxon name (royal-wolf)

Defnas *pl.* the people of Devon, Devonshire

Defna-scír Devonshire

Dena-mearc Denmark

Dene *pl.* the Danes

Denisc *aj.* Danish

þá **Deniscan** the Danes

Dinges mere unidentified portion of the sea between northern England and Ireland

Dorce-čeaster Dorchester, Oxfordshire

Dunnere an Anglo-Saxon name, possibly compounded of *dunn*, "dark," a word which may be of Celtic origin, and *here*, "army" (dark-army?)

Dyflin Dublin

Éad-mund an Anglo-Saxon name (fortunate-protection)

Éad-ríč an Anglo-Saxon name (fortunate-strong)

Éad-weald an Anglo-Saxon name (fortunate-powerful)

Éad-weard an Anglo-Saxon name (fortunate-guardian)

Éad-wulf an Anglo-Saxon name (fortunate-wolf)

Ealh-heard an Anglo-Saxon name, also *Healh-heard, Eolh-heard* (temple-brave)

Ealh-helm an Anglo-Saxon name (temple-protector)

Éast-Engle *pl.* the East Anglians, East Anglia, district comprising the counties of Norfolk and Suffolk

Éastre Easter

Éast-ríče the Eastern Kingdom, East Mark, the kingdom of the eastern Franks

Éast-Seaxe *pl.* the East Saxons, Essex

Ebreisc *aj.* Hebrew

Ecg-láf an Anglo-Saxon name (sword-survivor)

Ecg-wulf an Anglo-Saxon name (sword-wolf)

Engla-feld Englefield, Berkshire

Engle *pl.* the English, the Angles

Englisc *aj.* English

Éow-land Öland, an island off the coast of southern Sweden

Este *pl.* the Esthonians, the Balts, a Finno-Ugric people

Est-land Esthonia, the country of the Balts

Est-mere the Frisches Haff, a fresh-water lagoon at the mouth of the river Vistula, on the Baltic coast of northern Poland

Exan-čeaster Exeter, Devonshire

Falster Falster, a Danish island

Fastitocálon a name for the whale, derived from Greek (*aspidochelone,* lit. shield-tortoise)

Fearn-hám Farnham, Surrey

Finnas *pl.* the Lapps, a Finno-Ugric people

Fræna the Anglo-Saxon form of a Scandinavian name

Frésa/Frísa a Frisian

Frésisc *aj.* Frisian

Frísa *see* Frésa

Gadd an Anglo-Saxon name of uncertain origin, possibly meaning "comrade"

God-ríč an Anglo-Saxon name (god-strong)

God-wíȝ an Anglo-Saxon name (god-war)

God-wine an Anglo-Saxon name (god-friend)

Got-land Gotland, a Swedish island in the Baltic; Jutland, the Danish peninsula

Grimm-beald an Anglo-Saxon name (fierce-bold)

Hálgo-land Helgeland, a district in Norway

Hám-tún-scír Hampshire

Harald the Anglo-Saxon form of the Scandinavian name *Haraldr* (*hari-vald,* army-power)

Hǽsten the Anglo-Saxon form of a Scandinavian name

Hǽðum/æt-Hǽðum *dat.pl.* Haddeby, an ancient city in Schleswig-Holstein (lit. the heath people)

Héah-stán an Anglo-Saxon name (high-stone)

Healf-Dene the Anglo-Saxon form of the Scandinavian name *Hálf-Danr* (half-Dane)

Hrofes-čeaster Rochester, Kent

Humber the river Humber, in northern England

Ilfing the river Elbing, in northern Poland

Ióhann the Anglo-Saxon form of the New Testament name *John*

Ióséph the Anglo-Saxon form of the Bible name *Joseph*

Íra-land Ireland

Langa-land Langland, a Danish island

Læden Latin

Læden-ȝe-þéode the Latin language

Læden-ware *pl.* the Romans, Latin-speaking people

Lǽ-land Laaland, a Danish island

Léga-čeaster Chester, Cheshire

Léof-sunu an Anglo-Saxon name (beloved-son)

Limene the river Lympne, an old name of the East Rother, in Sussex and Kent

Lucuman an Anglo-Saxon name, composed of the name *Luca* and the diminuitive *-man*

Lunden/Lunden-burg London

Lýʒe the river Lea, in Bedfordshire, Hertfordshire, Essex, and Middlesex

Maccus a Celtic name

Mária Mary

Méore Möre, a district in Sweden

Meran-tún Merton, Surrey

Meres-íeʒ Mersea, an island on the coast of Essex

Mere-tún Merton, Devonshire

Middel-tún Milton Regis, Kent

Mierče *pl.* the Mercians, Mercia, comprises roughly the Midlands

Norðerne a Northerner, a Norseman

Norþ-Hymbre *pl.* the Northumbrians, Northumbria

Norþ-mann a Norseman, a Norwegian

Norþ-sǽ the Bristol Channel, between the south coast of Wales and Devonshire and Somersetshire

Norþ-Wéalas *pl.* the Welsh, Wales

Norþ-Wéal-cynn the Welsh people

Norþ-weʒ Norway

Odda an Anglo-Saxon name, possibly of Scandinavian origin

Offa an ancient and legendary Anglo-Saxon name of doubtful origin

Óht-here the Anglo-Saxon form of the Scandinavian name *Óttar*

Ord-héah an Anglo-Saxon name (spear-high)

Ós-bearn the Anglo-Saxon form of the Scandinavian name *Ás-björn* (god-bear)

Ós-ríč an Anglo-Saxon name (god-strong)

Ós-weald an Anglo-Saxon name (god-powerful)

Pante the river Pant, in Essex

Pedrede the river Parret, in Dorsetshire and Somerset-shire

Pleg-mund an Anglo-Saxon name (battle-protection)

Pryfetes-flód Privett, Hampshire

Réadingas *pl.* Reading, Berkshire

Sanctus Paulus the Latin form of *Saint Paul*

Sæfern the river Severn, in southwestern England

Scéo-burg Shoebury, Essex

Sciringes-héal Skírings-salr, an ancient trading center in Norway

Scónéʒ Skaane, a district in southern Sweden

Scottas *pl.* the Scots

Scyttisc *aj.* Scottish

Seal-wudu Selwood Forest, in Somersetshire

Seaxe *pl.* the Saxons, Saxony

Síd-roc the Anglo-Saxon form of the Scandinavian name *Sigr-tryggr* (victory-true)

Siʒe-beorht an Anglo-Saxon name (victory-bright)

Síʒen the river Seine, in northern France

Sillende Sjaelland, Zealand, a Danish island

Stúr-mere Sturmer, Essex, a lake formed by the river Stour

Súþ-Seaxe *pl.* the South Saxons, Sussex

Swéo a Swede

Swéo-land Sweden

Swíþ-wulf an Anglo-Saxon name (strong-wolf)

Temes the river Thames, in southeastern England

Ter-Finnas *pl.* the Terfinns, the Lapps occupying the southern shore of the Arctic Ocean, i.e., the Kola Peninsula and northern Norway

Trúsó Truso, an ancient city in northern Poland

Þur-stán an Anglo-Saxon name adapted from the Scandinavian name *Þórr-steinn* (Thor-stone)

Wǽr-ferhþ an Anglo-Saxon name (fidelity-mind)

Wéalas *pl.* the Welsh, Wales, the Celts

Wealh-ʒe-réfa Welsh-reeve, the sheriff of the Welsh Marches, a royal officer

Weonod-land the country of the Wends, a West Slavic people, now northeastern Germany

West-sǽ the North Atlantic

West-Seaxe *pl.* the West Saxons, Wessex

Wíʒ-ferhþ an Anglo-Saxon name (war-mind)

Wíʒ-helm an Anglo-Saxon name (war-protector)

Wíʒ-stán an Anglo-Saxon name (war-stone)

Wiht the Isle of Wight, Hampshire, on the Channel coast

Wil-tún Wilton, Wiltshire

Wil-tún-scír Wiltshire

Win-burne Wimborne, Dorsetshire

Winedas *pl.* the Wends, a West Slavic people

Wintan-čeaster Winchester, Hampshire

Wír-héal the Wirral, a peninsula in Cheshire, between the estuaries of the rivers Mersey and Dee

Wísle the river Vistula, in Poland

Wísle-múða the mouth of the river Vistula, in northern Poland

Wít-land Witland, possibly Latvia

Wulf-heard an Anglo-Saxon name (wolf-brave)

Wulf-mǽr an Anglo-Saxon name (wolf-illustrious)

Wulf-rǽd an Anglo-Saxon name (wolf-counsel)

Wulf-ríč an Anglo-Saxon name (wolf-strong)

Wulf-stán an Anglo-Saxon name (wolf-stone)